CREATING NEW FAMILIES

Tavistock Clinic Series

Margot Waddell (Series Editor)
Published and distributed by Karnac Books

Orders
Tel: +44 (0)20 7431 1075; Fax: +44 (0)20 7435 9076
Email: shop@karnacbooks.com
www.karnacbooks.com

CREATING NEW FAMILIES

Therapeutic Approaches to
Fostering, Adoption, and Kinship Care

Edited by

Jenny Kenrick, Caroline Lindsey,
& Lorraine Tollemache

Foreword by
Lionel Hersov

KARNAC

First published in 2006 by
Karnac Books
118 Finchley Road
London NW3 5HT

British Library Cataloguing in Publication Data

A C.I.P. for this book is available from the British Library

ISBN-13: 978-1-85575-935-0
ISBN-10: 1-85575-935-7

Edited, designed, and produced by Communication Crafts

Printed in Great Britain

www.karnacbooks.com

CONTENTS

ACKNOWLEDGEMENTS

First and foremost, we would like to thank the children and foster, adoptive, and kinship carers for the part they have played in the creation of this book. Through their collaboration with us, they have helped us to understand their dilemmas and needs.

We thank all the contributors to this book. In particular, we are very grateful to the parent, "Jason Andrews" (a fictional name), who wrote on behalf of his family, but who cannot be openly acknowledged for reasons of confidentiality. He provides a unique perspective on the value of the clinical work of the team to his family.

We are very honoured that Professor Lionel Hersov agreed to write the Foreword. He was an honorary member of the Fostering and Adoption team for several years. During that time we benefited from his wise advice based on his extensive experience of this field. We owe him a huge debt of gratitude.

We thank Dr Caroline McKenna for her valued advice in the preparation of Chapter 5. We thank Julia Granville for her help in providing case material for chapter 15.

The excerpt from "One Art" from *The Complete Poems 1927–1979* by Elizabeth Bishop is reprinted by permission of Farrar, Straus & Giroux, LCC.

We thank Diggory for providing the cover illustration.

We are grateful to Margot Waddell for her patience and encouragement. We wish to thank Christelle Yeyet-Jacquot, our editor at Karnac.

We also thank Klara and Eric King for their impeccable and thoughtful copy-editing, which turned a manuscript into a book.

We thank Sehra Khan for her generous and calm administrative support in preparing the manuscript of the book.

Jenny Kenrick, Caroline Lindsey, & Lorraine Tollemache

Margot Waddell

Since it was founded in 1920, the Tavistock Clinic has developed a wide range of developmental approaches to mental health which have been strongly influenced by the ideas of psychoanalysis. It has also adopted systemic family therapy as a theoretical model and a clinical approach to family problems. The Clinic is now the largest training institution in Britain for mental health, providing postgraduate and qualifying courses in social work, psychology, psychiatry, and child, adolescent, and adult psychotherapy, as well as in nursing and primary care. It trains about 1,700 students each year in over 60 courses.

The Clinic's philosophy aims at promoting therapeutic methods in mental health. Its work is based on the clinical expertise that is also the basis of its consultancy and research activities. The aim of this Series is to make available to the reading public the clinical, theoretical, and research work that is most influential at the Tavistock Clinic. The Series sets out new approaches in the understanding and treatment of psychological disturbance in children, adolescents, and adults, both as individuals and in families.

A volume that comprehensively examines the experiences and needs of looked-after and adopted children and their families and those in kinship care, long- or short-term, is long overdue. *Creating New Families: Therapeutic Approaches to Fostering, Adoption, and Kinship Care* describes work over many years based in the specialist

Fostering and Adoption team in the Child and Family Department of the Tavistock Clinic.

The complexity of the problems involved in the creation and support of new relationships and family constellations can only be recognized and addressed through an approach that is both flexible and focused, one that is familiar with the particular mental health and educational needs of those in the care system. This requires a dedicated multidisciplinary team of professionals who have the skills and resources to provide therapeutic interventions for adoptive, foster and kinship carers, children and young people, but also a wide variety of other interventions. These may include consultation to, and liaison with, for example, social services, schools, and adoption agencies. Represented in these chapters are the different ways in which the Tavistock team makes use of a range of theoretical models, be they systemic, psychiatric, attachment and cognitive behavioural, as well as psychoanalytic, to inform both assessment and intervention.

The sensitivity, depth, and wisdom shown in the work and therapeutic case studies described in these pages express, often in moving detail, what has been learned from long experience. The book offers enlightened and hopeful ways of engaging with the particular challenges and difficulties involved in creating permanence for those whose lives have been fractured, be it by neglect, rejection, abuse, loss—by any or all of these.

ABOUT THE EDITORS AND CONTRIBUTORS

Laverne Antrobus is a consultant child and educational psychologist working at the Tavistock Mulberry Bush Day Unit, a specialist unit that provides treatment and education for up to eighteen children aged 5–12 years. She also works at the Tavistock Clinic as part of a multidisciplinary team. She is particularly interested in working with parents and has run a number of parent groups.

Sara Barratt is a systemic psychotherapist at the Tavistock Clinic, where she is Chair of the Fostering and Adoption team, specializing in kinship care and work with families post-adoption. She is a clinical supervisor and teacher on the Tavistock Masters course and other systemic psychotherapy trainings in the United Kingdom and Malta. In addition she is consultant and trainer to local authority childcare staff and a therapist in general practice.

Hamish Canham was a consultant child and adolescent psychotherapist at the Tavistock Clinic and was Joint Organizing Tutor for the clinical training in child psychotherapy. He had a long-term interest in children in the care system, with a particular knowledge of residential care, and he wrote extensively about the field. He was a member of the Fostering and Adoption workshop and was Joint Editor of the *Journal of Child Psychotherapy*.

Louise Emanuel is a consultant child psychotherapist in the Child and Family Department, Tavistock Clinic, where she runs the Under Fives Service and is Course Organiser of the PG dip/MA in Infant Mental Health. She has a special interest in work with looked-after children and their carers and in consultation to organizations such as social services and childcare services, gained through previous posts working jointly with these agencies. She lectures abroad in Italy, South Africa, Ireland, Holland, and Israel.

Julia Granville is a systemic family psychotherapist and social worker in the Fostering and Adoption team at the Tavistock Clinic. She has over twenty years' experience working with families in the voluntary and statutory sectors. She has a particular interest and experience in working with adopted and looked-after children and their families and with families with non-traditional family forms. She has a small private practice working with couples, parents, and children.

Rita Harris is a consultant clinical psychologist and systemic psychotherapist. She is currently Clinical Director of the Child and Family Department of the Tavistock Clinic in London. She is a member of the Fostering and Adoption team, specializing in issues of contact for children with parents with whom they no longer live. She has developed multi-agency services in partnership with local authorities for the most vulnerable children, young people, and their families.

Lionel Hersov trained in medicine in South Africa, interrupted by Army Service in Italy in 1943–1946. He began training in General Psychiatry and Child and Adolescent Psychiatry in 1952 at the Maudsley Hospital and Institute of Psychiatry. He gained his M.D. in 1958 for research into "persistent" school non-attendance and school refusal. He was a consultant psychiatrist in the Children's Department from 1968–1984, when he retired to take up the position of Professor of Psychiatry and Paediatrics at the University of Massachusetts Medical School, Boston, Massachusetts. While at the Maudsley Hospital, he co-edited *Child and Adolescent Psychiatry: Modern Approaches* with Michael Rutter and Eric Taylor. He presided over the Tenth International Congress of the IACAPAP in 1982. In 1990, he began teaching specialist registrars in Child and Adolescent Psychiatry at the Tavistock Clinic and was appointed Honorary Distinguished Visiting Scientist. He still continues this work. His interest in fostering and adoption goes back years, and he has published papers on the topic.

Sally Hodges is a consultant clinical psychologist in the Child and Family Department of the Tavistock clinic, where she has worked for the last ten years. She has a special interest in working with children and adults with learning disabilities and is the main author of the book *Counselling Adults with Learning Disabilities* (2003). In addition to her special needs work, she works regularly with fostered children throughout court proceedings, with the aim of ensuring that their voice and preoccupations are properly heard.

Juliet Hopkins is an honorary consultant child psychotherapist at the Tavistock Clinic. She has published widely on aspects of child psychotherapy and has a special interest in problems in infancy. She is a senior member of the British Association of Psychotherapists and works in private practice.

Jenny Kenrick was until recently a consultant child and adolescent psychotherapist and Clinical Tutor for the clinical training in child psychotherapy at the Tavistock Clinic. She was a member of the Fostering and Adoption team and, with Lorraine Tollemache, was co-convenor of the Fostering and Adoption workshop. She has developed a particular interest in, and has written about, children in transition.

Caroline Lindsey is a consultant child and adolescent psychiatrist and systemic family psychotherapist. She worked full-time until recently at the Tavistock Clinic, where she previously chaired the Child and Family Department. She worked as a consultant to Camden Social Services for many years and subsequently established the Fostering and Adoption team in the Child and Family Department, together with Lorraine Tollemache. She was previously Chair of the Faculty of Child and Adolescent Psychiatry at the Royal College of Psychiatrists. She chaired the External Working Group on Mental Health and Psychological Well-Being for the Children's National Service Framework and is currently involved in a review of progress of CAMHS NSF implementation. She now works in a private and voluntary capacity.

Graham Music is a consultant child and adolescent psychotherapist at the Tavistock Clinic, where he works as a member of the specialist Fostering and Adoption team. He teaches and supervises on various Tavistock and other trainings, in Britain and abroad, runs the Child Development Research model at the Tavistock, and has a particular interest in linking attachment theory, child development research, and psychoanalytic ideas. He also has for many years developed psycho-therapeutic services in community locations, such as schools and GP practices, for several NHS Trusts in London. He is a member of the editorial board of the *Journal of Child Psychotherapy* and also works as an adult psychotherapist in private practice.

Margaret Rustin is a consultant child psychotherapist at the Tavis-tock Clinic, Organising Tutor of the Tavistock Child Psychotherapy Training, and Head of Child Psychotherapy. She has had a long-term interest in the experiences of adopted and fostered children and their parents. She has co-authored *Narratives of Love and Loss* (1987) and *Mirror to Nature* (Tavistock Clinic Series, 2002) with Michael Rustin and co-edited *Closely Observed Infants* (1989), *Psychotic States in Children* (Tavistock Clinic Series, 1997), and *Assessment in Child Psychotherapy* (Tavistock Clinic Series, 2000).

Miriam Steele trained as a child analyst at the Anna Freud Centre, where she was Director of the MSc programme in Psychoanalytic Developmental Psychology. Her long-term interest has been in bridg-ing psychoanalytic thinking and clinical practice with contemporary research in child development. She has carried out research based at Coram Family into the attachments of late-adopted (maltreated) children and their parents. She was an enthusiastic member of the Tavistock Fostering and Adoption workshop. She is currently Associ-ate Professor and Assistant Director of Clinical Psychology, Graduate Faculty, at the New School for Social Research in New York.

Lorraine Tollemache is an adoptive parent. She is trained as a teacher, a social worker, and a psychotherapist. Until recently she worked as a Senior Clinical Lecturer in Social Work in the Child and Family depart-ment at the Tavistock. She was a co-founder with Caroline Lindsey of the Fostering and Adoption team, and a co-convenor of the Fostering and Adoption workshop with Jenny Kenrick. She established train-ings for social workers in this field of work under the umbrella title of Children in Transition, and these are now part of the Tavistock MA in Advanced Social Work.

FOREWORD

Lionel Hersov

This timely and important book will appeal to professionals in CAMHS, social services, and other organizations who are asked to deal with the variety of problems arising in fostering, adoptive, and kinship families. At a time when the rates of mental health disorders in children and youth have substantially increased, a comprehensive account of multidisciplinary treatment approaches is long overdue, and this book meets the needs.

Current research has clearly shown that children growing up in poorly resourced orphanages or in dysfunctional and often drug-dependent families and who subsequently experience repeated breakdown in foster placements may develop inappropriate coping strategies. They struggle to progress educationally, socially, and emotionally. This, then, leads to problems even for the most well-meaning and involved families or parents, especially for those embarking for the first time on raising a family, as adopters or permanent carers.

It is the distilled wisdom and clinical experience of the members of the team and of a couple who have adopted that makes for fascinating reading for all engaged in similar work.

PREFACE

Caroline Lindsey

This book is the product of the work of both current and previous members of the Fostering and Adoption Team, now known as the Fostering, Adoption and Kinship Care Team, in the Child and Family Department of the Tavistock Clinic. Working with children who cannot grow up in their families of origin goes back many years in the history of the Tavistock Clinic. It originated in a working group convened to think about deprivation, eventually appearing in print as *Psychotherapy with Severely Deprived Children* by Mary Boston and Rolene Szur (1983). This group evolved into the Fostering and Adoption Workshop, a place where clinicians can discuss the children they are treating, predominantly with psychoanalytic psychotherapy. Caroline Lindsey began her career at the Tavistock Clinic, working part of the time as Consultant to Camden Social Services, which she continued until 1988. By this time she was convinced of the importance of providing assessment and therapeutic help, alongside the social workers, for the children for whose care they were responsible. The Clinic echoed this view when, in 1990, Lorraine Tollemache was appointed to a new post of Clinical Lecturer in Social Work, with a special responsibility in Fostering and Adoption. Together, Caroline and Lorraine began working with social services' referrals of children and families, where there were concerns about their psychological needs and about their placements. They established a network with other organizations. They were soon joined by a clinical psychologist, Clare Huffington, for one session. Shortly afterwards, a training course for social workers, "Children in Transition", was established, with an emphasis on the importance of familiarity with a range of theoretical frameworks for a full understanding of the needs of this group. A biennial conference was also initiated to address the interests of professionals in the field. Both these endeavours continue today.

The informal team gradually grew and was joined, in turn, by Rita Harris, Sara Barratt, Jenny Kenrick, and trainees from the various professional groups. Eventually, by 2000, it had sufficiently established its place in the Department to be recognized as a service in its own right, with well-established and valued relationships, both with the rest of the Department and with outside agencies, such as Coram Family. Later arrivals in the team included Graham Music and Julia Granville. Others have joined since. The emphasis in the team has always been on the important contribution that each profession and therapeutic modality makes to the task and the need for integration of thinking and intervention.

Great care has been taken by the authors and editors of this book to preserve the confidentiality of the families, whose stories have been drawn on to illustrate the work. Except when explicit permission has been obtained, all the details in the examples have been changed to ensure that recognition is not possible. However, as many families have similar experiences and there are often common themes running through the lives of those who care for or are cared for in alternative families, there may, inevitably, be some resonances with their own histories for those who read this book.

Editors' note

In the interest of grammatical simplicity, unspecified children have generally been referred to as male, and unspecified carers/therapists, etc. as female.

CREATING NEW FAMILIES

Introduction

Caroline Lindsey

There has been a growing recognition, in recent years, of the significant and varied needs of families for support, both emotionally and psychologically, and in material and financial terms, when they take on the care of other people's children. The emphasis on placing children in care for adoption when rehabilitation is not considered possible has also increased greatly following the initiative taken by the Prime Minister, so that there now is a target of 40% of children to be placed for adoption from care (DfES, 2000). This policy is contained within the broader context of a commitment to creating permanence for children and young people who cannot return to their birth families. In North America there has been a similar trend, with recent figures showing a 78% increase between 1996 and 2001 in children placed for adoption from care (Evan B. Donaldson Adoption Institute, 2004). Researchers have clarified what practitioners have always known concerning the extent of the largely unmet mental health and educational need of the young people in the care system (Meltzer, Gatward, Corbin, Goodman, & Ford, 2003). New services are now being set up to address these needs, both for looked-after children and for post-adoption support, within NHS, Social Care, and Education settings, often within multi-agency partnerships, including the voluntary sector. These services are recommended in the Children's National Service Framework (DoH, 2004) and will also be needed to fulfil some of the likely outcomes of the Adoption Support assessments that are part of the Adoption and Children Act 2002 provision.

Child Mental Health Services have always assessed and treated some looked-after and adopted children, those in kinship care, and their families; however, they have often been unable to give priority to their extensive and long-term needs. This book is intended to reflect the practice of the specialist, multidisciplinary Fostering and Adoption team in the Child and Family Department of the Tavistock Clinic. The team is firmly rooted in an approach that values interdisciplinary working for the contribution made by the thinking of each discipline to the overall endeavour with the child and family. It also places great importance on the multi-agency collaboration, especially with social services and education, without which no intervention with this group of children can succeed. The book represents the differing ways in which members contribute to the work of the team, with individual and joint accounts by clinicians of the ways in which their therapeutic practice has evolved and about the theoretical thinking on which it is based. It is hoped that the descriptions will be helpful and that practitioners will find a fit with their own experience.

Statistics relating to looked-after and adopted children and young people in England

The most recent data available as of November 2005 (DfES, 2005) refer to the year ending March 2005. There were then 60,900 looked-after children, an increase of 3% from 2001; 68% of looked-after children were in foster care placements, an increase of 9% since 2001; 8000 children had 3 or more placements, 30% of whom were 9 years old and younger; 2,900 unaccompanied asylum-seeking children were looked after, 69% of them living in London.

In the year to March 2005, 3,800 children were adopted—the same number as in 2004 and 38% more than in 1999/2000. The government target for adoption is to increase by 40% the number of looked-after children who are adopted by 2004–05, and to exceed this by achieving, if possible, a 50% increase by 2006. Of those adopted in 2004/5, 81% were placed for adoption within 12 months of a best-interest decision. Of adoptive placements, 93% ended in adoption. Of those adopted, 62% were between the ages of 1 and 4 years, and 28% were between 5 and 9 years. The average age at adoption, however, is 4 years 2 months—unchanged over five years. This latter statistic does have considerable importance: it represents the continuing delays in recognizing, early on in life, those children for whom remaining in their birth family is not going to be an option. The result is that they are placed late for adoption, with the consequent potential problems that this entails, which are described in this book.

The concept of permanence

It is self-evident that children living in birth families always have some key relationships that have been created biologically. But as a result of the high rate of divorce, separation, and re-constituted families, a significant proportion of children and young people in our society are also living with one parent and with siblings to whom they are not related biologically. In most alternative families, the new relationships are created not physically, but in language, through conversations. Kinship care is the exception to this, since in these families the agreement to care is based on the birth family relationship; but the commitment to the child is, as in the other alternative families, the outcome of conversation. While it is clearly the case that these alternative relationships can become secure and enduring, they carry a far greater risk of being destroyed than do biological relationships, as the same power of language that brings adoptive, kinship, and foster care relationships into being can also be used to end them. In other words, agreements to care for a child made through the long process of home studies and approval, Court Hearings, whether in adoption or care proceedings, followed by placement panel deliberations, and so on, can subsequently be overturned by conversations—for example, in placement reviews, in which there is always the option for one of the parties to say, "this must end". While this is less likely to happen in the case of adoption, the fault line is in-built into the foster-care review system, which must, by definition, question the quality of the relationship.

Professionals have tried to find words to describe the undertaking to offer children and young people a sense of continuity of relationship over time. As in other areas of psychological work, practitioners seem to tire of these expressions, and as they lose their meaning and freshness, new words are substituted in an attempt to bring renewed vigour to the endeavour. So, for example, the Children Act 1989 renamed the activity of keeping in touch with birth parents, from "access" to "contact", at the same time as it introduced the concept of the overriding importance of parental responsibilities over parental rights. The new term "contact" conveys the idea of a live relationship, feeling, touching, holding, interactional, and mutual, to which both people contribute. In contrast, "access" conveyed the notion of the rights of one person to another in a linear fashion. Similarly, previously practitioners had talked of adoption, short- and long-term foster care, and other forms of placement defined by their purpose, such as "respite". "Permanence" has now become the term used to describe all forms of care where rehabilitation to the birth family has been ruled out. We speak of "permanent placements" and "permanency planning". There is a need to remember, when talking about permanent placements, that what is meant is the establishment of relationships with new carers who will act as parents do, not simply a permanent place to live. Sometimes the placement is intended to be permanent, but neither the carer nor the child feels as if a significant or meaningful relationship has developed between them. The dictionary definitions of permanence include "remaining or intended to remain, indefinitely, lasting, designed to last indefinitely, without change, enduring, persistent, opposite to temporary". It is as if those who coined the phrase "permanence" intended to convey—or hoped to create—a reality of enduring relationships, irrespective of the different types of commitments inherent in adoptive, foster, kinship care, and special guardianship and in children's homes. The overarching concept of permanence carries the meaning that the child should experience lasting relationships, notwithstanding the fact that the legal frameworks defining the nature of the different alternative family or residential structures carry varying levels of responsibilities and rights. They also involve differing psychological commitments to each other for both adults and children and degrees of continuing contact with the birth family. Crucially, the creation of these new family-type relationships requires the support of a network of many other professional relationships, which need to be reliable and, ideally, also lasting.

Significant changes have been occurring in our society and in the social care system militating on behalf of and against creating permanence for the children and young people coming into care. These processes by which the achievement of permanency is either supported or undermined in current social work and clinical practice are considered next.

The mental health of children and young people in Great Britain

There have been a number of important recent studies (Collishaw, Maughan, Goodman, & Pickles, 2004; ONS, 2000, 2003, 2005), which have clarified the current state of child mental health in Great Britain, in both the general population and in looked-after children and young people. Collishaw demonstrated a common clinical impression: that the rate of adolescent conduct problems has substantially increased over the last 25 years in both girls and boys across all classes and family types. The Office for National Statistics studies (ONS, 2000, 2005) showed a worrying level of mental health disorder, in general, in 10% of 5–16 year olds in Great Britain. The ONS study of 2003 showed that the overall rate of diagnosable mental health disorder in looked-after young people up to 17 years in England and Wales is 45%; 37% had clinically significant conduct disorders; 12% were assessed as having emotional disorders, anxiety and depression; and 7% were diagnosed as hyperactive. Of the children and young people in residential care, 72% had a mental health disorder, 60% with a conduct disorder. These latter statistics are understandable, since only the most disturbed and disturbing young people are likely to find themselves in residential care. Those in kinship care had a lower rate of disturbance of 33%. The prevalence of childhood mental disorders tended to decrease with the length of stay in their current placement, from 49% of those in their first year to 31% in their fifth year of placement, which may reflect the importance of security of placement in ameliorating mental health problems. The relatively small number of children placed through fostering agencies had half the rate of disturbance as those children placed with local authority foster carers or at home on a care order, which may be a reflection of the specialist agencies' ability to provide a more intensive level of skilled support. Of the young people, 62% were one year or more behind with their schooling. Only one third of those with a significant mental health problem had been in touch with a specialist mental health worker. These data confirm the experience of carers and professionals that this group of young people is troubled and highly challenging and that skilled help is required to enable them to make use of a new placement.

Children adopted in infancy and not subject to neglect and abuse have only moderately increased, if any, rates of difficulties in comparison to children raised by their birth families. By contrast, research shows that young people placed for adoption late, from care, also have a significant rate of mental health disorder. Despite this, research has also shown that the majority (70–90%) of late-placed children can form satisfactory attachments with new parents, despite adverse early life experiences (Rushton, Mayes, Dance, & Quinton, 2003). Research at Coram Family (Steele, Hodges, et al., 2003; see Steele, chapter 3) has also shown the capacity of late-placed adopted children to develop secure attachments. The minority for whom this does not occur are children with a history of multiple abuse and frequent changes of carer, who show a lack of trust and avoidant or ambivalent relationships (Groze & Rosenthal, 1993). In a study of 61 young people aged between 5 and 9, newly placed from care with adoptive or permanent foster carers, who were followed up over the first year of placement, 73% had formed an attached relationship by the end of the first year. Those who did not attach were distinguished by a history of active rejection by their birth parents. The new parents of those children tended to be less warm and sensitive than the parents of the attached children. The level of psychosocial problems was significantly higher in the non-attached group on measures of conduct difficulties, emotional difficulties, and hyperactivity. They also showed more difficulty with the expression of feelings, especially of affection and pleasure (Rushton et al., 2003). This certainly accords with clinical experience in the adoption and looked-after children service at the Tavistock Clinic. The challenge of the severe conduct and emotional disturbance shown by these young people does not fall within the everyday experience of most parents and threatens the stability of many placements. The early life experiences of most of these children have almost guaranteed that their ability to form secure attachments will have been adversely affected. Nevertheless, they tell us that they seek and need a sense of belonging and continuity. This was movingly illustrated in a film of young people, entitled *Care Stories*, made with young care leavers in Haringey (Tavistock Training Publications, 2006). Their behaviour often belies this as they test their carers beyond endurance, being unable to trust, fearing and evoking rejection. The origins of lack of trust lie in their early life experiences, which have damaged the capacity for mutually satisfying interpersonal relationships in a deep-rooted psychological and biological way. Understanding this is essential to finding the means to going on helping and caring for them.

The social care system

While the poor mental and physical health of young people in care can be attributed to a significant extent to their early histories of neglect and abuse, deprivation, and family breakdown, as well as to genetic and biological causes, the outcomes of public care have been very poor. As reported in 1997, only 25% of care leavers had any academic qualifications; 50% were unemployed; 17% of young women were pregnant or already mothers (DfES, 1997), and 20% were homeless within two years of leaving care (Biehal, Clayden, Stein, & Wade, 1995). There is also a significant rate of foster-care breakdown and disruption of late adoptions. Triseliotis (2002) reported a disruption rate in adoption of less than 2% in the under 1s, 5% of pre-schoolers, and 15% between the ages of 5 and 12, rising to 33–50% in adolescents. A total of 6% of adoptive placements ended in another placement, as reported in the *National Statistics Bulletin* (DfES, 2005). There have been a series of initiatives, starting with Quality Protects, in 1998, to improve the quality of social care and to encourage the use of adoption when appropriate. By 1999/00 the situation had improved somewhat, so that only 34% of care leavers had any qualifications; by 2005, 50% were in that position. However, the overall figure of 59% of 19-year-old care leavers in education, training, or employment in 2005 shows an improvement of only 4% since 2004 (DfES, 2005).

Recently there has been an emphasis on the provision of better-joined-up care, involving social care, health and education, including the establishment of CAMHS looked-after children teams and post-adoption services. This has been encouraged by the recommendations of the Children's National Service Framework (DoH, 2004). There is also the ongoing Department of Health research project to deliver multidimensional treatment foster care, based on the Oregon model, to the most challenging young people. Results so far show reductions in offending, violence towards others, self-harm, sexual behaviour problems, and absconding. Placement in mainstream or special school has increased, and frequent non-school attendance has decreased. Behaviour difficulties in school are reduced (personal communication, Rosemarie Roberts, National Treatment Foster Care Centre, Maudsley Hospital).

Other intensive community-based interventions (CAMHS Innovation Projects; Kelly, Allan, Roscoe, & Herrick, 2003), based on good outcomes from the research of Hengeller (1999) and Kazdin (1997) have also been funded. There are also the many potential benefits of the new Adoption and Children Act 2002, including adoption support, placement orders, and special guardianship, which will all contribute to providing the resources and status that carers need in order to offer a child a sense that they have the capacity to parent them.

However, the current social care system delivers social work in a way that may be considered to be antipathetic to the creation of permanence. Over recent years, area offices have been split up into a series of teams: referral/duty/assessment; children in need; long-term, looked-after children, and leaving care teams. This means that because of their team structures, social workers are not able to remain connected to a child through the course of the placement. In addition, and probably related to their fragmented experience of social work, social workers are constantly moving on. Not only does this mean that the child has no constant social work figure, but it also leads to a failure to bear the child and his story in mind in a coherent and informed way. This may, then, be reflected by the child's own sense of confusion about the representation of himself. In the recent video referred to above, one young woman spoke of "an invisible package of papers", which she does not see but which tells a corporate story of her life.

Recent figures (DfES, 2005) show that it is now taking 15 months from best-interest decision to adoption for babies under 1 year and 2 years 4 months for those under 5 years. The development of concurrent planning for babies and young children—an initiative brought from the United States in 1998—provides continuity of care for the children in potentially permanent adoptive homes and intensive support for the birth parents. This method utilizes carefully selected carers who will, if the rehabilitation fails, go on to adopt the baby, but who also are prepared to work alongside the birth parents in giving them the best chance to care for their child. For example, in Brighton and Hove, where the project is owned by the local authority, all young children are placed either with their birth parents or in concurrent planning with project carers. Since it is known how damaging moving small babies is from the point of view of their capacity to make secure attachments, a system which promotes continuity of care should surely be utilized more widely (Monck, Reynolds, & Wigsall, 2003).

The foster carers and adopters

For the foster carers and adopters, the experience often parallels that of the child. There is lack of information about the child. This, together with a succession of social workers as well as several at the same time, with different and sometimes conflicting duties, can lead to great difficulty in grasping the meaning of a child's emotions and behaviours. They may feel a lack of skill and understanding to carry out the task. Feeling disempowered and challenged, together with a fear of failure and reluctance to ask for help, may lead to blame of the child, disruption of family relationships, and breakdown of the placement. Traditional child and adolescent mental health services (CAMHS) have often failed to recognize the differences between birth families and these families. Being treated as if they were the same as birth families and experiencing a lack of understanding of the challenge of the task of creating new relationships has often meant that foster and kinship carers and adopters have been unable to obtain the help they needed. Many CAMHS have also not had the skills or resources to give these families priority. Hence, the importance of the recent moves to create dedicated teams and staff.

It is clear that creating secure and enduring relationships for this group of young people requires people with the time and skill to provide a network of support for the carers and the cared-for, which includes education and training, counselling and therapy, and sufficient material resources.

Offering carers the opportunity to develop skills to parent behaviourally challenging children, using evidence-based parenting programmes, imparting understanding about the nature of the child's experience, and giving ongoing support to them while they implement it is a prerequisite to creating stable lives. Rushton, Monck, Upright, and Davison (2006) in a study funded by the DfES, have recently started to evaluate interventions based on these ideas. Similarly, offering children and young people the chance to work on their experiences in a range of ways is crucial for the success of their placements. We do not yet have a substantial evidence base to guide the work with this group of children. What is clear is that the complexity of their problems benefits from a multi-systemic therapy approach, involving the child, the family, and the school. This has previously been shown by Hengeller in the United States to be effective with delinquent young people and their families. As described above, treatment foster care with similar approaches is now being piloted in a study by the Department of Health (Chamberlain & Rosicky, 1995).

At the Tavistock Clinic we see children and families from many ethnic backgrounds and cultures, including asylum-seekers and refugees and internationally adopted children. We strive to ensure that our practice is culturally sensitive and informed. In this work, it is inevitable and essential to address matters relating to race, culture, and religion, since they underpin many of the personal themes involved in creating new families.

We have attempted to contribute to the development of new families by offering differing combinations of liaison and consultation with social services and education and adoption agencies, working closely with them whenever this is possible and providing detailed assessments of the children and families. Therapeutic interventions with the families and children include parent management training, parent/couple work, individual psychotherapy for the child and/or cognitive behaviour therapy, family therapy, consultation with school and family, and, where appropriate, psychoactive medication, for example for Attention-Deficit Hyperactivity Disorder (ADHD). We have found that this requires an integrated team with resources to work over long periods of time, where necessary. The team calls on a range of theoretical frameworks that inform this work, which are discussed in chapter 1.

PART I

THEORETICAL CONSIDERATIONS

There are many factors that contribute to the successful creation of a new family for children who cannot stay with their birth families. The contribution made by a child mental health service must be seen in the broader context of the wider community and in relation to post-placement support services. The range of resources that are or should be available have been addressed comprehensively by Argent (2003), but the availability of social work, with appropriate financial, legal, housing, and educational advice, is crucial.

Families who come forward to care for looked-after children do not necessarily see themselves as requiring psychological help and, by contrast, are likely to be assessed as well-functioning and capable of dealing with complex and challenging issues. However, it is now also absolutely clear that for many families help that addresses the emotional aspects of caring for looked-after and adopted young people is needed to ensure a successful outcome, especially for the most troubled. There is a need to develop knowledge and understanding of the impact of these children's earlier experiences on their development and behaviour and to acquire new and specific parenting skills, which may not have been relevant previously. Having been through the lengthy process that leads to achieving a child's placement, however, many families wish to be left to get on with the task of caring for the new family member without outside involvement. It is important that they will, as part of the process, have been helped to see that they are taking on a responsibility for which ordinary life does not necessarily prepare them well enough, and that accepting psychological support for themselves and their families is not going to be a sign of failure in any way. This means that it is an advantage if help can be provided in a non-stigmatizing manner and setting, as, for example, is work done by the voluntary organizations.

It is not just the parents who need help in adjusting to the demands made on them to care for the child, but also the child who needs help to adjust to living permanently in a family. The demands of ordinary family life for intimacy and reciprocity are very great for someone whose experience of close relationships has been one of rejection, abuse, and neglect. Families can more readily see that the child may need help with these issues but have a variety of responses, ranging from "we can help them ourselves" to "you deal with the child and leave us out of it". Our experience is that, almost inevitably, a mixture of interventions is required, which involve the family, the parents, and the young person, together and separately. It is crucial when asking them to engage on this work to convey the understanding that the family did not create the problems being presented, so that they do not feel pathologized and that their difference from other families, of being an alternative, not a birth family for this child, is recognized.

Children and their families may be referred at various points in the process from the point at which a decision has been made that they should be permanently placed—for example, transitional work—to work with families who are having problems after a placement has been made or after the adoption, sometimes several years later. All referrals are likely to have in common a high level of concern about the functioning of the child in more than one setting, usually both at home and at school, together with a recognition of the impact of the child's history on the ability to make new relationships as well as the ongoing effect of the birth family, whether in reality or in the mind. There is often a complex family–professional system, involving shared responsibilities, between social workers and family, with education always having an important role to play.

The issues being presented clinically are conceptualized using a number of theoretical frameworks. Each of these describes the difficulties from a particular perspective and also provides a guide to potential interventions. The team works together in an integrated way. The contribution of each discipline is respected, and the range of therapeutic modalities is seen as complementary. An attempt is made to see the problems of the children and their families from several perspectives and to create a "multiversa" (Maturana, 1988) rather than have one explanatory model to fit all. In the Tavistock team use is made of systemic, psychoanalytic, attachment, psychological, and psychiatric theoretical models to inform both assessment and intervention. We think it may be helpful to the reader if we set out these frameworks at the beginning of this book as we see them applying to work in the field of fostering and adoption. Each chapter within part I shows how the concepts described are particularly relevant to work with the children and their foster, adopted, and kinship families.

Caroline Lindsey

CHAPTER 1

A systemic conceptual framework

Caroline Lindsey and Sara Barratt

The systemic model has long been associated with seeing families in family therapy. Systemic practitioners have extended their practice more broadly into the wider domain of human systems, not exclusively focused on families, but applying the systemic approach also to work with individuals and couples as well as to training, consultation and liaison with professionals and agencies. A system is a name given to a set of relationships created between people characterized by a pattern of connectedness over time. Individuals in a system are seen to affect and be affected by each other in what is described as a circular way. This is in contrast to the idea that many hold, that one person affects the other unidirectionally—that is, in a linear fashion. Systemic therapists, however, also recognize that some people in a relationship may have, or be seen to have, more power to influence what happens than others—for example, parents often having more physical strength to impose their wishes on children. Systemic therapists intend to intervene to enable individuals to alter the balance of relationship between them, on the basis that the way the relationships are organized maintains or even creates the problems which are the source of their concern. Problems are not conceptualized as being located within the individual. Working systemically means that it is possible to choose to work, not simply with a family who live together, but to invite all those who are contributing to or have a role in constructing the problem that needs to be addressed: "the problem-determined system" (Anderson, Goolishian, & Windermere, 1986). The systemic approach is a crucial aspect of working with families who foster and adopt and with the professionals and agencies involved in their care. It offers a framework for understanding and intervening in the inter-relationships between the complex systems created for caring for children outside their birth families. Practitioners are seen as part of a new "co-created" system, which is formed between themselves and the families and other professional participants in the course of the conversations that they have together. The therapist actively participates in the creation of the story which emerges in the session, through questions which are asked or which remain unasked and by the interventions which are made. This contrasts with an idea that is sometimes held, that it is possible for therapists to act on the family from an outside, external position without being affected themselves.

Context

Context is a key concept. According to Bateson (1979), "without context, words and actions have no meaning at all". Context is defined, among other characteristics, by markers such as place, time, relationship, and language. The many varied contexts in which we live and work influence our behaviour, beliefs, and understanding of the meaning of our experiences and relationships, so that we may see ourselves and be seen by others as being different, depending on the context. For children who are cared for in alternative forms of families, the idea of family and family relationships is fraught with difficulty. There is no easy understanding of the meaning of everyday concepts, such as mother and father, daughter and son relationships for those young people who have experienced abuse and neglect at the hands of those people who are supposed to care for them and for whom, as they have moved from one place to another, home does not mean a place where you feel secure—"at home". In order to understand children's behaviour in these circumstances it is crucial to make no assumptions about the meaning of family life for them. Attachment theory (see chapter 3) describes a specific contextual relationship marker between caregivers and child. Bowlby (1969) described a system that ideally develops to create security in the face of fear and the unknown, in which the child experiences the parent as a figure of attachment who responds with appropriately sensitive caregiving. The pattern of attachment developed by the child is one of several aspects of the parent–child relationship.

In cases where the child has to move to a new home, it plays a crucial part in the way the pattern of future relationships evolves. Systemic therapists use the understanding that flows from attachment theory in working with relationships.

"The Coordinated Management of Meaning"

The "Coordinated Management of Meaning" (Pearce & Cronen, 1980) is a framework that conceptualizes the multi-layered levels of context in which we live our lives. The model is helpful in conceptualizing the complexity of alternative forms of family life. The levels include *the socio-cultural norms of society, family or team context, life script whether personal or professional, relationship context, episode, and speech-act* (Figure 1.1). Each level provides a context for every other level, reflexively. At times the meanings at one level are in contradiction with those at another level, which may account for the difficulties of individuals either in their personal or in their professional lives. It is with these contradictions of meaning in context that systemic therapists must concern themselves. Professionals working in this field may also experience contradictions between their personal beliefs and professional duties and agency role, which may affect their relationship with the family, other workers, and to the task.

The *socio-cultural level* of context powerfully defines the lives of families who foster or adopt, of the children as well as their birth families, since it includes the legislative framework by which the families are created, societal beliefs about parental entitlement, rights, duties and responsibilities, and the beliefs about parenthood and family life

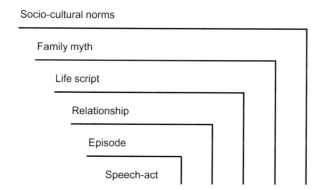

Socio-cultural norms

Family myth

Life script

Relationship

Episode

Speech-act

FIGURE 1.1.   The Coordinated Management of Meaning (Pearce & Cronen, 1980).

held by different cultural, ethnic, and religious communities. Professionals are also organized in their thinking and practice by their personal and professionally held beliefs and experiences. It is important for them to consider how ideas of difference in race and ethnicity, religion, class and culture, gender, age, and ability affect the meaning they give to their own lives and the families and colleagues with whom they work.

Within the level of what Pearce and Cronen term the *family myth* and to which Byng-Hall (1995) refers as *family script* are embedded the many different forms that make up the constellation of families in this field, referred to elsewhere as "a Family of Families" (Lindsey, 1993). Families hold a range of beliefs and patterns of relating, developed over generations, based on how they are brought into being and with whom. If we confine ourselves to considering foster, adoptive, kinship care, and birth families in relation to their sense of connectedness over time, it will immediately be apparent how different the experience of family life might be in each context for the child or young person. In the case of the first two, there is no mutually held family history over previous generations, joining child and parents, which in birth families and in kinship care is often the cement that holds otherwise precarious relationships together. The family's unique script is created by the intergenerational experience of family life and their specific cultural heritage, affecting the way they see the nature of parenting. The script plays a crucial role in the adaptation of those families who, for example, adopt as a consequence of infertility or the meaning of caring for a relative through kinship care.

The level of *life script* gives meaning to the family member as an individual, telling the story that runs: "I am the kind of person who. . . ." The life story of children in the care system usually contains a script of loss and rejection, of hurt, neglect, and abuse which often defines the way they perceive themselves and how they expect to be treated in the future. These experiences may lead them to see themselves as unlovable and blameworthy and to develop ways of behaving which address their need to be self-reliant and controlling of their environment. It may show in parentified behaviour, reflecting a story that they tell themselves, based on earlier experiences, that they need to take care of the parent, for whom they feel responsible. This then contributes to the way in which new *relationships* with foster and adoptive parents may form, based on the script, rather than, as everyone hopes, on the new opportunity for attachment. When a positive relationship between the new family members does develop, the young person may sometimes experience a conflict of loyalty and worry about the birth parent, based on earlier family ties and relationships. This may then give rise to often disturbing patterns of relating to each other—for example, tantrums, or withdrawal on attempts to offer affection or discipline—within the new relationship, which should be understood contextually. These disturbances can be described as *episodes*. Within this schema, the family relationships may define the meaning given to these patterns, and the family relationship, in turn, is defined by the episodes. Parents describe how they find themselves behaving in ways that they do not recognize, evoked by the child's repeated behaviour patterns, which defines their relationship in a potentially negative way. Often there are characteristic pieces of behaviour or ways of talking—*"speech-acts"*—which are meaningful to all the family members and may, in turn, define patterns of relating within the relationship. Ordinary everyday requests or reprimands may trigger verbal and behavioural responses based on the prior terrifying meaning of such communications for the young person. This may, then, lead to an escalation that resonates at all the other levels of meaning, of relationship, life script, and family life. It is often related to issues such as a refusal to eat or hoarding of food, for example, with parallel and significant meanings for both child and parent.

There are often potential contradictions in their role and task for professionals in the team. All child mental health work is contextualized by the socio-cultural framework, which includes the law of the country. However, in this field, professionals have frequently to move from a position where they have to take action—for example, in relation to child protection concerns—or to take a position by writing a court report—termed being in the domain of production (Lang, Little, & Cronen, 1990)—to a position where they are hoping to work therapeutically with a family, called being in the domain of explanation. Clarifying in which domain the clinician is operating is essential to enable practitioner and family to give meaning to their conversations.

Family life cycle

The idea of a family life cycle has been used in family therapy as a tool in conceptualizing the stages of family development. It can usefully be adopted for thinking about the stages that newly forming foster and adoptive families go through, including their decision to seek help. For many foster and adoptive families who are selected on the basis of their ability to function autonomously, the idea of asking for help may be in contradiction to their family script and is reached often only when they have exhausted their own resources. It is self-evident that the value of the life-cycle framework is to act as a guide rather than to create rigid expectations. An example of such a schema is presented in Table 1.1. The life-cycle concept enables the clinician to normalize the experiences that families are having, which seem different to what they had been expecting, based on what had happened previously in their birth family. For example, there may be issues of the timing of autonomous and independent behaviour and an expectation of when past wounds should have been healed. A commonly expressed concern by adoptive parents is why their child has not yet "got over" their trauma and "settled down". Being able to refer to an accepted "norm" of a much longer timescale required for children placed from care to adapt to their new environment is reassuring to parents. The explanation that the child's slow development may be to be expected, considering their past deficits of care, and is not a fault inherent either in the child or in their current parenting, reduces unrealistic expectations, guilt, and anxiety. The particular issues for fostered and adopted children can be embedded in the stages of the life cycle of the family. Key stages such as going to school, entering puberty and adolescence, and leaving home need an adjustment of family dynamics. Living in an alternative family brings other issues that have to be addressed over and over again during the course of these stages of development. These include, for parents and children, communicating to others about being adopted on going to school; for parents, dealing with questions about adoption, which change according to the child and young person's ability to conceptualize them; and for the young person the re-working of the question of why it happened to me and what this means for my identity.

Curiosity

Curiosity (Cecchin, 1987) as a therapeutic stance is central to systemic practice. Hypothesizing is used as a tool to guide the questions asked in the interview. The hypotheses attempt to include all parts of the system being presented. The therapist adopts a "not knowing" position on meeting the family. How is this possible, when the referrals received are full of highly charged and often definitive material? Clearly it is not possible or even appropriate to shed one's professional knowledge and experience in the context of a consultation, but we try to use what we know for the purpose of exploration, so that we continue to listen without making up our minds. We try to remain aware of a tendency to stop being curious once we think we "know" what is happening and of the risk of taking up a position of certainty, which may prematurely lead to solutions or opinions about the balance of relationships in the family—for example, colluding with the idea that one member is to blame. We attempt to facilitate people in becoming observers to their relationships within the family or team by asking questions about these relationships. These are known as "circular questions". Very often, this form of questioning allows aspects of relationships and their meanings to emerge in conversation for the first time.

Interventive interviewing

Circular questions are one form of the method known as interventive interviewing (Tomm, 1987) used by systemic therapists. There is a range of questions designed to enable people to consider their current dilemmas. These include discussing the benefits of changing or staying the same, the worst-case scenario, hypothetical situations, and exploring future and different possibilities for behaviour and relationship as if they were a reality. Embedded in these questions is an idea that changing relationships is a choice that is open to them, taking into account all the dilemmas of doing so or not. Asking these questions enables people to contemplate these choices, often for the first time, since they are usually preoccupied with the story of the past and the present.

Self-reflexivity

Working in this way demands a self-awareness that is referred to as self-reflexivity. The development of self-reflexivity is supported by working with colleagues in teams, who observe the therapy or consultation and comment on the interview, both in terms of content but more importantly in terms of the process between all the people in the room, including the therapist. This may happen using a one-way screen or with a colleague in the room. Teamwork also facilitates taking multiple perspectives in thinking about the situation. The views of the team members are shared with the group consulting with the team, who often include both family members and professionals. This may be in the form of the "message" given by the therapist or sometimes through the use of a "reflecting team" (Andersen, 1991), when members of the team join the therapist and the family to discuss

Table 1.1. Adoptive family life cycle

Stage	Adoptive parents' tasks	Adopted children's tasks
Pre-adoption	Coping with infertility and feelings of inadequacy as a man or woman, letting go dream of being a birth parent	For older children, trying to cope with loss of birth parents and uncertainty about future
	Helping own parents and siblings, and children (if any), accept plan to adopt	Coping with difficulty of knowing they will lose current foster parents
	Coping with prolonged evaluative assessments and anxiety of not knowing when they may be offered a child	Coping with anxiety about future adoptive parents
	Preparing for social stigma of adopting	
	Planning for lifestyle change, e.g. giving up job, change in relationship with partner	
	Coping with feelings about accepting a child who may not be "ideal"	
Infancy	Taking on the identity of an adoptive parent and finding acceptable role models	
	Developing realistic expectations	
	Integrating the child into the family	
	Persisting with affection and establishing secure attachment, even if faced by personal disappointment	
	Exploring thoughts and feelings about birth family	

Preschool	Beginning the telling process	Learning elements of adoption story
	Creating an atmosphere conducive to openness about adoption and talking about birth family	Questioning parents about adoption
Middle childhood	Helping child accept the meaning of adoption, including loss of birth parents, possible anger (especially directed to adoptive mother)	Coping with the adoption loss. Exploring feelings about being given up by birth parents, developing an acceptable story around this
	Helping child develop a positive view of birth family	Coping with stigma of being adopted
	Managing any contact with or communication from birth family	Validating dual connection to both families
	Coping with the insecurity that telling may engender, worry child may want to leave or not love adopters	
Adolescence	Helping young person develop own sense of identity including recognition of traits that may come from birth family; accepting difference from some of their values and style	Integrating adoption into a secure sense of identity
	Supporting search interest and plans and developing realistic expectations	Exploring feelings about search process, finding balance between idealization and vilification of birth parents
	Coping with adolescent rebelliousness with a sense of proportion, coping with feelings that young person may wish to leave home as soon as possible, thus rejecting the love they gave	Trying to understand extent to which feelings and behaviour are typical for adolescence and which may derive from being adopted

From Scott & Lindsey (2003), adapted from the scheme proposed by Brodzinsky, Smith, & Brodzinsky (1998).

the dilemmas they have heard about. This creates a transparency of thinking that facilitates families in hearing feedback, since during this process they are placed in an observer rather than a participative position. The team approach is helpful when addressing the complex and distressing situations that comprise work with families who foster and adopt. It makes it possible for all the different voices to be heard—of the children, birth parents, and carers, as well as professionals—and lessens the risk of the therapist being drawn in on "one side or another ". There has to be flexibility about the use of these techniques, however, since for some they are welcome and for others, for example, traumatized young people, it is important to offer the option of being seen on their own or with only two therapists.

Our experience in working with families who foster or adopt or offer kinship care is that it is important for therapists to be available over a long time. This is different from the treatments offered by child psychotherapists, which often set out to be long-term, ongoing work. Systemic therapists usually discuss the process of continuing or ending the work as it evolves with each family. The complexities that these families face and the pain and suffering of the young people is often enduring, so they are always having to re-work their relationships with each other as the young people grow and develop. The evolving life cycle for families in this situation makes it particularly important that therapeutic support is available over long periods of time, so that families can return for further work or remain in touch on an occasional basis.

Working with families should not mean either that the parents are interviewed in the presence of the children or that children are spoken to in the presence of the parents. There are times when children may play while their parents talk to the therapist and when the therapist enables the child to communicate with the parents by talking directly to the child. We hope to achieve a balance in enabling all members of the family to participate equally in the sessions and to feel that their point of view has been heard. This means that when working with younger children in the room, we need to go at a slow pace, incorporating their play into our conversation and using language that they understand. (See chapter 12 by Barratt for a description of how the systemic therapist addresses different parts of the system, enabling all voices to be heard, by seeing people individually, in couples, as well as in the family and with the professionals who are working with them in the community.)

Using a systemic framework for understanding the problems presented by young people and their families does not exclude the use of other modalities of intervention, such as the use of medication or cognitive–behavioural techniques or individual psychotherapy. Especially in this field, where problems are severe, complex, and enduring, it is often important to utilize a range of interventions to address specific symptoms—for example, problems of concentration using psychoactive medication and behavioural problems using parent-management training. Providing this intervention within an overall systemic framework allows the meaning of the intervention and its effect on the family members to be addressed, so that change in behaviour is thought about in terms of its meaning for family beliefs and relationships.

CHAPTER 2

Psychoanalytic framework for therapeutic work with looked-after and adopted children

Jenny Kenrick

Psychoanalytic child and adolescent psychotherapy as practised at the Tavistock Clinic has two main roots: one is its psychoanalytic theoretical base; the second is its base in the observation of infants and young children. These come together in practice with children and families. This chapter is to show the particular relevance of the theoretical base in our work with looked-after and adopted children and in our participation in the work of a multidisciplinary based team. The same frameworks inform work with both foster carers and parents.

Freud developed a new theory of man and of mind at the end of the nineteenth and early twentieth centuries. His new "science" challenged the prevailing views of mind, motivation, and the innocence of children. A medical, neurological model, it described impulse-driven behaviour in a quantitative way. Later he developed a formulation of mind, in which man is driven by conflict between the life and death instincts, under the influence of ego, id, and superego. He described transference and countertransference. It was left to his followers to elaborate his theories into more finely honed working clinical tools.

Melanie Klein saw her own developments of thought and practice as having their roots in Freud's work, an assertion hotly disputed in the famous Controversial Discussions with Anna Freud between 1943 and 1945. Each was bringing new clinical and theoretical formula-

24

tions derived from work with very young children. Klein observed the play of young children, the equivalent in her view of Freud's free association and in particular of dreaming, and interpreted what she saw to reveal the most primitive anxieties in the inner world of her patients. Anna Freud's work, emphasizing drive, together with structural and defensive theories, was also based on observations made of very young children, especially in the Second World War nurseries. The impact on these children of evacuation and separation from parents led her to emphasize the importance of including parents in the work with children, as well as thinking about the adaptations of the work to a range of different settings. All of this is very relevant to our thinking about work with looked-after children.

What emerged from the work of Klein and her followers was a theory of mind, and of development based on an *interactive* model. Her theoretical base is referred to as Object Relations Theory, as there must always be a relationship with another, sometimes referred to as an "object", which will in most cases be the mother. This is what Winnicott was referring to when he said, "There is no such thing as a baby" (Winnicott, 1952).

It is important to elucidate terms that are referred to in the chapters that follow. (For a range of examples see, in particular, Kenrick, chapter 7; Hopkins, chapter 9; Rustin, chapter 10; Emanuel, chapter 18; Tollemache, chapter 16; Canham, chapter 19.)

Projection is a widely used term; it has a particular relevance to our work in understanding the interactions both ways between children and their carers. Projection is the mechanism by which a person places unwanted aspects and emotions belonging to the self into another, normally in order to get rid of them. The danger for that person is that if, for example, he projects his own angry feelings into another, he can then experience that other person as actually being angry, or as being angry with him. This is a concept of extreme relevance for families, carers, and professionals in contact with deprived and disturbed children. In order to avoid a reactive response it is important for the other—usually the adult—to become aware that some of her feelings may emanate from the child. This may help prevent her from actually becoming the angry person responding to the child in ways that the child may over time have come to expect. Projection of positive feelings can, conversely, lead to more positively developing relationships.

Projective identification was used by Klein (1946) to describe a particularly powerful form of projection. Klein saw it primarily as evacuative. Later theorists came to the conclusion that, like all forms of projection, its aim is communication of states of mind to another. In projective identification that other may experience a changed and often disturbing perception of herself. Bion (1952) described it thus: "The analyst feels he is being manipulated so as to be playing a part, no matter how difficult to recognize, in someone else's phantasy." Following Klein, later theorists used the spelling "phantasy" to differentiate unconscious from conscious "fantasy". In the first place projective identification is used by the infant before he has words to communicate his earliest states of mind to his mother. She will feel his feeling—that is, the upset mother will be feeling the child's distress and will then try to do something to relieve it. If this process proceeds well, then the infant/child/patient takes in both the connection to the mother/therapist and her capacity of understanding and trying to make sense of his experience. Over time he will take in a developing capacity of his own to tolerate a wide range of emotion and experience. However, if the mother cannot tolerate the projections of her child, either because of her own state of mind—for example, depression—or impingements on it, such as domestic violence, then the child will not develop a sure base for making sense of his own experiences of life. Indeed, a base can be formed for an anxious and persecutory view of his experience of relationships and of the world.

The relevance of this process for deprived and disturbed children, who may have had limited experience of early receptive and containing mothering, is clear. In therapy with children who are using projective identification desperately, whether to get rid of unbearable feelings or in the hope of achieving communication, it can be very helpful to describe and to name, in quite a simple way, the feeling as the therapist experiences it—for example: "There seems to be a very sad feeling around at the moment." In particularly powerful states of projective identification the child may seem to be trying to force himself intrusively into the mind and body of the therapist. This can lead to states of fusion and confusion of mind that go beyond ordinary communication, while also being communication of a very disturbed state of mind.

From Klein's theory of projective identification Bion (1962) developed the powerful notion of *containment*, which we can understand in terms of the earliest development of the infant and his need for a receptive and responsive mother/object, as just described. The mother needs to be able to bring to her own mind a capacity for "reverie", so that she can take in and think about what the infant has projected, and then to return to him his feelings in such a way that they are bearable, usually expressed initially by some function of physical care. She needs to have detoxified the original projection so as to mediate against the infant being left in a state of "nameless dread". In our work with children and families it is crucial that professionals are able to hold a containing function so that more benign experiences of relating and feeling understood can develop. It can involve a lengthy period of surviving projected feelings, of frustration and doubt, until the child or family is able to apply their own mind to understanding and modifying, rather than evading anxieties.

With looked-after and adopted children we are aware of the *defences* they employ, often to survive in the face of both overwhelming impingements on their development and the anxieties that may result.

Splitting between good and bad can be a defence to preserve a good object. We often encounter this as a positive, and sometimes idealized, view of birth parents in the face of the reality of experience. The "bad" aspects of the actual and internalized parents may be projected onto and located in the foster carers or adoptive parents. To challenge this defence, which can make caring for the child in the present so difficult, can be to confront the child with feelings of loss and despair greater than the child is able to manage, and could lead to *acting out*. This can be seen as a defence against the pain of thought and thinking. It can lead to behaviours which are difficult to manage in substitute home or in therapy. These behaviours may seem at times to have a *manic* quality. They can then appear to be symptoms of ADHD; but we will frequently see them as defences against the anxieties of depression, thinking, and reality. Some children seem to hold themselves rigidly together by such manifold defences that they can appear stupid and even to have specific learning difficulties. Indeed, they may be unable to process their thoughts and feelings in their minds, for thought for some children seems to lead inevitably to just the painful realities they strive to avoid. Attacks on *linking* their thoughts can result in inhibiting their true possibilities for development. These attacks become an attack on qualities and capacities of mind.

Many looked-after children are actually helpless and have little say in their own destiny or in changing adverse experiences. Some of these children may develop *omnipotence* as a defence, particularly to avoid experiences of separation and dependency: the "I can do it" . . . "I don't need you" . . . "I don't care" child, who is in fact feeling just the opposite. Often these feelings are directed at adoptive parents who can feel particularly rejected by the contemptuous child. For them it may be difficult to see the vulnerable child behind the defence.

Child psychotherapists are particularly aware of the *inner world* of the child and will want to bring their understanding of it both to the team and to the network. Klein described it as follows: "The baby having incorporated his parents feels them to be live people inside his body in the concrete way in which deep unconscious phantasies are experienced—they are in his mind 'internal' or 'inner' objects". At the same time his perception of external relationships and experience is "altered by his own phantasies and impulses" (Klein, 1940). An understanding of the conflicts and complexities of the child's inner world can help us to make some sense of his apparent reluctance to embrace new opportunities for relationships and experiences. It can be bewildering for a child placed in a warm adoptive family when his inner world is filled with hostile and disruptive figures. This kind of disturbance, rooted in early experiences and phantasies, can prevent a move to the more secure attachments that all hope for in permanence. Attachment research (see Steele, chapter 3) has added to our understanding of how the earliest attachments, identifications, and all that contributes to the inner world of the child persist in spite of the development of new attachments and more positive identifications, which will modify these earlier introjects. We have to think about the constant interactions of these when seeing how difficult it can be for a child to build up a secure and solid feeling of his own identity (see Rustin, chapter 10).

There are two main types of *identificatory processes* that determine the development of a sense of self and identity. The first is *adhesive identification*, the term used by Meltzer (1975) to describe a very thin form of identification, like a copying of aspects of another. It also represents a very early failure in the development of projection and projective identification. Bick (1968) used the term "second skin" to describe defences against these early failures (see Emanuel, chapter 18). The characteristics of such identity will normally collapse under any form of pressure. Adhesive identification can be seen for example, in girls attempting to adopt a pretty Barbie kind of identity, often masking more aggressive characteristics, or in boys adopting tough, macho characteristics, often an attempt to deny feelings of intense vulnerability. These demonstrate the defensive function of adhesive identification. *Introjective identification*, on the other hand, is a positive process, dependent on a good-enough early experience of containment, which results in taking in and identifying with the qualities of an object, so they can become a part of a solid feeling of identity. This is part of a healthy process of development.

In our work with looked-after and adopted children we use these among other conceptual frameworks for building understanding of the complexities and conflicts of their lives. From such understanding gained interactively with our patients the work to develop capacities for thinking and the development of mind can proceed. Here Klein's theory of *position* is helpful, as positions are not rigidly fixed, as were Freud's points of fixation. With Klein, an individual may oscillate between positions at different developmental life crises, such as in adolescence. Each position carries its own constellation of anxieties and defences against those anxieties and the turbulence generated by change and development. The *paranoid–schizoid position* is characteristic of the infant's earliest stages, when he perceives the mother both in relation to her functions and to the parts of her body: eyes, breasts, nipples. The anxieties of this position are predominantly of a persecutory nature for the infant who, until he has had enough of the good experience of containment, cannot see the parts except in a polarized way: all good (present), or all bad (absent and persecuting). In order to sustain an experience of a good breast (present/pleasure of feeding) the infant splits off the experience of the bad breast (absent/pain of hunger). While the split serves to preserve the idea of a good breast, he can also feel more persecuted because of this very polarization. With enough good experiences of the containing mother, the infant is able to begin to conceptualize an idea of an absent breast/object that contains the certainty of returning—that is, the idea of the mother who is present in his mind even while she is absent in fact. Feelings of deprivation and the persecution of separation are thereby reduced. These are characteristics of the *depressive position*, when the idea of a mother who is both good *and* bad, more integrated, becomes possible. The infant then develops feelings of concern for the damage he has done in phantasy to the mother with his aggressive feelings when she was absent and a wish to repair the damage. He feels concerned for his mother. The negotiation of the two positions requires the capacity to tolerate the pain of the knowledge of responsibility for what one has done to one's object. This is particularly difficult for children who have had limited experiences of containment and who may themselves have been damaged by painful or violent enactments by others. In therapeutic work one has to distinguish carefully between the genuine reparative gesture of the depressive position and the apparent gesture that may, in fact, be more placatory, deriving from fears of retaliation from the therapist as the recipient of the aggressive phantasy. Klein helps us to understand the use of defences against the turbulence of change that we observe so often in our patients.

The Kleinian development takes us away from an emphasis on curing symptoms to a development of mind, and to the building of inner resources that can help the individual face the inevitable vicissitudes of living.

Klein described a subtle interaction between internal conflicts and the impingements of the external word. She described that interface at which we are constantly working with deprived and emotionally damaged looked-after and adopted children: we seek to find meaning for the complex emotional interactions of their lives and understanding of the interrelationship between individual infantile anxieties, deriving from a child's earliest relationships, and the earliest and often repeated environmental failures of care and interactive development.

The majority of the children discussed in this book will at some level have been subject to *trauma*. This can be a single incident—such as abandonment, witnessing the murder of a parent, or an attack on the child—or the impact of more cumulative trauma, such as repeated sexual or physical abuse, or the frequent moves that many will have made while in the care system. All will have been subject to abandonment in some degree. The effect of trauma on the child will vary depending on his earliest relationships and the stability or lack of it in his early life. Graham Music (chapter 4) discusses the neurological changes that can take place as a result of trauma. The child psychotherapist may encounter children who have been deeply fragmented by traumatic experiences; how much would depend on the developmental stage of that particular child. Too often we encounter children whose stories of sexual abuse have not been believed by adults or have not been legally proven to have taken place. When the child experiences adult denial of his actual or emotional truth, there can be a serious problem for that child, who can be left with deep self-doubt, or with enduring rage, cynicism, and lack of trust in the adults who are supposed to care for him. It is a task of the child psychotherapist to help the child to make some sense of his actual emotional experience. Inevitably there will be mourning for the damage done to him and grief at loss, as well as a need to be able to own feelings of justifiable outrage, rather than remaining afraid of the power of his rage.

In developing her therapeutic skills, the child psychotherapist relies upon the experience both of her own psychoanalysis and of infant observation as part of her training. These come together all the time in the consulting-room as she differentiates between feelings that are projected into her and those that are her own, deriving from her own experiences. The crucial importance of the therapist's own pathology not in any way imposing on a patient can be particularly appreciated when the therapeutic work is with a highly vulnerable group of children and young people whose development and understanding of the meaning of life will often have been impinged upon by the complex needs, preoccupations, and pathology of their parents and carers.

In the therapeutic setting the emotional impact of the child and his perturbations and states of mind on the therapist can be used for thinking about his inner world. It is an interactive process of the infant/child with the mother/therapist, informed by Bion's theory of containment. The work of the therapy brings into the relationship the mind of the therapist continually trying to make sense of what is happening now, in the light of what is known of the child's earliest relationships and experiences. The therapist is also developing an understanding of the transference and countertransference. *Transference,* first described by Freud (1912b), has come to be used to describe what a patient projects into the therapist from his unconscious phantasies, based upon what or whom the therapist represents for him in his inner world at a specific moment. It brings together unconscious phantasy about the past and the actual experience of the past in the present relationship with the therapist. In the therapeutic work the therapist is able to describe this complex dynamic as it refers to how the patient sees her. The exploration can modify some of the toxicity attached to past events and phantasies, as the patient sees that the therapist can survive and indeed carry on thinking about problematic issues. *Countertransference* used to be seen as an inhibition to an understanding of the patient, but it is now seen as one of the therapist's main tools of understanding. It refers to the feelings evoked in the therapist in response to the patient and has to be scrupulously differentiated from what is evoked in the therapist from her own internal experiences. What evolves in the therapeutic encounter is a process in the present resonating with the internal world of the child. What may be new for the child is that his conflicts of love and hate can be thought about in the therapeutic encounter in new ways that will not—as perhaps has so often happened in the past—have to involve enactment.

A way of working with a child develops from a combination of psychoanalytic and developmental methodologies that are described in some of the following chapters. What the therapist brings to the work of the multidisciplinary team is the child's view of himself and his situation. This is a view that is often, in the thick of the problems of working networks, at risk of slipping from its proper primacy. Thus the inclusion of the child psychotherapist in consultation to the network can be crucial. A view of the child and his inner world can be established during initial assessment of the child and on a continuing basis when the child is in therapeutic treatment. An assessment will often help to establish whether a child is interested in the process of thinking about himself. Can he bear to make use of the new experience offered by the therapeutic relationship to begin to change or to drop some of his defences against thinking about himself and his situation? This is a central dilemma for both child and therapist. Many children have developed quite rigid systems of defences that have helped them literally to survive adverse experiences. However, when these defences have involved escaping from thinking about the intolerable by the use of behaviours that have to be managed, the child's developmental thrust may become perverted or severely limited. Here is an example of the care that has to be taken by the psychotherapist: to observe and to think about the child in the room; to have theory in mind but not with a rigidity that might leave the therapist less open to the impact on her of the child and his state of mind; to apply careful thought to what to say to a child, what words to use, when to say anything at all; how carefully to approach the child's defences at any particular moment. She also has to think about how intensely a child for whom the bonds of intimacy may be perilous can engage in therapeutic work. There can be a particular difficulty when the therapist has knowledge of the family history of a child, or of plans for a new placement that the child himself does not consciously know. She has to work at that fine interface between the child's internal and external realities. She must also relate appropriately to the interface between the views of the child and those of the networks surrounding the child. She can then hope to represent, without jargon, the "wishes and feelings" of the child about decisions that have been taken on his behalf by the adults in his world.

CHAPTER 3

The "added value" of attachment theory and research for clinical work in adoption and foster care

Miriam Steele

Our work often brings us into contact with children whose parents were unable to care for them, leaving others to assume this duty. They have often endured multiple separations and losses. It was children like these who first inspired John Bowlby to devote his career to studying and understanding the impact upon children of maternal deprivation. In a report for the nascent World Health Organization, Bowlby commented on how mental health depends on children receiving continuous care, from which both mother—or mother-substitute—and child derive an enduring sense of joy (Bowlby, 1951). During the 1950s, at the Child and Family Department he helped to establish at the Tavistock Clinic, Bowlby convened a study group aimed at elucidating the importance of the parent–child relationship. Among his many colleagues was Mary Ainsworth. She conducted longitudinal studies of infants and their mothers, which identified sensitive and responsive care as the vital ingredient in promoting secure or "healthy" infant–parent relationships and, in turn, a solid sense of self within the child that would launch him towards trusting relations with others, and a sense of competence in pursuing cognitive and social goals. Bowlby drew on Ainsworth's developmental research, cognitive psychology, control theory, and evolutionary theory to advance a theory of attachment in three volumes, *Attachment* (1969), *Separation* (1973), and *Loss* (1980).

Attachment theory

There are four main assumptions that convey the essence of Bowlby's (1973, 1980) conceptualization of attachment relationships: (1) intimate emotional bonds between individuals have a primary status and biological function; (2) the way a child is treated has a powerful influence on a child's development and later personality functioning; (3) attachment behaviour is to be viewed as part of an organizational system that utilizes the notion of an "internal working model" of self and other to guide expectation and the planning of behaviour; and (4) attachment behaviour is resistant to change, but there is a continuing potential for change so that at no time in a person's life are they impermeable to adversity or to favourable influence.

All of these are central considerations in understanding the aetiology and experiences of children in care. Bowlby (1973, 1980) postulated that humans are biopsychologically motivated by the need for attachment and that our survival is inextricably linked to and dependent upon the capacity to establish and maintain emotional ties to others. Operational from birth and evident across the life span, especially at times of crisis, the "instincts" of crying, reaching out, and holding are the functional expressions of a biological imperative with evolutionary origins. Evidence has accrued that infants are born with a capacity and motivation to relate to those delivering care to them and so are oriented from birth to relate to their social environment. (Stern, 1985; Trevarthen, 1979). Related to this biological basis of the attachment system we have compelling evidence from research in neuropsychology that qualities in the environment impact on the physiology of the brain—namely, that the brains of infants who are maltreated look different from those who have been well nurtured. (Perry, Pollard, Blakeley, Baker, & Vigilante, 1995).

Bowlby was emphatic that we need to account for the actual experiences that infants and children endure and to try as much as possible to keep in focus what has probably happened to them. For children in care, this is of paramount importance. Skilled assessments need to be made in order to reach appropriate, better informed decisions about the care they need. These assessments must take into account both the reality the child experienced and the representations of those experiences. Lieberman, for example, posits that "current life experiences for parent and child need to be carefully elucidated to determine the relative contributions of exposure to trauma *and* of intersubjective transmission in infant maladaptive functioning" (Lieberman, 2004).

The idea of an internal working model of self and attachment figure(s), which organizes thoughts and feelings regarding relationships and guides expectations regarding the nature of future interactions, arose out of a synthesis between classical psychoanalytic thinking and cognitive psychology. Bowlby pointed directly to the notion that we each carry within ourselves a representation of the self and the other, and the self in metaphorical conversation with the other. The challenge for adults interacting with children—whether they be natural parents, adoptive parents, teachers, or childcare workers—is to recognize that these mental representations that underlie the child's attachment behavioural system have developed out of the many interactions the child has had, often with a range of caretakers, who displayed a range of functioning. Erratic, chaotic, irrational behaviour follows from the internalization of erratic, chaotic, irrational, and often aggression-tinged parenting.

Bowlby was emphatic that while these internal working models once formed are resistant to change, change is possible throughout one's lifetime. The move into an adoptive placement thus represents a most dramatic intervention. However, Bowlby gave expression to the challenge faced by these children and the mothers who adopt them:

> once a sequence of behaviour has become organized, it tends to persist and does so even if it has developed on non-functional lines and even in the absence of the external stimuli and/or the internal conditions on which it first depended. The precise form that any particular piece of behaviour takes and the sequence within which it is first organized are thus of the greatest consequence for its future. [Bowlby, 1973, p. 201]

Clinically relevant advances in attachment research

Two advances in attachment research are of particular significance for clinical work in adoption and foster care: the Adult Attachment Interview and the delineation of the Disorganized/Disoriented Pattern of Attachment in infancy as observed in the Strange-Situation paradigm.

The Adult Attachment Interview (AAI) outlines individual differences in how parents *represent* their childhood history (Main, Kaplan, & Cassidy, 1985). The goal is to elicit from the adults narratives about their childhood experiences that reveal their state of mind with regard to attachment. The quality of the childhood experiences and states of mind regarding attachment can be two very different entities—that is, it is not whether the childhood experiences were positive or filled with adversity but, rather, the evaluations of these experiences that are deemed vital. Main and her team of researchers found that they could correlate the parents' responses to the Adult Attachment Interview with their child's behaviour in the Strange Situation (see Main, Kaplan, & Cassidy, 1985; Steele, Steele, & Fonagy, 1996). It is remarkable that the two instruments—one focused on behaviour (in the infant), the other on linguistic qualities (in the adult)—could be connected to such a highly empirical degree.

The majority of (middle-class) parents observed by Main, Kaplan, and Cassidy (1985) were what they described as coherent or *secure–autonomous*. These parents were able to speak of both positive and negative features of childhood experience in a way that convincingly conveyed a valuing of attachment. These parents were those with the highest probability of having babies who responded to them in a secure manner at 1 year of age in the Ainsworth Strange Situation (Ainsworth, Blehar, Waters, & Wall, 1978). Other parents insisted they had difficulty in recalling childhood attachment experiences, showing a tendency towards defensive idealization of the past and leaving the listener/reader with an impression of neglect or rejection in their experience—stored implicitly but not readily available to awareness. These parents' state of mind with regard to attachment, termed *dismissing*, has been shown to be highly correlated with having babies who avoid them, move, or turn away in the reunion episodes of the Strange Situation (Ainsworth et al., 1978; Main, Kaplan, & Cassidy, 1985; Steele, Steele, & Fonagy, 1996; van IJzendoorn, 1995). A third classification, which also typifies some incoherent narratives provided in response to the AAI, are those said to have a *preoccupied* state of mind with regard to attachment. These interviews move astray by speaking too much about negative—often overly involving—aspects of the past that intrude on present functioning such that the speaker often seems highly angry, and their infants in the strange situation also seem angry or petulant, a pattern of infant attachment termed *insecure resistant* or *ambivalent* (Ainsworth et al., 1978; Van IJzendoorn, 1995). Another significant feature of Adult Attachment Interviews, especially those from clinical populations, suggests a lack of resolution of mourning of past losses or trauma. Parents who produce interview responses classified as "unresolved" have been shown to be prone to having infants who are disorganized in the Ainsworth strange situation (Main & Solomon, 1990), with one probable mechanism of influence being frightened or frightening behaviour by the caregiver towards the child (Main & Hesse, 1990; Schuengel, Bakermans-Kranenburg, & van IJzendoorn, 1999).

There is great interest in the AAI stemming from the robust predictions it has been shown to have with regard to infant patterns of attachment (Ainsworth et al., 1978), as these early patterns of relating have long-term associations to mental health in later childhood and beyond. For example, organized and secure infant–parent attachments are strongly associated with later development, including emotional regulation (Parke, Cassidy, Burks, Carson, & Boyum, 1992; Sroufe, 1990), ego resilience (Losel, Bender, & Blinsender, 2003), peer competence (Lieberman, Doyle, & Markiewicz, 1999; Youngblade & Belsky, 1990), altruistic behaviour (Zahn-Waxler & Smith, 1992), acquisition of social skills (Emde, Biringen, Clyman, & Oppenheim, 1991), development of morality (Park & Waters, 1989), cognitive growth (Sameroff & Emde, 1989), and academic success (Cowan, Powell, & Cowan, 1998).

Parents' AAI responses and infant–parent attachment have also been shown to link with verbal and nonverbal behaviours of school-aged children (aged 4–8 years) in a widely used and previously validated task, broadly known as the attachment story-completion task (e.g. Steele, Steele, et al., 2003). In this task children are presented with story beginnings or "story stems" depicting an attachment dilemma (e.g. what to do when you have hurt yourself as a result of engaging in behaviour that one's parent has prohibited) and asking the child to "show me and tell me what happens next". As with the AAI, researchers study the content and style of responses made by children in order to infer the relative accessibility in the child's mind of an attachment figure who can be counted on for support and understanding. A more direct spin-off of the AAI has been interview measures that ask parents to describe in detail their relationships with their children. In my own work with adoptive families (see below) we have used the AAI, a version of the story-stem task we call the Story Assessment Profile (Hodges, Steele, Hillman, & Henderson, 2003), and the Parent Development Interview (Aber, Slade, Berger, Bresgi, & Kaplan, 1985). Before detailing this work, it is useful to consider in some detail the phenomenon of attachment disorganization because this is almost invariably a part of the history of all children in care.

The creative and clinically relevant discovery of attachment disorganization came from observations that some of the infants being filmed in the original Strange Situation were showing odd behaviours that simply did not fit within the system for classifying attachment behaviour first articulated by Ainsworth and colleagues (1978). These children appeared not to have an organized strategy for dealing with the stresses the paradigm engendered, perhaps freezing or crying uncontrollably, and so were described as disorganized–disoriented (Main & Solomon, 1990). The infant displaying a disorganized pattern appeared to view the parent as frightening (Main & Hesse, 1990), suggesting the infant was uncertain of which behaviour would be appropriate in the presence of the parent. The attachment figure "is at once the source of and the solution to its alarm" (Main & Hesse, 1990, p. 163). The incidence of disorganization ranges from 13% to 87%, depending on levels of risk to the parent–child relationship—that is, child maltreatment or parental psychopathology not surprisingly dramatically increase the risk (Lyons-Ruth & Jacobvitz, 1999). Careful home observations of mothers and their infants were coded (Main & Hesse, 1990) for frightened or frightening behaviour in the United States and by Dutch colleagues Schuengel, Van IJzendoorn, Bakermans-Kranenburg, and Bloom (1999) who found correlations between maternal frightening behaviour and disorganized strategies in their infants. Karlen Lyons-Ruth and colleagues expanded the set of behaviours observed between mothers and babies to include maternal helpless or hostile behaviours. They found that extreme parental mis-attunement to infants' attachment-related communication and the display of competing caregiving strategies that both elicited and rejected infant attachment feelings and behaviours predicted disorganization in these infants (Lyons-Ruth & Jacobvitz, 1999). Features of what Lyons-Ruth describes as "parental affective communication errors" (Lyons-Ruth, Yelin, Melnick, & Atwood, 2003) include calling to the infant while physically backing away.

The other side of these communication errors can be seen in the child. In some cases children seem to develop a capacity to "mis-cue" their caregiver, giving signals that they are not in need of comfort or care, thereby making it unlikely that their caregiver will respond appropriately to their distress (Cooper, Hoffman, Powell, & Marvin, 2005). Children with problematic attachments frequently miscue their caregivers, masking their underlying attachment needs by looking away, moving away, or openly rejecting the parent. At the same time, these children's needs to explore and develop a genuine and joyful sense of autonomy are often compromised by their urgent and highly defended preoccupation with unmet attachment needs. The more insecure the dyad, the more intense is this cycle of miscuing and misunderstanding.

Special features of the child in foster care
and late adoptive placements

The research on insecure and disorganized patterns of infant–parent attachment and the observation of affective errors so often expressed by their parents, with mis-cuing by their children, is of special interest in terms of the parent–child relationship with children in care. Parents/carers of such children often remark on the similarly confusing behaviours they exhibit to their caregivers, such as conveying a sense of lack of interest or rejection of comfort, despite it seeming probable that such nurturing is also urgently needed.

Mary Dozier has researched the developing relationships between foster carers and the infants placed with them and has also highlighted features akin to the literature on miscuing (Dozier, Higley, Albus, & Nutter, 2002). Even following a disruption in care during the first 18 months of life, babies appear capable of organizing their behaviour around the availability of new caregivers. Dozier found that a baby can show attachment security with a foster carer, depending upon the foster carer's attachment state of mind as evidenced by a correlation between the carer's Adult Attachment Interview and the baby's Strange Situation classification. This research highlights how the foster parent who is autonomous and secure with respect to her own attachment history is better able to understand the child's need for defensive miscuing and is able to look gently beyond this rejection by the child and initiate a series of new interactive practices that serve to let the child know—perhaps for the first time in his life–that it is safe to express attachment needs. As the child learns through repeated interactions that there is now someone available to meet these needs, he begins to show proximity seeking and contact maintaining when distressed, and correspondingly discovers new energies for exploration of his environment.

Adoption as intervention

For these kinds of reasons, children do remarkably well in adoptive families relative to their earlier experiences (Brodzinsky, Smith, & Brodzinsky, 1998; HodgesSteele, Hillman, Henderson, & Kaniuk, 2003). The opportunity to grow up in an adoptive family provides a nurturing and reparative family experience, which can help to redress the impact of earlier adversity (Hodges & Tizard, 1989; Howe, 1998; PIU, 2000; Tizard & Hodges, 1978; Triseliotis & Russell, 1984). It has often been said that adoption offers children the most intense form of intervention that exists (O'Connor & Zeanah, 2003). As more children who show a high prevalence of emotional and behavioural difficulties as sequelae of their earlier maltreatment experiences are placed for adoption, there will be an increased need for services, including detailed assessments that can help parents and professionals address children's particular needs. It is against this background that we initiated a study looking at assessments of adopters of hard-to-place children and the children placed with them from an attachment perspective.

Attachment Representations and Adoption Outcome Study

The study,[1] conducted with Jeanne Kaniuk (Coram Family) and Jill Hodges (Great Ormond Street) represents one of the first to look at intergenerational patterns of attachment in non-biologically linked parents and children. The study highlighted the specific characteristics that each member of the parent–child dyad brings to this new and developing attachment relationship. The study was longitudinal in nature, so that the changes in the child, both in terms of his behaviour and his thoughts and feelings about attachment relationships, could be tracked over time, from the beginning of the adoptive placement to one and two years into the future. The main sample comprised 65 children who were "late-placed", between the ages of 4 and 8 years. Another group of 55 children comprised our "early-placed" comparison group placed before their first birthday, but who at the time of their first assessment were of identical age as the late-placed children. The study included the assessment of fathers alongside mothers. There are no studies to date that have addressed the important issue of how fathers may contribute to the attachment process for children whom they adopt. (For a detailed account of the findings to date from this study, please see Hodges, Steele, Hillman, & Henderson, 2003; Hodges, Steele, Hillman, Henderson, & Kaniuk, 2003; Hodges, Steele, Hillman, Henderson, & Kaniuk, 2005; Steele, Henderson, et al., 2006; Steele, Hodges, Kaniuk, Hillman, & Henderson, 2003.)

Selected findings

1. *Changes in children's story-stem responses*

    a. All children in the late-adopted group showed progressively more "secure" representations in their story-stem narratives across the two-year follow-up. However, alongside these secure representations there was also evidence that the negative representations (catastrophic fantasy, extreme aggression, bizarre/atypical responses) persist. This important finding highlights the way in which positive representations are formed, presumably reflecting the more positive caregiving the children are receiving in their adoptive homes, while the negative hard-to-extinguish representations continue to exist alongside the development of new representations (Hodges, Steele, Kaniuk, Hillman & Henderson, 2005).

b. Compared to the children who had been adopted within the first 12 months of their lives, the late-adopted, maltreated group showed more of the negative themes (avoidance and disorganization). The difference between the two groups, especially in terms of themes of extreme aggression and bizarre/atypical responses, did not diminish over the two-year period. (Hodges, Steele, Kaniuk, Hillman & Henderson, 2005).

2. *Adult Attachment Interview results*

a. In the distribution of Adult Attachment Interview classifications of the adoptive parents, there was a higher proportion who were Secure (72%) as compared to the typical population of 56%. This is important in terms of it highlighting good practice among the Coram Family social workers in their assessment. There were, however, 18% who were Dismissing and 10% who were classified as Unresolved with regard to loss/trauma, which has implications for post-adoption support (Steele, Hodges, et al., 2003).

b. Children placed with mothers *or fathers* who were classified Secure on their Adult Attachment Interviews were most likely to show reduction in their negative story stems across the two-year follow-up period as contrasted to children placed with parents one of whom was classified Insecure or Unresolved (Steele, Hodges, et al., 2003).

3. *Experience of Parent Development Interview*

This interview (Aber et al., 1985), modelled after the AAI, focused on the present representations of the new relationship with the child.

a. Mothers who provided Adult Attachment Interview narratives that were classified as Unresolved with regard to loss/trauma were less likely to express positive responses when discussing their newly adopted child and expressed, instead, more negativity, despair, and lack of satisfaction with the placement (Steele, Henderson, et al., 2006).

b. Mothers who responded to the Parent Development Interview with themes of despair and lacking in satisfaction with the adoptive placement were more likely to have children respond to the story-stem assessments portraying child aggressiveness and parents placed in a child-like position (Steele et al., 2006).

Conclusion

It is clear that an attachment framework, based both on John Bowlby's theoretical formulations and the extensive and impressive empirical data underpinning our current understanding of attachment relationships, has much to offer those working with looked-after children. Access to training in the state-of-the-art assessment measures cited above is becoming more and more feasible with, for example, several trainings a year in the United Kingdom of the Story Stem Assessment Profile (Hodges, Steele, Hillman, & Henderson, 2003) and training on the AAI also being conducted worldwide. Clearly, not all practitioners will have access to such specialized training. However, familiarity with the empirical findings emerging from studies using these measures offers new understanding of the complex nature of the forming of new attachment relationships, especially complicated in the worlds of fostered and adopted children. Knowledge of the many features that the coding systems have highlighted as differentiating groups of early- versus late-placed children, for example, may ultimately prove very valuable in the matching of adopters to children in care. The attachment framework and assessments described in this chapter have also begun to highlight the process of the building-up of attachment representations in the children as they embark on these new relationships. Moving to the level of clinical interventions will surely become the next vista where an attachment framework has the unique capacity to serve as a secure base from which to proceed.

Note

1. The Attachment Representations and Adoption Outcome Study was generously funded by the Glasshouse and Tedworth Trusts of the Sainsbury Family Trusts.

CHAPTER 4

The uses of a neuroscientific perspective

Graham Music

In the last decade neuroscience and developmental research have-
provided convincing evidence about the impact of early experience
on later development, and in particular of the impact of trauma
and neglect on the developing brains of young children. This has become a powerful explanatory tool to be used alongside other bodies
of thought, such as attachment theory and both psychoanalytic and
systemic therapy, to make sense of the plight of many children who
have been adopted or fostered and their families. We now have neuroscientific explanations for why such children provide such a huge
challenge to their carers and the systems around them, for why all too
commonly we see in these children symptoms such as aggressive and
self-destructive behaviour, being impervious to ordinary affectionate
care, impulsiveness, the inability to regulate emotions, and the other
signs described all too clearly in this book.

Much has changed since the early days of psychoanalysis, when it
was believed that traumatic early experiences, such as of sexual abuse,
were repressed, leading to all manner of malevolent symptoms that
were cured by helping people to remember the traumatic episodes.
We have since discovered that cure and changing symptoms are not so
simple, and that the basic explanations used in those days were somewhat off the mark. In particular, our understanding of the fine details
of how early experience affects children is much more advanced, as is

43

our understanding of how certain experiences affect different parts of the brain. More is now known about how different areas of the brain link up, and how some brain functions may be more to the fore at different points in a child's life. We know now, for example, that levels of stress in a mother as early as pregnancy affect the unborn child (Field, 2004), and that the stress hormone, *cortisol*, released by pregnant mothers, will cross the placenta and impact on the developing foetus. We know that infants who have consistent and attuned caregiving develop the ability to "self-regulate", whereas experiences of either neglect or trauma might not be consciously remembered but will affect not only behaviours and attitudes, but also the very structure of the brain as well as the *HPA axis*, a central part of the neuroendocrine system that controls reactions to stress, particularly through the releases of hormones. This is a system that humans share with many organisms from way back in evolutionary history.

The human is born with literally billions of neurons, but at birth the connections between the neurons, neuronal pathways, and synaptic connections are not formed. Such pathways will take different shapes, according to the kind of early experiences one has. Neurons that are unused, that do not form pathways that a child's experience deems useful, are "pruned" and wither away. Schwartz (2002) quotes a figure of 20 billion synapses pruned every day between childhood and early adolescence; he says that like "bus routes with no customers, they go out of business".

Experience is filtered through ready-formed pathways, just as water will naturally flow down already formed channels. Once an expectation is formed, it remains, and the world is experienced according to such preconceptions: children expecting to find the world terrifying will have a terrifying experience of the world. The phrase "cells that fire together wire together" has been described as Hebb's law, after the ideas of the neuroscientist (Hebb, 1949). Hebb's law describes the process whereby particular neuronal pathways form at the expense of other potential pathways and become standard ways by which one expects an experience to follow another experience if they have previously gone together. If the presence of adults triggers either fear or dissociative processes, as it does in many fostered and adopted children, then these children's fear responses will, in all likelihood, also be triggered with other more benign adults, such as adoptive parents. The human brain, and particularly the infant brain, is malleable to an extent. Schore has described this as the "neuroplasticity" of the human brain. The period from last trimester of pregnancy through to the second year of life is very crucial, although thankfully some plasticity remains throughout the lifespan.

Particularly important is our understanding of the different kinds of memories that we have and how these affect us. To simplify matters, we can divide memory into two basic kinds. One is often called *declarative* or *explicit memory* and is concerned with memories of facts and events that can be explicitly recalled and spoken about. Consciously recalling a date or name would fall into this category, as would remembering the details of ill-treatment at the hands of a parent and the kind of memories of traumatic events that Freud had initially suggested that we help people to recall. The other kind of memory is generally called *procedural* or *implicit memory*. This is a kind of knowledge that includes "how we do" things: both skills such as riding a bike or playing an instrument, and also memories of how relationships are likely to go, based on previous experience. More often than not these are the kind of memories we are faced with in a therapeutic session, and of which carers can often receive the impact. For example, the child who expects violence or abuse might scornfully push away a kind gesture by a carer, an expectation based on an earlier and not necessarily conscious memory of an abusive carer.

Research has shown that by about 6 months of age children of depressed mothers act in a depressed way even with non-depressed, attuned adults (Pickens & Field, 1993). Such expectations of how relationships are likely to go are based on procedural memories and can also be described in other ways, such as Bowlby's idea of "internal working models", and Stern's (1985) concept of RIGS (Representations of Interactions Generalized). In psychoanalysis a transference might be seen as just such an expectation of how relationships are likely to pan out, being based on what can be called "internal object relations". Such preconceptions of how relationships are likely to unfold are not conscious but are based in procedural memory, as if inscribed viscerally in our central nervous systems. The child who expects no parental care may not cry out when hurt; the child who expects violence and abuse may well be hyper-alert and jumpy, irrespective of who he is with; the abused child who re-enacts sexual acts, or the violent victim of violence, is often enacting procedurally that which he cannot consciously recall. The brain circuits to do with violent reactivity will be to the fore in such violent children, and those to do with self-regulation and processing emotional experience might be little used and not available.

Adopters and foster carers often struggle to understand why they are treated with such suspicion and disdain by the children in their care, or why they are lied to, stolen from, not entrusted with intimacy and private thoughts, all of which are likely to be based on behavioural patterns and expectations laid down in procedural memory but far outside consciousness.

Not only do, for example, infants of depressed mothers act differently from other infants, but it has also been found that their brains are organized differently from other children (Beebe & Lachman, 2002), and such research has important implications. Children who are fostered and adopted have often had extreme experiences of abuse, trauma, and neglect, and some writers, such as Perry et al. (1995) and Schore (2003), have shown how their brains are different as a result of their experiences, in that some areas are more developed and others less so. We now have strong evidence for how this happens. Many interested in neuroscience (e.g. Pally, 2000; Schore, 2003; Siegel, 1999) have shown that the human brain is "experience-dependent", which means that it develops differently depending on what kind of experience it receives.

Schore and others have pointed out that it is primarily the more primitive parts of the brain that are most active in infancy. He stresses the importance of the early months and years of life, when huge developments are taking place in the right side of the brain. The right side of the brain can be seen as the seat of emotional processing, along with other elements of the limbic system. The part of the brain that deals with logic and thinking, the left brain and parts of the cortex, are in evolutionary terms relatively new and are, in fact, not "on-line" to a great extent in the first couple of years, when many vital neuronal pathways and synaptic connections are forming. Similarly, the part of the brain that contextualizes explicit or declarative memories, the hippocampus, is also not active in the first year or so of life. In other words, massive developments are taking place before the human mind is able to consciously remember actual events.

These early years are vital. Just as the rat pup that is licked by its mother will cope better with stress as it gets older, so a parent's good emotional and physical contact with its infant is an inoculatory factor in its growing up. With loving contact all manner of helpful and calming chemicals, opiates, and hormones are released in both mother and infant. Schore argues that in this process the right brain of the mother is in communication with the right brain of the infant, and this connectedness is forming the synaptic connections and neuronal pathways. When early experience is of trauma or neglect, then quite different chemicals are released. Blood pressure is higher, the stress hormone cortisol is released, as is adrenalin, heart rates are increased, and these high stress levels can become the infant's natural way of being. A small almond-shaped part of the brain called the *amygdala* is vital in such processes; it is the organ that responds to fear and is very ancient in evolutionary terms, being present in pre-mammalian creatures. From our primordial history we are primed to be alert to danger and to respond in microseconds to any threat. The amygdala is the organ involved in this process. The kind of startle response we all might have to a loud noise might be an example of the amygdala in action. Infants and children subjected to trauma might have an amygdala on constant hyper-alert. Perry (e.g. Perry et al., 1995) has taught us a great deal about the impact of trauma on brain development, and he has written of how such children can barely relax at all, are frequently constantly "on the move", and are often given a diagnosis of ADHD. Such children seem to see and suspect danger where other children might sense none. When working with such children it is often hard to work out what the trigger is to some sudden outburst or switch in mood or lashing out—behaviour that often leaves a carer feeling helpless and desperate, not to say hurt, rejected, angry, and bewildered.

Such behaviours are often based on procedural memory, which is more likely to be linked to the amygdala, as well as other more primitive parts of the nervous system, such as the basal ganglia. The other memory system, declarative or explicit memory, is more linked with the hippocampus, which is barely active in the first year or so of life. The kind of hyper-alertness that we so often see in the kind of children described in this book is one typical procedurally based response to stress and trauma, and it can also be described physiologically in terms of a heightened sympathetic nervous system. Such children are not able to regulate their own emotions and need help in what Greenspan (1997) has called "down-regulating". This inability to regulate and process emotions is common in those children who are diagnosed as "disorganized" in attachment terms, and this group makes up a large sample of children who are fostered and adopted. Emotional regulation in an infant, child, or adult does not, of course, just happen. At birth an infant can more or less regulate things like its body temperature, breathing, or heartbeat, but it requires another person, usually the mother, to regulate its emotions. Slowly over time the kind of early care received becomes the basis for self-regulation and so becomes a crucial factor in forming the personality. Traumatized children who have a heightened sympathetic nervous system might be said to be struggling to manage their emotional climates as best they can. However, what starts out as a natural response to a stressful situation can become an impediment to ordinary everyday living. The constantly hyper-alert bodily response might be compared to those over-zealous soldiers still fighting an enemy years after the war is over.

There is an opposite response by the nervous system to stress and trauma, an activation of what is called the *parasympathetic nervous system*. When the parasympathetic nervous system is activated, the body goes in the opposite direction and closes down, rather like a creature playing dead in front of a predator. Blood pressure becomes very low, as does the heart rate, and the mind goes into a kind of "shut-down". This is another common response to serious trauma and can also give rise to physiological and emotional responses that can form the basis of the personality long after the original traumatic incidents have finished. In fact, the left side of the brain—the bit of the brain that specializes in logical thought, conscious memory, and such—can often shut down when faced with trauma. At such times the survival mechanisms of the right brain take over. This is why many victims of trauma cannot consciously remember what happened to them. It is not that the memories were suppressed so much as that the part of the brain that would do the remembering has been shut down. This gives rise to the phenomenon of *dissociation*, in which people can seem to be cut off from their own experiences. It might be another explanation for why many of the children we are thinking about in this book do not achieve much academically. They have learnt to cope either by being hyper-alert to danger, which impedes ordinary relaxed concentration, or by going into a shut-down dissociative mode in which the thinking part of the brain becomes inactive. Such processes can also, of course, be described in terms of the basic survival responses of fight/flight and freezing, seen in so many mammals. As described earlier, in trauma the left brain can shut down, while the links between the left and right hemispheres are less strong. Indeed, trauma victims have been shown to have a smaller *corpus callosum*, the part of the brain that joins the left and right hemispheres, as well as having an enlarged amygdala, and there is some evidence that their hippocampus can atrophy as a result of exposure to trauma.

As well as trauma, severe neglect can also lead to atrophy in certain parts of the brain, leading to severe developmental delay and serious deficits in the ability to empathize, to regulate emotions, and consequents deficits in the capacity to manage intimacy and ordinary social interaction. Studies of extreme cases of deprivation, such as children adopted from Romanian orphanages who were terribly neglected (e.g. Rutter, 1998), have shown the impact of such early deprivation not only on the behaviours of the children, but on their actual brains as well. Much research (e.g. Dozier, Stovall, Albus, & Bates, 2001) seems to be converging to demonstrate that children who are adopted very early—particularly in the first year to 18 months—have a far better prognosis than those adopted later.

This might all sound rather gloomy, and, indeed, when working with such children, we have good reason not to be overly optimistic. We know that the behavioural patterns that are established early can be very difficult to shift and that once an experience is burnt into the circuits of the amygdala, it is there forever. It is useful to caution against simplistic notions that a good dose of love is all such children need to help them back into society's mainstream. There are other worrying preconceptions that similarly need to be banished, such as that "it is best to just forget about the past", as well as the idea that children have to be made to consciously learn about their past as a way of letting it go—a kind of enforced therapy and mourning. Both are dangerous, as we must always bear in mind the dreadful experiences such children have suffered, yet, similarly, we must never force a child to face a factual truth about his life before he is emotionally ready to do so. This is a subtle and complicated process, and these children and the professionals around them often need specialist and experienced help to begin to get them back "on track".

However, change is possible, if it is sometimes the result of slow and painstaking work. One way this can happen is through therapeutic work, and, indeed, Joseph LeDoux (1998) has argued that therapy is

> another way of creating synaptic potentiation in brain pathways that control the amygdala. The amygdala's emotional memories are indelibly burned into its circuits. The best we can do is to regulate their expression. And the way we do this is by getting the cortex to control the amygdala.

As described before, the amygdala is the seat of our primitive fear responses and reacts in a fraction of a second to any perceived danger. Experiences will often be filtered straight to the amygdala via the thalamus. However, there is a slightly longer route whereby experience is filtered via the thalamus to the cortex, which is the thinking, more cognitive bit of the brain. Thus the "direct route" can be mediated by benign new experiences. For example, a loud noise might cause an initial startle in a war veteran who then allows himself to become aware that the noise was simply a carpenter hammering next door, and he then relaxes. Therapeutic work can enhance such processes, building up the capacity to interpret experience in new and less frightening ways, and this is but one way in which change can take place. Other by-products of therapeutic work are likely to include a better link between left and right brain (a better-functioning corpus callosum), better thinking capacities, greater ability to form a coherent narrative about oneself and to regulate one's emotional life, an enhanced ability to tolerate dependency and difficult emotions without acting out, as well as the ability, of course, to form and manage attachments better in general.

What is hopeful about the neuroscientific evidence is that change is certainly possible throughout the lifespan. We might never erase the old experiences and their related brain circuits, but we can build new experiences, new expectations, new circuits in the brain. There are, of course, some important "windows of opportunity" when major developments take place and the brain is changing rapidly. Particularly important are the first few years of life, and also later adolescence, when the brain is similarly growing and changing. However many clinicians, professionals, and carers have facilitated and borne witness to genuine change and development in the personality of these children, and many chapters in this volume, while often using a different language, demonstrate just such developments.

CHAPTER 5

The role of psychiatric assessment and diagnosis

Caroline Lindsey

The work of a specialist multidisciplinary CAMHS team assessing and treating looked-after and adopted children necessitates in almost all cases consideration of whether a diagnosable mental health disorder is present, especially given present knowledge that suggests that this is so for almost 50% of looked-after children (Meltzer et al., 2003). The well-known, strongly expressed antagonism to the making of diagnoses is based on a belief that damage is done to children by the process of labelling and a fear of the stigma associated with mental illness. However, the dangers of disadvantaging children and young people, their parents and carers, and the professional network by the failure to recognize a significant mental health problem outweighs these concerns. There is therefore a clear role for a child and adolescent psychiatrist in participating in the diagnostic assessment process undertaken by the multidisciplinary team. In addition to the significant level of mental health difficulties in this group of looked-after and adopted children, they also are more likely to have physical disorders, including epilepsy, speech and language disorders, developmental delays due to both organic and environmental factors, such as enuresis, conditions such as foetal alcohol syndrome, and other forms of learning difficulties (Meltzer et al., 2003). There is, therefore, an additional role for the psychiatrist in identifying physical health problems and referring young people, if needed, for investigation and further assessment by a paediatrician or, where appropriate, for a psychological assessment.

The process of diagnosis

The diagnostic process requires a full assessment of all aspects of the child's functioning, including the presence of a psychiatric disorder, developmental status, intellectual level, medical conditions, psycho-social adversity, and of their adaptive functioning, which is how far the problems interfere with everyday life. Making a diagnosis in this fullest sense, which allows a formulation of the child's difficulties to be articulated, enables the clinician to say something to the family about what is known concerning the causation, prognosis, and effective treatments of the problem. It is crucial that the diagnosis is set within the context of everything that is known about the child, since otherwise it will make no sense to the family and other involved professionals. This means taking the birth and current family situation into account as well as the experiences of adversity that the child may have gone through. However, many of the common conditions that affect children who have been in the care system have similar symptoms. It is not always possible easily to disentangle the effect of severe trauma, deprivation, abuse, and neglect on the child's mental state. In this regard, it is important to mention the complex area of attachment difficulties (see Steele, chapter 3) which often coexist with serious psychiatric conditions, but which may sometimes be accorded a diagnosis of an attachment disorder in their own right.

It is important for the families of these children to have information concerning a possible diagnosis, since it may offer them an explanation for the child's behaviour or mood and may guide both professionals and carers to intervene appropriately to help them. It may enable parents and schools to be more realistic about their expectations of the child and support the application for additional resources to help the child through the identification of their special educational needs, known as the "statementing" process.

There are two systems of multi-axial diagnostic classification in use, which are very similar in most aspects: the International Classification of Diseases, ICD-10 (WHO, 1993) and the Diagnostic and Statistical Manual, DSM-IV-TR (APA, 2000). There are three main diagnostic groupings: emotional disorders, disruptive behaviour disorders, and developmental disorders, as well as other, less common conditions.

Often children have more than one condition, known as co-morbidity: for example, many of the young people we see may have coexisting Attention-Deficit Hyperactivity Disorder (ADHD) with conduct disorder and with depression. We frequently see children with symptoms of anxiety and depression, who may have suicidal ideation. Many abused children suffer from post-traumatic stress disorders: the flashbacks they experience give rise to a range of disturbed behaviours, which are difficult to understand without the knowledge of the condition. They may also present with eating disorders and self-harming behaviours. Severe relationship difficulties need to be distinguished: whether they arise from disturbing early life experiences, which have profoundly affected the capacity to trust and relate, resulting in attachment difficulties, or whether they arise in the context of one or more disorders, including autistic spectrum disorders and depression, which can, of course, coexist.

The child's mental health problems inevitably impact on family and parental functioning, sometimes to a severe degree. Parents, often mothers who may have the key caretaking role, may develop depression or physical symptoms. Both parents may find themselves responding to their child's challenging behaviour and rages in uncharacteristically angry and uncontrolled ways, resulting in escalating episodes of conflict. These states of mind affect, in turn, the capacity to parent effectively and may induce further experience of despair, fear, and insecurity in the child. Substitute carers, who have had childhood experiences of abuse, may find that these are re-evoked in unexpected ways, which makes them psychologically vulnerable when looking after abused and neglected children. Parents in all these situations may need help in their own right.

Monitoring outcomes

All CAMHS are now expected to audit their outcomes, which requires the use of tools that will identify the mental health of the young person on referral and subsequently. The Tavistock Clinic is part of the CAMHS Outcome Research Consortium (CORC), which is developing a model of outcome evaluation. It currently uses the Strengths and Difficulties Questionnaire (given to parents, children over the age of 11 and teachers to complete) (www.sdqinfo.com), the Child Global Assessment Scale (completed by practitioners), and the Experience of Service Questionnaire (CHI-ESQ, given to children over 9 and their parents). Another scale for use by clinicians is the Health of the Nation Outcome Scales (HoNOSCA), and there are other tools for assessing specific conditions, such as the Conners Rating Scale for ADHD and the Moods and Feelings Questionnaire for depression. These audit processes are not yet sufficiently sophisticated to capture the complexity of the difficulties experienced by many children and young people seen in the team. In addition, in common with all other CAMHS, there are difficulties in getting families to complete follow-up questionnaires. Nevertheless, they are helpful in beginning to characterize the children seen, from a diagnostic perspective, in assessing the extent to which their functioning is being impaired by their disorder, and in monitoring progress and outcome, where these data are available.

The role of heredity

One frequently asked question concerns the hereditability of psychiatric disorders suffered by the birth parents. In addition, the general intellectual functioning of many of these birth parents is often at the lower end of the average range, and learning disability is not uncommon. There is no automatic transmission of any of these traits to any one individual child, but as a group they are at high risk. Disorders that are genetically transmitted include bipolar disorder, autistic spectrum disorders including Asperger's syndrome, and severe hyperactivity/ADHD (hyperkinetic syndrome). If both parents suffer from schizophrenia, the chances that the child will inherit it are 50%. It is important to note that antisocial disorders and alcohol and drug dependency are also not only socially determined. On the other hand, milder hyperactivity/ADHD often has a socially determined component, and is common in children who have spent a period in care (Roy, Rutter, & Pickles, 2000) as well as in severely deprived adoptees (O'Connor, Rutter, and the English and Romanian Adoptee Study Team, 2000). Bohman and Sigvardsson (1980) looked at the adolescent outcomes of children who had been adopted before the age of 2. Although genetic factors influence children's outcomes, the greater part of poor outcomes may be prevented by ensuring a good upbringing, even in children of high-risk parents. It is therefore important for new carers and parents as well as clinicians to get as much information as possible on the birth parents' psychiatric and criminal history. Since the majority of permanently placed children are from high-risk backgrounds, they will be especially sensitive to both their original and their new family environment. In order to maximize good outcomes for the child and not expose the child to further risk, the new parents need to become particularly skilled in managing their child's behaviour.

Psycho-active medication

The use of psycho-active medication as treatment for some of the diagnosed disorders in this population is, like the diagnosis itself, a subject of controversy at times. A limited number of medications that have been shown to be beneficial are available for use for children and young people. As with all drug treatments, some have side effects, which may be significant. The young people's problems are complex. Medication can make a contribution to an improvement, alongside psychological, social, and educational interventions. It may be necessary to have a trial of medication in order to explore what difference, if any, it makes. This may be especially important when parents and young people are experiencing great difficulties. Leaving severely disturbed young people untreated may create such a strain on the placement that it is at risk of breakdown.

The conditions that we tend to see and for which medication is offered and is effective are ADHD, depression, and psychotic states.

The stimulant, methylphenidate, in various preparations, short- and long-acting, is the treatment of choice for marked or severe (hyperkinesis) ADHD. Treatment with methylphenidate should not be used in children under the age of 6. It should be used only after a thorough assessment which has looked at the child in home and school settings. Strategies for behavioural management need to be introduced, which attempt to help the child to focus and attend in school, both before treatment begins and afterwards, in order to maximize the beneficial effects resulting from the medication. Once the right dose is found, if the diagnosis is correct, the effect is obvious (Taylor, Dopfner, & Sergeant, 2004). There is a reduction in restlessness, an increase in concentration and capacity to work, and an increase in thoughtfulness, with less impulsiveness. As far as we know, it does not have any harmful long-term effects, although it may cause weight loss and growth retardation, which must be carefully monitored. When methylphenidate does not appear to work, in the context of a clear diagnosis, there is a range of alternative medications to be considered, including atomoxetine, recently approved by the National Institute for Health and Clinical Excellence (NICE, 2006). In the children and young people whom we tend to see, ADHD is often only part of the picture, often complicated by the presence of anxiety and severe behavioural difficulties. Apart from providing help with parental and teacher management strategies, psychotherapeutic work should be offered alongside the medication.

Psychological treatments are the first choice for depression unless it is very severe at the outset. But the use of antidepressants is advocated by the recent NICE clinical guideline (NICE, 2005) if, after three months, there has been no improvement in moderate to severe depression in young people over the age of 12 years. Only fluoxetine (Prozac) is recognized as a medication for depression in young people. Use of other preparations needs to be discussed with child and adolescent psychiatrists. The guidance is clear that medication must only be given in conjunction with psychological therapies. In addition to support for cognitive behaviour therapy (CBT), interpersonal therapy, and brief family therapy approaches, NICE refers to the evidence arising from research conducted at the Tavistock Clinic and elsewhere, which showed effectiveness for both systemic family therapy and individual child psychotherapy (Tsiantis et al., 2005).

A proportion of the young people whom we see present with serious mental illness, sometimes complicated by alcohol and substance misuse. In early and mid-adolescence, it is not always possible to be confident about a diagnosis such as schizophrenia, and a very careful assessment, sometimes necessitating an inpatient admission, is required. Where the diagnosis seems likely, the newer antipsychotic drugs tend to be used in psychoses such as schizophrenia because they often have fewer unpleasant side effects, which make patients more likely to take them. Nevertheless, there are still concerns about the risk from these drugs of substantial weight gain, metabolic disorders, and movement disorders in the long term. Despite these risks, the effect of these illnesses is so severe that the use of medication, with monitoring, is often necessary to reduce symptoms such as delusions and to improve social functioning. Again, as in the case of other psychiatric disorders described, it is always important to offer close therapeutic and social support and therapy where it is possible, alongside the use of medication.

There are also exceptional circumstances where a traumatized young person shows such a degree of psychological disturbance and challenging behaviour, with a risk of harm to self and others, that there may be a case for considering the use of one of the major antipsychotic tranquilizers such as risperidone. This may, together with other interventions, enable the situation to be contained (Reyes, Buitelaar, Toren, Augustyns, & Eerdekens, 2006).

Decision making about the use of medication requires the full involvement of parents, children, and young people. There is a great deal of information available to support this process, as well as parent support groups (www.medicines.org.uk).

Conclusion

In working with children and young people who are fostered, adopted, and in kinship care, it is useful to take a "both/and" position as opposed to an "either/or" stance in relation to the use of diagnosis and psycho-active medication. The "both/and" position permits the possibility of providing both psychotherapeutic approaches and psychiatric perspectives to assessment and treatment for young people and their families.

CHAPTER 6

Psychological assessment of looked-after children

Rita Harris & Sally Hodges

Whereas placements are being considered for children, or indeed when the functioning of a child in care is a cause for concern, the multidisciplinary team will often turn to the psychologist for a view about this. This chapter briefly outlines the range of assessments that are undertaken by psychologists and underlines the importance of drawing together information about the child from different sources and perspectives. The field of psychological assessment is wide. This chapter draws attention to the complexities involved in the process of assessment rather than providing a detailed account of the assessment tools used.

Both clinical and educational psychologists are trained to undertake psychological assessments. The main difference between them is that educational psychologists tend to focus on the child in an educational setting (although they do always take into account a child's background or home environment), whereas clinical psychologists are trained in understanding emotional, learning, and behavioural experience across the age range, through childhood to adulthood and old age. Clinical psychologists who work with looked-after children tend to specialize in this area through further training and clinical experience, as is the case with the psychologists attached to the Tavistock Clinic Fostering and Adoption team.

When is a psychological assessment considered?

In the Tavistock Clinic, we would consider carrying out a psychological assessment under many circumstances. Perhaps a child is under-achieving in school, or appears to be struggling with a particular aspect of the curriculum, such as arithmetic or reading, or has problems with the ability to attend and concentrate, which may fluctuate. Children's behaviour may be significantly unusual in certain environments, or they may demonstrate behavioural difficulties, such as aggression or extreme anxiety, in some situations. They may show marked social and communication difficulties or be overly affectionate with strangers.

Psychological assessments aim to complement the wider multidisciplinary assessment. We would consider the psychologist's findings alongside those of other team members, in order to get as complete a "picture" of the child's needs and strengths as possible at the time of assessment, taking into account that functioning is also dependent on environment.

What is a psychological assessment?

Often psychological assessments are equated with cognitive or attainment tests, where a child's intelligent quotient (IQ) is given as a score and his abilities are given in terms of ages (such as a reading age or writing age). However, psychologists are trained in a much wider range of assessments, and part of the psychologist's task is to decide which kind of test or assessment would be most helpful in the understanding of the child's presentation and functioning.

Cognitive and attainment tests are, of course, a core tool in psychological assessments. These are tests that have been standardized, so that it is possible to give a child's results as an "age-related norm"—a score that tells us where a child is in direct comparison to their peer group. Among the best-known of these assessment tools are the Wechler Scales, which are regularly updated with age-related norms for many different cultures and countries. The most up-to-date UK edition is the fourth edition, which consists of 15 subtests that explore a wide range of a child's cognitive abilities, such as memory, processing speed, verbal comprehension skills, and visual perceptual skills, among other skills.

There are other kinds of attainment tests that look at specific areas of functioning, such as reading or writing ability, memory functioning, visual coordination, and so on. Psychologists normally first carry out a more general assessment to understand a child's profile of strengths and weaknesses. Then specific assessments are used to explore further those areas that have been highlighted in the main assessment. Sometimes these assessments address specific "presenting difficulties" or areas of psychological difficulties, such as attention, social, and communication difficulties, concerns about a possible diagnosis of depression, anxiety, or autism, or perhaps specific difficulties such as problems with executive functioning (forward planning and organizational skills).

With pre-school children, psychologists are able to draw on a range of developmental assessments, which again are standardized, but assess a wider range of developmental abilities, such as motor and fine motor development, alongside cognitive development.

The Tavistock Clinic's psychologists are also trained to carry out projective assessments. Projective "tests" are assessment tools that explore emotional functioning and profiles, so rather than focusing on problem areas, they explore the full range of a person's preoccupations, fantasies, and experience of relationships with significant others. Projective assessments utilize ambiguous stimuli, such as picture cards, drawings, or stories that allow children to "project" aspects of their functioning and their experience of relating to others. They are not "tests" as such, as they do not have right or wrong answers, but they can give very helpful pointers or directions for further exploration. Projective assessments are difficult to implement and analyse. Psychologists need much practice and supervision when learning to use this kind of assessment. The skill in using projective assessments is in the analysis, in the close observation of the child's behaviour, and in the understanding and awareness of the child's relationship to the psychologist in the assessment situation. The absence of certain behaviours is also important information—for example, when a child avoids talking about the parental figures in drawings or becomes incoherent when describing a picture that depicts aggressive or potentially violent behaviour. This kind of assessment can give enormously helpful information when completed in conjunction with other assessments, as they give some understanding of the emotional processes that can lead to difficulties in functioning and vice versa. For example, projective assessments may highlight anxiety about failure or about being negatively judged, which may help an understanding of why a child might easily give up in the cognitive assessment. It is also well established that emotional difficulties can lead to cognitive difficulties, and the two areas of functioning have a complex and interdependent relationship (Hodges, 2003; Sinason, 1992). Assessing as fully as possible a child's psychological functioning will give the multidisciplinary team the best chance of helping the often vulnerable children and their adoptive or foster families.

Emma

Emma was a 5-year-old child referred to the Fostering and Adoption team at the Tavistock Clinic. She had been born prematurely to a substance-using teenage mother and was quickly placed for adoption. Following two stable foster placements, she was finally placed for adoption at the age of 2½ years. At the time of placement, she had a number of physical difficulties, including poor fine and gross motor control, and she was viewed as having learning difficulties, particularly in relation to absorbing new information and developing social relationships. With the care and attention of her new family, over time, her physical difficulties receded, but her apparent learning and social difficulties did not. When she was 5 years old, we were asked to assess Emma and her family and, if necessary, help them to engage with the appropriate education services. Emma was assessed using both cognitive and projective tests. What we found was that she was a child who, despite indications to the contrary, was in fact of higher-than-average ability for her age across all the areas assessed. However, what also emerged was that her limitations appeared to be linked to her social communication and emotional difficulties. These had resulted in a degree of controlling behaviour with which, once it was understood, her family and school were able to work. The assessment demonstrated that she had a high anxiety level and a powerful drive to control others and to "be in charge". This explanation was helpful to the family and school, as it was possible to shift the emphasis of support and treatment from her cognitive functioning to her emotional and social difficulties. A treatment plan that focused on these areas was put in place, and Emma's learning difficulties gradually improved.

Psychological assessment relies heavily on the skills of the assessor, and observational skills are critical—observation not just of the child's behaviour, but also of how the child makes the psychologist feel and behave, that is, the ability to observe the impact of the child on oneself.

A psychologist's tools are not just the assessment materials, but their own contribution and skill in the assessment process, which can make the difference between a helpful assessment and one that does not reflect a full understanding of the child.

The use of psychological assessment with fostered and adopted children

There is frequent concern expressed by both professionals and families about the cognitive functioning of children referred to our team. While it is common for children whom we see to have reached their physical milestones within the average time-frame, they often underachieve at school and present as having learning difficulties. It is not unusual for teachers to report these children as being isolated, distracted, and lacking in confidence. In this situation, we try to understand how much of the child's difficulties are organic, due to brain damage, and how much they are emotionally disturbed, and how this is impacting on their learning capacity. It can also be the case that children are of normal intelligence but have missed large amounts of schooling. In our experience, being able to offer parents an understanding that their adoptive children do not have permanent organic damage or that their behaviour is not evidence of a learning disability can help them refocus on the emotional issues involved in their children's difficulties. Poor school performance can often be a distraction from what are complicated emotional difficulties and a poor fit between carer and child expectations of interpersonal relationships. Children who have lived with several different carers may arrive at an adoptive family with little expectation that their new family will properly commit to them. This may be in sharp contrast to the expectations of adoptive carers, who enter the relationship with the strong hope that the child will develop a sense of belonging. In this context, children and carers have the potential to be disappointed and confused by each others' behaviour. Being able to consider and perhaps explain some of a child's difficulties in functioning in terms of their early life experiences can make the difference between a successful and a failing placement.

Conclusion

This chapter concerns the psychological assessment of a particularly complex group of children and young people. The early and often repeated trauma through multiple placements may make it difficult to understand the patterns and interrelatedness of their difficulties. The emotional well-being of children or young persons impacts on their ability to concentrate and learn. For their carers and teachers, the behaviour of these children can be frustrating and difficult to understand, hence compounding their sense of isolation and poor confidence. Psychological assessments can play an immensely valuable role in helping those caring for and working with these children and young people to understand their strengths and their very real limitations, at particular times and in particular contexts.

We feel that detailed and well-considered psychological assessments are a critical component in the wider assessment provided by the multidisciplinary team. Psychological assessments, together with information gathered by seeing the family as a whole and the child individually for a psychotherapeutic assessment, help in the understanding of a child's presentation, which, in turn, makes it easier to plan for their needs, both at home and at school.

PART **II**

PSYCHOTHERAPEUTIC WORK
WITH CHILDREN

Since the work described by Boston and Szur (1983) and the research of Boston and Lush (1994), the Tavistock Clinic has promoted the importance of working with children in transition, both for their own well-being and development and to ensure, as far as possible, the permanence of placements.

Jenny Kenrick describes particular problems for looked-after children before they have been permanently placed and also some aspects of their characteristics of personality. She discusses technical problems of working with the children at the interface between their internal and external realities.

Sally Hodges provides a different model for work with children in transition. She describes the value of using cognitive behaviour therapy with children in order to help them develop self-regulation following severe trauma. She details the model and gives examples of its application.

Juliet Hopkins' chapter focuses on the disorganized/controlling attachment pattern as seen in the psychotherapy of two late-adopted children. Caught in experiences of "fright without solution", they show long-standing resistance to forming new attachments. Hopkins suggests reasons why this may be and shows how, as the children developed more positive attachments to their therapists, so their attachments to their adoptive parents grew. She also touches on what can often seem to be an imponderable problem: why children appear to remain so attached to "bad objects" in their early relationships. (For other views see Steele, chapter 3, and Music, chapter 4).

Margaret Rustin discusses the difficulties for looked-after and adopted children in establishing a sense of belonging and of identity. When this process has to take place after disruptions of continuity of care and separations in the child's early life, the task is more complex—especially, as she shows, for the adolescent. Her clinical illustrations evoke the intimacy of the therapeutic relationship and show how the therapist uses her countertransference to inform and to develop the work with the child. Rustin describes the development of a sense of identity and belonging for the individual, but it is also useful to refer to Barratt (chapter 12), who describes the development of belonging in a family.

Jenny Kenrick

CHAPTER 7

Work with children in transition

Jenny Kenrick

Ryan

When I go to collect 6-year-old Ryan from the waiting-room, I am struck by a picture of a boy in a real transition. He is sitting next to his social worker, surrounded by a pile of luggage. When he sees me, Ryan picks up a duffel bag, which he drags along the corridors to the therapy room. Having arrived in the room, he tips up the bag, and his toys spill out onto the floor—first some soft toys, and then cars and games. I feel that he is showing me his most precious possessions, all that he has at this moment. He hands me one of his soft toys—I find I am glad to hold onto its softness at this poign-ant moment. Ryan starts to play with his cars, telling me about the ones that are his best. Gradually I talk to him about how he seems to be carrying his luggage with him today; that I know he has come from one foster home and is moving to another after he has seen me. He tells me that he liked where he was, it was quiet there. He pauses and seems to reflect. I say that it sounds as if it was a place he liked to be, and it was perhaps quite hard to leave. He nods in agreement.

But thinking any more about loss and his feelings about his situa-tion quickly becomes too difficult. He finds that his spectacle case is empty. "Where are they?" The idea of loss cannot be thought

67

about. Action follows as he runs from the room back to the social worker. He seems fearful that he has lost her too. I explain this anxiety to her, and she is immediately in touch with Ryan's feelings. Ryan is able to return to his therapy session.

I start this chapter with a description of a very particular moment in a child's life. It provides an opportunity to bring into focus some of the specific problems for children who have not yet been placed in permanent alternative homes. It is also a useful description because it shows, albeit briefly, that for Ryan there is a social worker actively involved in the process of his life, one who knows and understands this little boy very well. Pre-eminently with children in Ryan's situation, the professional network of services needs to be working and thinking together in the interests of the children, for these are children whose earliest experiences may well not have been of a parent or parents who are able to come together in such a way as to think creatively about their child's needs. Their own unmet needs may have predominated over the consideration of the needs of the child—which was probably a reason for that child entering the local authority care system in the first place. I write as a child psychotherapist, working within the theoretical and conceptual basis described in chapter 2. I also write as a child psychotherapist in a multidisciplinary team. Individual work with a particular child will only be one part of the work for that child. Although a central message of this book is to show how professionals from different disciplines and theoretical positions come to work together, I intend here to think about some of the characteristics of children in transitional care—characteristics that apply also to adopted children, who will largely come from the looked-after child population, especially now that the greater number of children being placed for adoption are older, not placed at birth. (Margaret Rustin develops some of these themes in chapter 10.)

With children in transitional placements, moving through the care system, often with many moves through different foster or institutional care homes, each with its own different culture, one is constantly working at an interface. The one that I am most concerned with in this chapter is the interface between the child's inner world and his external experience. The inner world is built up from internalized interactive experience from the beginning of a child's life, felt by him to consist of real figures. But these are influenced by the child's own phantasies. What we see with many looked-after children is that in place of a more benign inner world—the sum of mainly benign care and interactive experience—their inner world may consist of cruel, abandoning figures. Real experience of abandonment and cruelty only serves to fix the phantasy. When a child's internal and external expectations are of negative care and experience, it is not difficult to see how complex systems of defences may build up. These can seriously affect what use a child may be able to make of different opportunities of care and why finding a good new family may still lead to failed and disruptive experiences for all concerned. His current interactions will be profoundly affected by the sense he has made of his earlier interactions. Too often a child may seem to be gripped, against his own best interests, by what Freud described as the repetition compulsion.

Some characteristics of looked-after children: Early adverse conditions and the impact of trauma

Children who are looked after on their way to some permanency of placement in adoptive, long-term foster, or residential homes will usually have been subjected to some level of early trauma. My definition of trauma at this point is of the impact of external events which impinge on the child and his development and on circumstances necessary for his development—examples could include assaults while still in the womb from the mother's drug or alcohol abuse; levels of physical or sexual abuse, perhaps from a very young age or over a considerable period of time; the impact on their minds as well as their bodies of being children of mentally ill parents. All involve the absence of thoughtful parental containment such as will lead to a proper capacity in the child to think thoughts and to make sense of his experience. Early experiences may carry a particularly persecutory quality in the present.

Ellie

Ellie, aged 10, was in long-term foster care. When she saw her foster mother walking in front of her holding her 3-year-old niece by the hand, Ellie's anger and distress overflowed. During an assessment, she was able to tell me of her memories of how, when she was very little, she used to walk down the street behind her drunken mother—there was no Mum available to hold her hand. It was at that moment, behind her foster mother, that the pain of the realization of what she had *not* had became unbearable.

Trauma can be extreme and may return in flashbacks. I think these moments often come when the child finds himself *alone* in the face of experience that he is unable to process for himself—that is, the crisis is both of the event revived and of the lack of containment, such that the child experiences a moment of "catastrophic anxiety" or "nameless dread", as they have been variously described.

Pat

An example from the psychotherapy of 10-year-old Pat in long-term foster care. At moments of intense anxiety in the child, her child psychotherapist found that she repeatedly had a picture in her own mind—a single frame of the child standing at a doorway looking into a white room. It was a powerful communication to the therapist, which we came to understand, over time, as a projection of a traumatic moment when the child was alone, unable to process her experience. This moment was when she saw her mother cut her father's throat. The room, in fact, was red with his blood.

We know from our work with the bereaved how quite often an image, perhaps of a loved one at the moment of death, may seem to intrude, to take over, and to make it impossible for a prolonged period of time to recover another and other memories of that person; to provide a balance to the fixed picture of the traumatic moment. So it can be for children fostered or adopted who have little or no experience of a containing mind with any continuity in their lives, to help mediate the impact on them of traumatic experience.

Lack of a sense of continuity of experience

This will be at an internal level and is likely to be reinforced by external factors to which I have referred earlier. I am thinking here about what the attachment theorists refer to as reflective self-functioning and the importance of the development of internal narratives of self, which add meaning to life. This is why, I feel, that the repeated and often very abrupt moves that children seem to have to make while in transitional placements become cumulatively so damaging. They are effectively traumatic and extremely prejudicial to the development of the child. I have written about this form of cumulative trauma elsewhere and at greater length (Kenrick, 2000).

Kris

A child, Kris, with whom I worked over a number of years, had had three such sudden moves about which I knew. One took place when he was 4: his foster father committed suicide, and Kris was immediately removed, thereby losing both a loving foster father and mother—she was too distressed to hold on to Kris' distress, and the new foster family to which he was removed knew little of him or what had happened. In that home he was later physically abused and removed immediately the abuse was disclosed. He was later in a short-term placement—one that did not expect too much of him but in which, I felt, his more negative and angry feelings became rather split off. They seemed to have become projected and lodged in the son of the family, who resented Kris and who one day hit out at him so badly Kris was kept off school to hide the bruises. Again he was removed abruptly, of course, for his own safety. But each time he was left confused and with his own more negative view of himself reinforced.

Unfortunately, in some cases social services departments are unable to provide continuity of workers. In many areas, staff shortages and current demoralization can too often lead to a child having frequent changes of social worker. Who, then, really holds his history, beyond the facts? How can a child, then, be helped to attach meaning to facts? Ryan, of whom I spoke earlier, was fortunate. His social worker was dedicated to remaining available to Ryan on his complex journey. She was an important aspect of his continuity of experience through the too-often repeated disruptions of his life.

The precarious and uncertain quality of experience

An example of play in a psychotherapy session of a 7-year-old boy demonstrates the quality of these factors.

Ricky

Ricky bursts in to the room, rushes to his box, flings things out behind him onto the floor, tears off his t-shirt, all with many an s___ and a b___. He takes out the scissors and puts them in his mouth. He takes them out again and says, "Where's the Sellotape?" I say that I expect it's in his box. It's not. He says it's gone. I take up the implication that he feels I haven't looked after it or kept it safe from the other children who come in the room (a major preoccupation of Ricky's). He is on the floor looking for it. He finds a loose thread of carpet and tears at it. He cuts it off with the scissors, rolls it up, and, tipping his head back, pours it into his mouth. I feel myself gagging from the dryness of the experience. He slowly pulls it out: "It's a snake." Then he spits it in the bin. I say that it seems as if he is spitting out something very nasty—the horrid, dry, stuck-in-his-throat snake. There is no time to explore further, as he leaps on the desk and then onto the windowsill—forbidden, as I remind him. He stands above me, swearing at me, and starts to spit at my face and on my hair. His face is screwed up with rage. I differentiate between the spitting *out* of the horrid feeling into the bin and the spitting of his angry feelings *at* me. "No", he says. "I'm still spitting out."

Later he moves to the sink and after throwing a handful of water over me—I talk to him about how I am to be the one who is to know what it feels like when something happens out of the blue, when you least expect it—he begins to play with the water. He takes out a small bucket and fills it with water. He dips his face in it, stands up, and shimmers with a delighted expression. "It's going down my back, down my trousers." He puts his hands in the water and looks almost in wonder at the lights and the bubbles in the water. "Look." I say I am looking. He looks at me to check that I am. Then he plunges his face in the water and starts to blow bubbles. He lifts up his face and then shrieks at the water. I comment on the two different moments: how he really seemed to be having fun with the bubbles, but it seemed hard to think it could last. The fun just seemed to change into shout and noise and be lost. He puts his head back in the water and blows some more bubbles.

In this extract from a not untypical session with Ricky we can see how profoundly he is all over the place, tied up in knots of undifferentiated feelings. Unable to feel that he has any certainty of finding what seems lost—out of sight, it is gone forever, or, more likely, I have let someone steal it. This is a more persecutory aspect of his anxiety. I struggle to hold on to something that he hears, and he is then able to make his own contribution: "No, I'm still spitting out." It's a thought, not just an action, a behaviour like most of what had happened in the session up until then. Then later he settles and begins to play. It can even begin to be fun, and an experience he can explore—the different things he begins to do with the water. But the noisy shout, like an uprising of an internal perturbation, threatens to spoil it. It is hard for him to hold on to a good experience for very long at a time.

Many of the children we see do not have the capacity to develop meanings through creative play, but they may become increasingly resentful, cynical, despairing, and even apparently hardened in their hedonism in the face of the repeated disruption of what attachments they may, precariously, have held.

Use of projection and projective identification

Often our main access to any understanding of the emotions of such children may be through our own feelings—carer or therapist—while we are with them. As far as we can, we need to explore within ourselves what a child is projecting into us. Then we need to seek to establish what in this feeling comes from within ourselves and what seems to be a communication from the child.

Sid

The therapist of 12-year-old Sid had moments of sheer terror in sessions. After kicking or spitting at her for a time, Sid would come quietly up behind her and touch the back of her neck or her bottom. She would feel paralysed, for a moment unable to respond, the frozen potential victim. She learned from exploration of these moments how Sid really wanted her to know what it feels like to be the helpless victim, unable to resist the sexual assault that had so often in his early life come on him from behind. Equally chilling for her was when the assault became more violent, following what seemed to be more gentle interactions between them. She really was in projective identification with a sadistically intruded-into child.

In Sid's case, the therapist felt changed within herself by the experience in the therapy room with him. She was not normally a frozen victim. This was a case of projective identification. She was the recipient of the communication and was able to work over the experience in her mind and to begin to be able to talk to Sid about it. Often, like the crying baby signalling its distress to its carer, the projections will be less powerful, even of a more benign state of mind. However, carers who have looked-after children frequently find themselves irritated or enraged or saddened by behaviours of children. And that may be the point. It is the rage or the sadness which lies behind or fuels the behaviour that the child needs someone to know about; or he needs to evacuate these feelings into another in order to be rid of them in himself—the child who may leave an adult impotent with rage while he leaves the room smiling, literally without the original feeling any more. It is lodged in someone else. Where the strength of feeling cannot be processed, we have to remember that some children seem to be remorseless in projection of violent and furious feelings, rage felt in the carer may erupt, and a cycle of violence may follow in which the adult can become the actual abuser. When the carer is feeling overwhelmed, a pause to explore to whom the feelings really belong may help to prevent or to limit enactment. Hence the need for foster carers to receive a level of support in their work with very difficult and disturbed children (see Emanuel, chapter 18). I feel very strongly that foster carers and also residential workers are in an invidious position, because as employees of the local authority they may feel that their status and job will be jeopardized if they are open about the difficulties they encounter with a particular child. But, on the contrary in my view, honest laying-out of these difficulties should only be helpful to gaining greater understanding of a child and thus making a real contribution to his care.

What's wrong with me?

Children like those described above are often left feeling "what's wrong with me?" "What did I do that made all this happen to me?" This can be a particular concern for those children who are the only children of their families to be placed in the care system and out of their families. Research by Quinton, Rushton, Dance, and Mayes in *Joining New Families* (1998), has provided evidence of this.

Sammy

Sammy, aged 8, born as a result of his mother's brief liaison with a very violent man, was the only one of her children she felt she could not manage; he was too like his father. In his therapy, he constantly felt that I was about to reach my "that's it" point and that I would eject him forever, in order to take on a new baby/patient whom I would really love. In fact, Sammy, for all his irritating habits and destructiveness, was a most endearing child. Over time, he felt that he did have a place with me. He stuck a paper with "Sammy's Room" on it on the window; he now felt he had an exclusive place, both in the sessions with me and in his foster home. He had laid claim to both, and he felt more secure from that position to repel all potential borders from outside. But he could have remained stuck with feelings of grievance, so hard to shift when there is a basis for them in reality.

Destructive, hateful, contemptuous relationship with mothers — longing for an exclusive and intimate relationship

It was work with some adopted children that particularly highlighted for me problems that many of these children have in developing secure maternal relationships. It can seem that the rage and despair that are left with them as a result of what is unquestionably abandonment, often compounded by abuse or neglect by their birth mothers, can continue unabated in children as they attempt to develop new relationships. Attachment is contemptuously turned away from: "You're not my birth mother." . . . "You never had a baby." . . . "You're stupid." Parents can become divided from one another. Mothers hated can feel hate towards a child, and many adoptions are close to breakdown when referred to mental health services. I think these difficulties are present for children before they are permanently placed but may only emerge more floridly and viciously when a child is permanently and potentially more securely placed. Then the early idealizations of placement break down. Because life in foster care may be so uncertain and precarious, carers may only have flashes of this contempt and hatred. But sometimes they will be the recipients of the projected feeling, and I think this can be an explanation for some foster-care placement breakdowns. The carer does not feel able to really like or to warm to the child.

Contempt can also mark a longing for more exclusive and close relationships. It also deflects from the pain of the disastrous quality of the relationships.

Jane

Jane, aged 7, whom I recently saw in an assessment, attacked and repelled her foster mother. But she showed me in her play with the toy kangaroos that when mother and baby became separated, they could only look at each other through impenetrable glass. They would never be able to reach each other. "It's very sad", she said. Indeed it was; the longing was intense and could begin to be thought about with Jane. At the same time that Jane was longing for intimacy, she was also terrified of it.

This is true of many of the children we see in psychotherapy who, as they experience a development of a more trusting and closer relationship, may seem impelled to destroy it. For some of them, intimacy has inevitably led, in the past, to inappropriate sexual relations. They cannot, without help, differentiate such experience from the possibility of more enduring and deeper relationships.

One can see these difficulties as a contribution of splitting processes, which are part of early and of normal development for children. However, with some children in transitional placements the splitting process is maintained long after those splits would have become more integrated for children in more ordinary family situations.

Jeb

For 8-year-old Jeb, who had spent five years shuffled between different foster placements, the one apparent certainty that he held on to among many confusions was that his mother had wanted to keep him with her, but he had been taken from her by social services, and she was still trying to get him back. The fact that she had neglected him, often leaving him alone for many hours, was no fact for Jeb, at least consciously. However, his anger was directed onto different foster mothers who, he said, never gave him enough food, or even the food that he liked, and were too busy with the other foster children. He was projecting into them the anger that somewhere within himself he felt against his birth mother for her neglect. Jeb's anger and resentment made him a difficult child for his current foster carer to look after or to like very much. Effectively, Jeb was maintaining a split between his idealized birth mother and the denigrated foster mother to whom he was very contemptuous.

Defensive processes

We all make use of defences for our survival. Some children need more of them to survive than do others. Those who live in a hostile environment, or who are afflicted by severe mental disorders, may need them more than most. Neurologists are charting the impact on the development of the brain of certain responses (e.g. Perry et al., 1995), which can, in turn, mean that over time a particular trigger will lead to a particular behavioural response. A classic example is the observation of how the individual may respond to traumatic threat by either fight/flight or freeze responses.

One response that we observe frequently with children who have had actual experiences of abandonment, abuse, and neglect can be a flight from thinking. Some will take flight into delinquent or destructive behaviours (acting out; literally, here, putting out their states of mind into their environment). Others may show hyperactive states. Some, of course, suffer genuine ADHD states. But for others the hyperactivity can be fuelled by and defensive against acute states of anxiety. I gave an example at the beginning of this chapter, when Ryan encountered thoughts and feelings of loss and fled from the room. Later in the session he started to attack both me and the fabric of the room, so that no further real thought was possible for either him or me. This is an example of what Henry (1974) called "double deprivation": when a child who is already deprived deprives himself still further by cutting himself off from the possibility of more positive experiences and relationships (e.g. with his therapists or carers). If an aspect of thinking is about making and holding links in mind between people, events and various levels of things—what we might call being open to making sense of things or to understanding—then many children we see seem actively to attack these links. The attack, in essence, is an attack on the first coming together of the creative link between the parental couple. Some children feel, most sadly, that there never was such a creative link for them. Ellie, referred to above, knew her mother was a prostitute and she could not name, nor was it known, who her father had been. This was a source of real depression and negative identification for her.

Tom

Cutting links in his mind was a problem for Tom. He was a "good" boy, placed, with his brother, with a view to adoption. He did not cause too much trouble in his new family. He seemed to fit in, but in a rather chameleon-like way. The family brought him for therapy because the foster mother found that he evoked in her a level of rage that she had previously not experienced (i.e. the projection into her was of a quality that seemed to change her, thus being a projective identification). It emerged that Tom had complex feelings about his birth family and the abandonment of himself and his brother, while other children remained in the family. "If you don't think about it, you don't have feelings." But he cut off, projected into his foster mother, the rage that he feared would break up his world, as it seemed it might have done earlier. When his feelings had a place in his therapy, he could begin to think about his birth family and to mourn its loss. He began to realize he could have two families. Then he could begin to attach himself to his prospective permanent family in a more real and less adhesive way—he became much more alive in himself, albeit as a rather stroppy adolescent. Tom also demonstrated the problem for many children of having many families in mind (see Rustin, chapter 10).

Children do not only have to relate internally and to make sense of birth and subsequent foster families in fact and in phantasy, but with increasing emphasis on contact they may have regular, if intermittent, actual meetings with some or all of the key figures in their lives. This can, of course, can be enormously helpful to some children, though it is always a complex process to negotiate. For some children, perpetuating contact can be quite abusive: being made to have contact with those who had abused them. They may need to be helped not to have actual contact. This must always be a complicated decision, unless the needs of the child can be of paramount importance over the needs of parents. Although that is both desirable and obvious, it may not be easy when faced with very needy parents.

Working with the defences of children who may need them more than do many others is a delicate balance to achieve. We need to approach the defences with respect and care. As therapists, carers, social workers, we have to carry the irresolvable ethical dilemma: do we ultimately help, or do we leave a child more vulnerable, if we begin to open him up to the real pain of his existence? When we see a child so caught up in defensive behaviours as to prevent him making use of his talents, of his thinking mind, or accessing new experiences, whatever we may wish for him, we can only proceed at his pace, with what he can bear. But, at the same time, we have a responsibility not to fail to notice those moments when a child begins to take a courageous new step forward: when omnipotence begins to become potency; when the child can begin to feel he has made some impact on his carer or therapist, who may be made glad or sad because of him. Often we do miss that moment of shift because it is so minimal at first, or because we, like the child, are risking becoming fixed in our expectations of what might be possible.

Some children remain very hard to get through to, and they seem unable, even with help, to reach out towards thought or change. For some children, it can seem that what they know is preferable, however catastrophic, to what is not known. That can be the balance they seem, fearfully, to choose to hold on to. Yet some children show resilience and courage against all the odds in the face of continuing difficulties which can be quite inspirational to those who have direct contact with them. I think of some of the children who, after many moves of care placement, seem to retain some hope that leaves them to attempt, yet again, to form a new attachment.

For children in transition, the move to permanency can be the time when there can be an implosion or explosion of aspects of the child which are already known about, as well as of those which may be less clear—as, for example, the contempt of maternal figures. I think this may be one of the reasons that these moves often seem to be negotiated at great speed. The network may fear that if the child has too much time to think, he might turn down a really good chance of a permanent new family. This can be true for children who may have had so many moves of placement already that they may have become deeply cynical about the idea of the often-called "forever family". For them it can seem that nothing is forever. Forever is when things break down. The time of negotiating is one of another interface: transitional/permanent. If the move can take place with time and thought given to all involved, it can help a new placement to start off with more chance of success. The family the child is leaving also need special consideration. It is helpful if all involved in the child's network can work collaboratively at such a time. Another factor that is emerging as important in research from Coram Family is that for new families and for children where there is less emphasis on an expectation of an instant adhesive attachment on placement, real attachments can grow at their own pace and may lead to more securely based new placements that have a better chance of permanency.

Some therapeutic and technical considerations

It used to be accepted wisdom that children could not start psychotherapy until they were living in a permanent and supportive family environment. Practice has shifted, partly because of increasing understanding of the needs of the children before they have stability of placement. The request, not just for therapeutic assessment of the children, but to provide therapy on a longer-term basis can, to my mind, be reasonable. Therapeutic provision can offer a child some means of escaping the rigid grip of defences and acting-out behaviours which can lead to continuing breakdown of placements. Many children are able to engage in contact with someone who seems able to understand the impact of their rage and despair and to continue to bring a thoughtful mind to the child's emotional predicaments and dilemmas. Children are often referred for therapeutic help because their destructive and aggressive attacks make it difficult for any carers to hold on to them. Over time in therapy it is often the despair, at times of suicidal proportions, that can be the most difficult aspect of these children to have to sustain in the work. To do that requires strength, resilience, and courage on the part of both child and worker. Until this process is under way, it may not be possible for a child, deprived and abused, to begin to differentiate rage from what may be the more justifiable outrage at the events and feelings about the past. Only then may a child begin to develop a new relationship to that past. Then, less burdened, he can begin to reach out to take advantage of new opportunities. Although the Adoption and Children Act is laudable in aiming to move children more rapidly through the care system to the permanence of adoption, I think it does not allow for a core of children whose far from "ordinary" experiences have been so damaging to their development that without considerable help they will only be adopted at extreme risk both to themselves and to their new families.

Hunter (1993) reported on a group of children in care with whom she had worked before they were permanently placed. She found that the average length of psychotherapy treatment she was able to offer them was one-and-a-half years—time enough for a considerable amount of work to take place.

One aspect of the children's lives with which we are well able to work is *uncertainty*. Neither they nor we know what or when the next move will be, nor for how long we can work together. There can often be uncertainty about whether a child will be brought for sessions on a regular basis. Transport and escort arrangements can be difficult to establish and maintain. However, I think we should seek to establish as much certainty as is possible with a supporting network at the outset of therapeutic work. As well as practical arrangements, the anxieties of some in the network about what psychotherapeutic work involves must be respected, and some of the myths which may persist about psychotherapy must be addressed. Many believe that it involves only a raking-up and confronting of actual events of the past, whereas it is about that subtle interface as encountered in the present interactions of the therapeutic relationship.

The main tool of the child psychotherapist is working and thinking as the session unfolds with the transference and countertransference: that is, understanding the inner world from the present relationship of the child with the therapist. Some children have, as I have suggested above, great difficulty in experiencing the intimacy involved in such a relationship. The therapist has to watch most carefully over the "temperature" of a session. Was it because, as with Ryan at the moment of his encounter with feelings of loss, there was a moment of longed-for emotional intimacy that proved unbearable and that made him run from the room? Was it a moment such as psychoanalyst Wilfred Bion describes (1959) when "the patient feels he is being allowed an opportunity of which he has hitherto been cheated; the poignancy of his deprivation is thereby rendered more acute and so are feelings of resentment at the deprivation"?

A concomitant of the need to monitor closely what one's patient is able to explore emotionally in today's session or in a specific part of the session is the need to think carefully about both timing and wording of what the therapist says in the sessions. A particular way of wording a thought or interpretation could be taken as criticism by the child and would instantly increase levels of persecutory anxiety. With a particularly vulnerable child it might be more appropriate to move very gradually to the transference interpretation. It may be preferable initially to describe what is happening in the child's play—in the transitional area of play. That is to say, there may be a description or observation of how the baby pigs are being attacked by the lions. Then it may be possible to comment on the fierce and terrifying feelings while this is happening. That may be as much as a particular child can manage. But a language of emotions is being developed. It can be possible, through use of the therapist's countertransference, to describe and even to explore prevailing states of mind, such as an overwhelming feeling of sadness that does not seem commensurate with the action of the play.

While the analytically trained child psychotherapist will have both transference and countertransference in mind, the work of Betty Joseph (1989) and Anne Alvarez (1992), among others, has helped us to see that it can be more useful for the therapist to hold the projections from the child within herself—to be the container who explores those feelings in herself (Bion) and can use them to understand the child, while still describing them to the child in herself. In other words, it can be more important, sometimes over a considerable period of time, not to return the projection to the patient as belonging to him too quickly, otherwise there as a risk of increasing the persecutory anxiety and thus of the recourse to non-thinking defences. One has to know one's patient. But one is also faced with dilemmas about interpreting too late, missing an opportunity for development, or too soon, risking losing one's patient. This can seem complex, and it is. It is good to be reminded by Hoxter (1983), writing with simply expressed profundity:

> the "thinking" [about the child] . . . does not require to be intellectu-
> ally demanding, it entails rather the capacity to bear experiencing
> the child's feelings and one's own accompanying feelings until they
> have undergone a process of internal modulation, enabling the adult
> to make a response in keeping with what the child has communi-
> cated, rather than a reaction directed by the adult's own emotions.

One of the tasks of working with looked-after children is to help them to differentiate one feeling from another. All children are at times over-whelmed by the strength of their feelings. If this can seem a usual state for a child most of the time, if outbursts of feeling can actually risk the loss of all they have—their present foster home, for example—children may initially be alarmed at sorting out their feelings. A better-known state of confusion and of feeling less may seem preferable. But over time, and with the experience that expression of feelings can lead towards understanding, a child can ultimately feel less fearful, even less "mad".

Joanne

Joanne, 10 years old, was relieved when she realized that she could feel angry with her foster mother, who did not accompany her to her session because she was attending a review on another foster child. She found she could know the anger and find that it would not destroy the foster mother, who would be—and was—at home for her when she returned from her session.

An issue that frequently arises is one of confidentiality of the child's material from their psychotherapy sessions. Some parameters are set by Child Protection procedures and can be supportive to workers, in that there are times when information must be shared. There is a duty on all of us of care for the child. Now that child psychotherapists are involving themselves more in the external world of their child patients by attending reviews or writing court reports, there is a need to be extremely respectful of what emerges with a child in the course of the therapeutic session. The child psychotherapist is in what can be a unique position in being able to represent the views of the child at a profound level. This may help a professional network to hold on to the real wishes and feelings of the child when planning for him, without being deflected by others' agendas. Some children, when they are honestly informed of this role, can really value it. It can show them that adults can come together thoughtfully in their interest. They can be pleased that their therapist takes time to talk to their teacher. Some may, of course, still be too ill, too damaged, or suffering too much from persecutory states of mind to appreciate this. We have to move out into the external world of the child with care, carrying a particular responsibility, as we do, for more knowledge of his complex inner world. We are truly working at an interface.

CHAPTER 8

Cognitive behaviour therapy

Sally Hodges

T his chapter outlines the basic principles of cognitive behaviour therapy (CBT) and how CBT can be adapted for children who have been fostered or adopted and their families. Children are usually placed into care either because their families of origin have decided that they cannot parent them or, more commonly, because outside agencies have concerns about the quality of care provided to them. Children who are looked after by others have, by definition, experienced trauma. This trauma has often been considerable and over a long period of time. Looked-after children can present a very real challenge for psychological treatment. They are likely to have undergone multiple traumas such as emotional or physical abuse and then the loss of their family and home (even though relationships may have been difficult) and often multiple placements. They can be extremely emotionally damaged by their difficult life experiences and sometimes also by the subsequent events related to moving into care.

CBT is a task-focused, time-limited, and collaborative approach to treatment. It might be considered that the deep-seated and complex damage often seen in fostered and adopted children does not indicate short-term highly structured treatment. It might be argued even that CBT could not offer much more than a "sticking-plaster" approach. CBT is a treatment that offers a gradual and staged approach to a child's difficulties, some degree of control and partnership in treatment sessions, and treatment that focuses on the child's priorities and anxieties and can impact on aspects of the core damage caused by abusive life experiences. Because it is a time-limited treatment, it can be provided when the long-term placement has yet to be finalized and further uprooting may be unavoidable. The containing structure of CBT can also be helpful in the early stages of adoption, when traumatized children may find it very difficult to settle and the placement is jeopardized owing to their presenting difficulties. For these reasons the CBT approach must be given merit in work with fostered and adopted children. The very ethos of CBT is that it focuses on the child's own priorities, anxieties, and preoccupations, working in partnership with the therapist, in order to develop a set of skills that can be drawn on in times of distress. This allows for a greater sense of ownership, control, and agency in the child's treatment. For these reasons, CBT with fostered and adopted children and their families can provide a meaningful, realistic, and helpful approach to managing their difficulties.

The use of CBT with children is a relatively young field, especially compared to the field of CBT for adults, and there is a dearth of knowledge about how to apply cognitive–behavioural treatments to fostered and adopted children. This chapter explores the literature that relates to this developing area and considers how to make use of CBT theories with this client group.

The development of cognitive behaviour therapy

The term cognitive behaviour therapy is used to describe a wide range of therapeutic approaches from behavioural treatments to cognitive therapy and many treatments that encompass aspects of both. Contemporary CBT draws on a range of cognitive and behavioural theories and approaches. It has come a long way from its more behavioural origins dating back to the 1920s (Watson & Raynor, 1920). At this time learning theory suggested that behavioural change could be achieved by providing variations of rewards and punishment (positive and negative reinforcement), with little regard for involving the patient in their treatment. The cognitive aspect of CBT owes its origin mostly to the work of Aaron T. Beck in the 1970s (Beck, 1976). Beck was influenced by the growing understanding of the role of cognitive mediation in learning (e.g. Bandura's social learning theory, 1977). This work seriously challenged the presumption that behaviour and emotions could be changed purely through behavioural treatment.

Cognitive treatments quickly became popular, as they allowed for the patient to have a sense of involvement and active engagement in their treatment.

Beck's cognitive therapy was initially developed for adult mental health difficulties such as anxiety, depression, and anger. Beck's treatment was verbally sophisticated and required the capacity to self-report, motivation to engage, as well as the capacity to understand complex ideas and relationships.

Since Beck's early work, as many as 17 variations of cognitive therapy and CBT have been developed. The range of client groups to whom CBT is applied has also widened considerably: CBT has been developed to address difficulties across the age span and across intelligence levels, and it has been refined to work with children and adolescents (e.g. Friedberg & McClure, 2002; Reinecke, Dattilio, & Freeman, 2003) and with people with learning disabilities (Stenfert Kroese, Dagnam, & Loumidis, 1997).

Most contemporary CBT draws on elements of both cognitive and behavioural treatments, though the term CBT is also rather typically loosely used to include purely cognitive treatments. It has also been used to include elements of cognitive reframing, thought stopping, positive imagery, problem solving, psycho-education, coping skills training, relaxation training, and graded exposure. This chapter focuses on the CBT that has evolved from the work of Beck (1976) and Ellis (1962), where cognitive restructuring is the central component of treatment.

What is cognitive behaviour therapy?

In essence, the theory of CBT is that psychological distress arises from, and is connected with, unhelpful, dysfunctional, or distorted cognitions—thoughts—as well as images and perceptions. That is to say, it is not distressing events in themselves, but the meaning that the patient attaches to them, that causes the difficulties. This perspective does not negate that dreadful events can, and do, happen to people, but that how they perceive them can either exacerbate or reduce their psychological distress in relation to the event. The treatment aims to improve psychological well-being by teaching more adaptive thinking strategies and systematically practising these (*cognitive restructuring*).

Cognitive distortions arise from core negative self-attributions or beliefs that generate *negative automatic thoughts* (NATs)—for example, the thought "Jane (foster mother) did not smile at me when I came in from school so she must not like me" (automatic thought), can follow on very quickly from "I am a bad person and therefore unlovable" (cognitive distortion). It is considered that automatic thoughts occur unbidden and lead to a range of cognitive distortions, which, in turn, lead to negative emotion (thinking that I am not liked leads on to depression and anxiety), and a cycle is set up whereby feelings reinforce thoughts and vice versa. Typical cognitive distortions or thinking errors include: all-or-nothing thinking (you are either clever or not; I'm not clever, therefore I must be stupid), jumping to erroneous conclusions, mind-reading (she did not smile at me, so she thinks I'm not worth knowing), and labelling one's self rather than one's behaviour. The aim of treatment is to help the patient to challenge these thinking patterns, in part through behavioural evidence, but also to identify the core negative beliefs and then to develop more healthy thinking patterns and strategies.

Patients are taught that emotions, cognitions, behavioural responses, and physiological responses are all connected. They learn that how one interprets or thinks about both the event but also the physiological experiences that accompany an event (such as sweating and rapid breathing) impact on how one feels about the situation and then, in turn, on how similar events are interpreted in the future. The core aim of CBT is that patients are taught to recognize their thinking patterns and, with this, their typical cognitive distortions. They learn to develop effective cognitive *challenges* or learn to make alternative *inferences* from events. This can be done through cognitive and behavioural *experiments* and *homework tasks*. Alongside this work, patients are taught methods for managing their physiological symptoms, such as breathing and relaxation exercises.

As stated, CBT is a relatively short-term, structured treatment. Typically, the child will be taught the principles behind CBT and then be encouraged to talk through distressing situations, initially with the therapist. As the child's understanding and competency increases, he will be encouraged to record events at home and, eventually, to "self-treat". The treatment is focused on the patient's self-perceived difficulties (i.e. at the start of treatment the problems as seen by the patient are listed and then placed in a hierarchy), so engagement in the work tends to be high, and, on the whole, patients are motivated to engage. This is not to minimize the less conscious feelings patients have about change and the possible meanings of symptoms. Cognitive therapists remain mindful of the impact of their relationship with the patients and of the impact of unconscious processes, but their primary focus is to work with the problems as directly and overtly presented by the patient. Therefore, CBT tends to empower patients, and the problem-orientated treatment "makes sense" to the patient, increasing compliance.

A typical CBT session will include the following:

1. setting an agenda for the session;

2. talking together about aspects of CBT theory, to enable a development of the awareness of the importance of underlying beliefs in determining thoughts;

3. time spent on developing the understanding of the relationship between child's thoughts, physiological experiences of distress, and behaviour;

4. reviewing the child's diary or talking about his week, looking at themes in his thinking patterns to identify negative automatic thoughts;

5. developing thought challenges or alternative thoughts;

6. practising challenges through playing, talking, and role play;

7. developing homework tasks based on developing strategies from the previous week and the content of the current session.

In order to consider the application of CBT, it is helpful to look at brief clinical examples.

Anita

Anita, who is 11 years old, is living in foster care with a couple and their two older girls (age 14 and 16). She had been placed in foster care while a permanent placement is sought for her. Anita's mother's partner sexually abused Anita over a period of several years. Anita's mother refused to believe any allegation she made, choosing to remain with her partner in the face of compelling evidence that abuse had taken place.

Anita is a quiet, thoughtful child, who initially appeared to have settled into her foster placement, getting on well with the older girls. However, her foster carers have asked for her to receive some input as she has recently become increasingly irritable and demanding, and they feel that this is out of character. When meeting with Anita, she did not identify her behaviour as a problem, but she wanted to talk about her difficulties in getting to sleep at night. She described how she had been suffering sleeping difficulties and anxiety attacks at night.

Through a CBT approach, Anita has been exploring her thoughts around her night time fears. Perhaps not surprisingly, it became apparent that night time noises around the house were making her anxious and distressed. Her fears were explored in depth. Hearing a noise at night would make her heart beat faster, and this would make her feel that there was something wrong with her, which, in turn, increased her somatic symptoms of anxiety. Anita was able to keep a diary of the situations that lead to anxiety (lying in bed at night) and immediate antecedents (hearing people walking around downstairs). She was able to recognize the thoughts that were going through her mind in such situations, such as, "I'm not really safe, Brian could still come and find me." Anita was able to see the link between her perception of noise and her fear, and her somatic experiences and her cognitions, but she struggled with identifying her core negative beliefs until the therapist used a less threatening medium of a recent story line in a soap opera, where a child had been abused by a family member. Anita was able to talk about how the child in the programme had been thinking, and she commented that the child in the soap opera should have just told her abuser to go away. We reflected on how the child was in a vulnerable position and the abuser was in a position of power, but she still struggled, saying that if the child had been firmer, it would never have happened. She was then able to make a link between her own situation and the TV programme. It became more apparent to Anita that she saw herself to blame for her situation, and eventually she was able to say clearly that, at heart, she believed that it was her fault that she was abused as she had not said "no". One of her core negative beliefs related to her experience of feeling that she was to blame for her situation, which led to her high anxiety level: "It was my fault, therefore it will happen to me again." Anita was then able to develop some cognitive challenges to her intrusive thoughts, through looking at evidence for her beliefs. These were easier to generate when considering the child in the soap, for example: "She is only a child, how could she stop him?" "Her behaviour did not encourage his abuse." Anita was able to develop cognitive challenges to her core negative beliefs that eased her distress at night.

Aaron

Aaron is an 8-year-old boy whose parents are both long-term drug and alcohol abusers. Social services have been working with the family over the last four years to try to improve Aaron's and his younger brother's, Mark's, experiences. However, after extensive work, the children are still presenting at school very often late, dirty, unkempt, and hungry. Aaron and Mark have been placed in foster care while an intensive parenting assessment takes place.

Aaron has been very angry. He deeply misses his parents and has been quite oppositional with his foster carers, destroying their property and being quite verbally abusive. He was offered 10 sessions of CBT. Initially he used the session to express his anger, but when asked how he wanted to change in his life, he was able to generate a hierarchy (get back home, help my Mum, get social services off our backs, get into the school football team). Using this as a basis for the work, Aaron was asked to focus on the aim "get social services off our backs". We were able generate lists of why social services might be worried about Aaron (and Mark), and he was able to self-generate some alternative thoughts from "they just want to make life difficult" to "they are doing their jobs; I don't like it, but if no one looked out for children, children who really need help might never get it". Gradually his anger ratings decreased from 9 out of 10 to 4 out of 10. He was also able to think about his anger towards his foster carers. He was able to identify thoughts about how he felt he would be disloyal to his own parents if he liked them, and that if he became happier, it would be used as evidence that he was unhappy at home. Aaron was able to think about his experiences, and while he refused to keep a diary, he was prepared to allow his foster mother to come into the beginnings of sessions, so that they could both describe difficult incidents between them over the previous week. CBT did not remove Aaron's anger but gave him the skills to think about different perspectives or challenges to his angry thoughts.

Application of CBT to fostered and adopted children

Although there is a large body of research evidence on the efficacy of CBT, the majority of the work has been focused on adult work and on specific presenting problems, such as depression and anxiety, in isolation. There is a growing body of research evidence for CBT with children, but very little on CBT with children who are looked after by others. This is probably for the most part owing to "being in care" not being a presenting problem as such, but an experience that unfortunately some children go through. By the very nature of their situation, there are likely to be multiple changes in these children's lives, including possible moves, new schools, loss of family of origin, and so on, making it very difficult to put changes down to treatment rather than any other factor. Often children who are fostered or adopted have been traumatized or abused in previous settings, and the kinds of difficulties they may present with can be wide-ranging. This makes it difficult to compare like with like: responses to life experiences can be very specific to the particular child.

It may be helpful to consider research evidence to particular life events that tend to be associated with being either fostered or adopted. Given that experience of neglect or abuse are the most common reasons for being fostered or adopted, it would give some indication of the usefulness of this approach with fostered and adopted children to consider the impact of CBT on children who have been abused. In a study of 229 children aged 8–14 years, Cohen, Deblinger, and Mannarino (2004) found that CBT reduced PTSD symptoms in children who had been sexually abused more effectively than did child-centred therapy. This study found that the improvements in anxiety and depression levels were maintained in the CBT treatment group at both the 6-month and 12-month follow-up (Cohen, Mannarino, & Knudsen, 2005). Ramchandani and Jones (2003) systematically reviewed the literature for treatment of children who had been sexually abused and found that, in the 12 studies they reviewed, CBT produced the most positive results, particularly for younger children. Runyon, Deblinger, Ryan, and Thakkar-Kolar (2004) have reviewed the research regarding treatment of PTSD in children who have experienced physical abuse and neglect. They found that the majority of studies established that CBT with the carer and child together is the most effective, and more specifically that CBT for the carer alone is not as effective as including the child in the treatment. This means that providing the carer with CBT to manage the child's symptoms is not as helpful as using CBT methods with the child and carer together.

There have been a number of studies that look at CBT group work for fostering and adopting parents (see also Granville & Antrobus, chapter 14). Groups for parents and carers tend to focus on the development of positive parenting strategies through methods similar to the CBT work with children—that is, exploring beliefs about situations, looking for evidence for negative beliefs, and identifying behavioural antecedents or triggers. Groups practise together but also reinforce learning through individual homework tasks. Recently Rushton and colleagues (2006) have reported on the process of systematically looking at parenting programmes for adoptive parents, where they are directly comparing a CBT approach with an educational/illuminative programme. The CBT approach is based on the Webster–Stratton programme, and the educational/illuminative programme is focused on learning to understand the meaning of children's behaviour in the context of their past experiences. This study is aimed to provide some evidence as to the usefulness of parenting programmes for adoptive parents, an area that has not attracted much systematic research. One study that did attempt a systematic assessment of this area is that by Macdonald and Turner (2005), who looked at the impact of CBT training of foster carers. Interestingly, they found no differences in placement breakdown or the frequency and severity of behavioural problems in the children, but the foster carers in the CBT group demonstrated increased confidence in dealing with difficult behaviour. They hypothesize that the apparent lack of support from social services and perhaps the measures selected fed into the somewhat unexpected results.

What can we draw from the literature on applying CBT to children?

Children as young as 5 or 6 can benefit from CBT if proper thought is given to the presentation of the theory and method. For younger children, visual prompts are very helpful, such as using emotionally animated faces, drawings, or photographs, placed in order of degree (e.g., very upset, a little upset, neither upset nor not, a little happy, very happy; or frowning/distressed through to smiling) in order to help children think about changes and feelings in relation to specific events. Very young children will struggle with being able to "think about thoughts", and the work is more likely to be play-based. As children get older, they will be more able to recognize and consider their thinking patterns. With developing cognitive functioning, it will be more possible to consider using more representational materials such as analogue scales, like those designed by Lindsay (1991), which can be used to represent degrees of feelings through graphic representation of lines to increasing size blocks. Creative use of a "feelings thermometer" can be effective in identifying changes in the intensity of feelings. From the age of 7 to 9 (depending on cognitive development), straightforward numerical analogue scales can be used. Using analogue scales can be helpful in graphically understanding the degree of the child's distress or difficulty, and can be very helpful for the child in highlighting areas of change. For example, a child may be asked to rate his distress when considering a particular negative thought and then asked to rate his distress when focusing on a challenge or alternative thought, allowing for greater recognition of changes in feelings.

Thought bubbles can be helpful to younger children, and diaries organized into thought bubbles can be an extremely effective way of recording events, as well as a child's response to them. Events and thoughts can be represented in drawings or modelled in clay, not just written as words. Some children respond well to role playing, and using puppets or dolls to act out situations can be easier or less anxiety-provoking. Others may respond better to reversing the roles of child and therapist, with the therapist describing the thoughts they imagine the child to be having. Media, television programmes, storylines from popular children's books or television programmes can be productive in helping children recognize common thinking errors, and it can feel "safer" thinking about someone else's problems.

Much of the literature regarding using CBT with abused children suggests that involving carers improves the outcome. It may be helpful to include carers in all (or part) of the session for several reasons: the carer may be able to help remind the child of events that troubled them, they may be able to help the child to find the most effective form of communication and to generalize what he learns in the session into the wider environment. Whether or not to include a carer will be depend on individual children and their situations, though the younger the child, the more likely it is that carers will need to be included in at least some of the session.

Implications for working with looked after children

Children who have been through distressing events are likely to have emotional and behavioural difficulties as a result, and the damage can be so deep that the straightforward limit-setting and boundaries that parents have to provide on a daily basis with their child is not nearly enough. Getting these children and families the most effective kind of help can be hampered by many factors, such as temporary placements and parents looking after many needy children and not having the time or capacity to manage lengthy interventions or many appointments. Child factors are also important, such as the reluctance to engage in treatment and real difficulty in thinking and staying with any relationship, including that of a therapeutic relationship. All of the above factors can mean that a short-term, structured, and problem-led focus can be more achievable and meaningful to children who are looked after and to their carers.

CBT can therefore be an obvious treatment choice. It can provide children and their carers who would not otherwise be able to access psychological treatments with the possibility of change. It is a short structured treatment that can appeal to both children and families, and it is orientated to the child's problems and undertaken in partnership with the child and the carers.

CBT also provides us with a treatment methodology that is compatible with other ways of working, such as family therapy, play therapy, or counselling. Aspects of CBT can be drawn on in family therapy, such as keeping diaries or challenging negative thoughts. In the Tavistock Clinic we have successfully combined CBT and individual psychotherapy: for example with a young boy who had been very traumatized and whose behaviour was out of control, one of his weekly analytic sessions was swapped for a CBT session—he had two psychotherapy sessions a week—for a short period of time. This enabled him to regain some control over his behaviour and then, in turn, making it possible for the intensive work to continue. CBT has developed in a flexible way, enabling therapists to draw on aspects that will be most helpful to the children who are looked after and the carers with whom they work.

CHAPTER 9

Individual psychotherapy for late-adopted children: how one new attachment can facilitate another

Juliet Hopkins

One of the risks of adopting children in care is that they may perpetuate their deprivation by rejecting the loving care offered them. Clinical experience shows that when this happens, it can sometimes be possible to facilitate children's attachment to their new parents by involving them in individual therapy.

This chapter aims to describe the difficulties inherent for these deprived and rejected children in making new attachments and to consider how a new relationship to a psychotherapist may help these children to take the risk. Concepts from psychoanalysis and from attachment theory are used to understand the therapeutic process.

In order to explore these issues, I bring examples from the psychotherapy of two children—Max and Pauline—who had each been adopted at the age of 4 years but who had not bonded with their respective adoptive parents.

Max and Pauline

When they started therapy, Max was 9 years old, and Pauline was 14.

The early histories of these two children were typical of children placed in late adoption and do not need for present purposes to be individually specified. Enough to say that after two or three years in their birth families, where they suffered both abuse and neglect, they experienced several foster home placements before joining their adoptive families. Both sets of adoptive parents were caring, concerned, and thoughtful people who supposed, as many adoptive parents do, that they could undo the adverse effects of their children's early experiences within a year or two.

The problems that late-adopted children are liable to present after placement are as well known to social workers as are their typical early histories. Max and Pauline developed a pattern fraught with particular difficulty. They were hostile and rejecting, defiant and rebellious, at home and at school. At home, Max did not like to be touched, held, or cuddled: he escaped outside at every opportunity. Pauline also could not give or accept affection, though she liked to hang around her adoptive mother while being obnoxiously rude. Both children were failing at school, where they could not concentrate and were repeatedly disruptive. Max was a bully in the playground; Pauline had no friends and sometimes truanted.

Children like Max and Pauline, who appear to care for no one, and to turn to no one when hurt or distressed, are often said to be suffering from an "attachment disorder". They do not enjoy a selective attachment to anyone. Although there are varying opinions about what constitutes an attachment disorder, what is not debatable is that such children commonly manifest the signs of a "disorganized/controlling" attachment pattern (Lyons-Ruth & Jacobvitz, 1999) with all its characteristic perplexing, contradictory features.

The disorganized/controlling attachment pattern

Children who enter the care system have experienced abuse and neglect at the hands of their care-givers, the very adults to whom they are attached and on whom they depend for their safety and well-being. Their parents have been actively abusive, drug-addicted, or mentally ill, with consequent frightening and unpredictable behaviour.

Main (1995b) describes how maltreatment by the attachment figure places the infant in an irresolvable paradox in which it can neither approach the frightening parent, nor shift its attention, nor flee. She summarized the subjective experience of this irresolvable conflict as "fright without solution". This invites an obvious comparison with Winnicott's "unthinkable anxieties" and Bion's "nameless dread". The fear that is unthinkable and unnameable is likely to be the threat to the infant's very survival by the actions of the parent.

The effects of exposure to "fright without solution" are already apparent in infants 1 year old. In the Strange Situation test when these infants are first frightened by separation and then reunited with their care-givers, their behaviour reveals that they cannot trust their care-givers to provide a secure base. Impulses to fight, flee or freeze conflict with the urge to approach the care-giver, and the result is manifest in the disorganized and contradictory behaviour characteristic of a disorganized/disoriented (D) attachment (Main & Hesse, 1990).

Fright cannot be borne for long without solution. As "D" infants grow up, if abuse and neglect continue, they master their helplessness to achieve safety with their care-givers by developing powerful defensive strategies which characterize the disorganized/controlling attachment pattern. They become extremely controlling of adults, most often in a punitive way. The punitive need to control adults can become the basis of opposition and defiance, as it did with Max and Pauline. The aim is self-sufficiency. Bowlby (1980) explained how the defensive processes associated with this attachment pattern lead to "segregated systems"—extreme forms of dissociation that separate attachment information from consciousness. Attachment behaviour, feelings, and thoughts become disconnected from consciousness and from each other but continue on occasion to break through in fragmented, irrational, and unpredictable ways. In order to maintain their defensive strategies, these children become hyper-vigilant: any sudden or unpredictable change is liable to trigger behaviour that may seen totally disproportionate and irrational.

Therapy

Although children like Max and Pauline are often regarded as too emotionally damaged to be suitable for psychotherapy, there has been a long tradition of treating them at the Tavistock Clinic. In 1983 Mary Boston and Rolene Szur published their ground-breaking book on *Psychotherapy with Severely Deprived Children*, which drew on the experience of some 80 children in care who had received psychotherapy. Many of these children had experienced both abuse and neglect. The book described the steady progress that most of these children could make "provided the therapist could stick it out in the difficult phases".

Although adoptive parents may not appear to be contributing to the problems that their adoptive children present, it is essential for them to have help and support while their children undergo the upheavals of therapy. Understanding their children's difficulties and their own painful and sometimes violent feelings towards them can make a vital difference to their children's capacity to change. Both Max's and Pauline's parents were determined to overcome the impasse that existed between their children and themselves and make good use of the opportunities offered to them for interviews at their clinics.

Issues of control: testing the limits

Attachment theory is concerned with survival, with the dimension from protection and safety to danger and fear. The therapist aims to provide safety and to be experienced eventually as a secure base, but this poses a colossal threat to children whose only sense of security resides in the stability of their defensive system (Hamilton, 1987). A therapist who offers sensitive attention directed towards recognizing and empathizing with the child's feelings and intentions threatens to arouse the longing for care that segregated systems keep actively at bay. The therapist needs to play it cool, since sensitive understanding may generate acute anxiety and lead to a major explosion of all the defensive operations at the child's disposal, as it did for Max and Pauline.

Max was a big, athletic 9-year-old with a crop of blond hair. His twice-weekly therapy with Mrs J began with a wild display of extremely provocative and disruptive behaviour. He could not stay in the therapy room but escaped all over the building, climbing up and down the banisters of the stairwell in a way that courted serious danger. He threw toys and water at Mrs J and out of the window. He created havoc in the toilets. He broke into drawers and grabbed the phone to dial 999 to have Mrs J arrested.

Pauline was a plump teenager who dressed in black and red—"the devil's colours". Her dress and swaggering posture conveyed a threat in spite of her small size. She, too, began her twice-weekly therapy by alarming her therapist, Mrs T, promising to give her a bloody nose. The sense of alarm spread through the clinic as Pauline insulted the receptionists and overturned the clinic's flower vases. Like Max, she projected into others her terror of being trapped into a new abusive relationship.

Underlying Max and Pauline's wild behaviour was a powerful need to be in control, to maintain their defensive systems, and to regulate the emotional distance with their therapists. Max soon discovered that he could always have the upper hand. When he leapt onto the forbidden window ledge and started to kick the glass, he knew Mrs J would rush to stop him, so he could leap past her and bolt out of the door. Discovering that he could go when he chose helped him to feel safe enough to stay for longer. Pauline was able to exert the same reassuring control by refusing to come to some sessions and leaving others early. Knowing she could do this allowed her to continue. Children cannot feel safe when they have control over adults, but children who have experienced "fright without solution" cannot feel safe when adults are in control either. Their disruptive behaviour invites adult control, which they both need and dread. An escalating battle in which adult and child outdo each other to gain mastery may result. It requires much testing by the child to discover that the control offered by a particular adult may be safe to accept.

A new developmental opportunity

After two months of outrageous behaviour Max discovered Mrs J's refusal to play the roles that he had automatically assigned to her, as a rejecting and punitive adult or as a helpless, defeated child. She was not going to imprison him, send him away, surrender, or let him walk over her. He appeared to have discovered what unconsciously he may have been seeking—that therapy offers a new developmental opportunity (Hurry, 1998), a relationship in which to externalize the aftermath of adverse and abusive experiences, experiences such as "fright without solution".

Boston (Boston & Szur, 1983, p. 9) describes how children in care make "endless evacuation into therapists of chaotic, confused and unwanted feelings". Naturally, young children cannot talk about their experiences of rejection and abuse, when they may not even recognize that these are what they have had. Their hope of recovering from the impact of these experiences is to externalize them with someone who can safely tolerate being hated, humiliated and helpless without retaliating or collapsing, and, more than that, who can tolerate being experienced as deliberately cruel and abusive. Those who deal intimately with these children have to accept the many negative ways that the children perceive them while also tolerating the powerful negative emotions that the children arouse in them.

Developing attachment

Bowlby (1980) predicted that children like Max and Pauline, who had retreated into emotional self-sufficiency after suffering loss, would reject new attachments but betray the existence of their segregated attachment systems in isolated thoughts and actions.

Max provided a classic example of this prediction by becoming very possessively attached to the therapy room and the clinic—"*My* room" and "*My* clinic"—while maintaining that he hated Mrs J. This development of an initial attachment to the territory rather than to the therapist is common in deprived and abused children. For Max it proved to be the beginning of a new and very gradual growth of positive feelings for Mrs J. After six months of treating her with extreme contempt and heaping her with playground obscenities, he allowed her to become first the woman he loved to hate and then the woman he hated to love. His tone of contempt began to mellow as he became a pop singer who crooned songs in which words of love were replaced by terms of abuse. After a couple of terms these songs sometimes conveyed quite an affectionate feeling. Affection leaked out in other fragmented ways. Instead of physically avoiding her as though she were contaminated, Max now brushed against Mrs J and asked her to catch him when he jumped off the furniture. His parents reported their awareness that Max was now ambivalent about therapy instead of wholly against it.

Pauline claimed, "I never care, so I'm never hurt. I don't get attached to anyone". However, she, too, betrayed the existence of her hope for attachment to Mrs T at the same time as she claimed to hate her: she refused to leave the session when time was up, consciously intending to annoy, but clearly also conveying that she hadn't had enough. Soon she was telling Mrs T of her dream to be part of a couple—a couple who shared their lollies and drinks together.

Moments of sharing confidences like this alternated with threats and insults. These sudden oscillations between contradictory moods, characteristic of the disorganized/controlling pattern, are extremely confusing to adults who feel they "never know where they are", with the child. Segregated systems deprive children of a sense of continuity. The children are often unaware that their moods have switched.

Over time, Pauline grew friendlier as she began to imagine that Mrs T shared all her own interests in teenage fashion, film, and music. She gave her black lipstick and nail varnish so they could look alike. She now wanted an attachment but intended it to be entirely on her terms, with Mrs T experienced as a reflection of herself, not someone with independent opinions and a life of her own.

Imagination and play

Imagination is rarely well developed in children who have been through the care system. Some of them have been too frightened to allow their imagination to develop at all. They cannot tell stories or enact symbolic themes. Others, like Max, spend most of their play time simply messing about but can also play out some fantasies, which are usually of the catastrophic nature described by Main and Cassidy (1988), who observed that these fantasies were characteristic of children with disorganized/controlling attachment patterns.

> For example, Max used baby dolls as bait for sharks. He made ambulances run over people and he drew attractive restaurants that led to torture chambers. Parallels can be seen with earlier experiences he had had when supposedly protective and nurturing figures did abusive things.

> Pauline's imagination also contained classically catastrophic themes of violence and destruction, murder and suicide, but, more hopefully, it also contained an idealized group of celebrities and their families who befriended her. The details of these celebrities' encounters with her were so vivid that at times she seemed to believe they were true. Thus her imagination had provided her with idealized conflict-free relationships and protected her from the acute ambivalence inherent in developing an overt attachment to her adoptive parents, whom two of the celebrities clearly resembled.

As attachments develop, so play and imagination change and become both more varied and more positive.

Max began to bring collections of cards and badges to show Mrs J, and soon this friendliness developed into a desire to play games of imagination with her. For months he chose to play the part of a robot that Mrs J was required to bring to life. Pauline, too, compared herself to a robot, "I don't feel anything. I'm a robot". The robot theme seemed to express both children's inner emptiness and their sense of being repeatedly taken over by dissociated "robotic" impulses beyond their control.

Following the robot play, Max's repertoire widened and ranged from quite childlike games involving physical contact to more age-appropriate activities like doing magic tricks and playing hangman.

Once children are secure enough to express themselves in a range of symbolic themes, "play itself becomes a therapy" (Winnicott, 1971) and progress accelerates. However, progress is never easy. The growth of new attachments is liable to be impeded by the tie to earlier attachment figures. A loyalty conflict results.

Loyalty conflict

Both psychoanalysts and attachment theorists are united in giving significance to loyalty conflicts and to the subjective safety of the link to familiar internal objects, even when this may involve the repetition of negative experiences.

Like most deprived children, Max made very few references to present or past life at home or at school. However, he told Mrs J several times that he did not want to be adopted and that he hated his new mother when she came "to choose" him. "I was all right until they took me. I was free." Chillingly, his few references to his adoptive family were all in terms of "they" and "them", not "we" and "us". He didn't want "them", he told me, he wanted to go back to his foster home, a home in which he was thought to have been neglected. He said his foster parents "were great 'cos they didn't bother me". The tag he chose for himself, which he managed to engrave in numerous places in Mrs J's room, was the letter "B", the initial of the name of his birth mother and of his foster parents. He covered the "No Smoking" signs in the clinic with "Yes Smoking" signs, and it was not difficult to guess the fact that his birth parents and foster parents had smoked and that his adoptive parents disapproved of it. This clash represented the nub of the problem. If Max accepted his adoptive family's values, he would have to give up his identity as a tough, independent, streetwise kid and recognize his failure to be the good, cooperative child that his new parents wanted.

Fairbairn (1952) described the tie to bad objects; he explained how a new mode of relating is felt to involve not only a guilty betrayal of the early relationship but a fear of the loss of the sense of self. A negative therapeutic reaction may sometimes be understood as a return to the residual security inherent in previous attachments, however unsatisfactory, rather than facing the sense of betrayal and loss inherent in developing new relationships.

Pauline's loyalty conflict was even more apparent than Max's. She had always refused to call her adoptive parents "Mummy" and "Daddy". "They aren't my parents, they never will be". Behind this rejection was an agonized longing to be their child and an irrational fury that they had failed to give birth to her but had allowed her to suffer for years at the hands of her birth parents. By dressing sensationally in the devil's colours and asking to be known as "Lucifer", she tried to make a virtue of her identification with her birth parents' badness. "My parents hated me. Everyone will always hate me." She believed that her evil feelings were due to inheriting her father's genes and so could never be modified. She felt safe clinging to her identity as a powerful, bad, go-it-alone teenager and threatened by the therapy that challenged this view of herself.

Both children's rejection of their adoptive parents' affection and acts of kindness is a reminder that good experiences with adoptive parents may be too poignant to accept, lest acceptance should unleash intense rage and grief about past privations. Pauline also felt bound to reject the privilege of being adopted into a wealthy home. She identified with having nothing and no one and was destructive of her own and her parents' possessions. Perhaps, like some children, she would have found adoption easier in a home offering more distant relationships (Steele, Hodges, et al., 2003) and fewer privileges.

Changes during therapy

Max's relationship to his adoptive parents improved gradually during his two years of therapy. He began to refer to his relationship with them as "we" and "us" at about the same time as he achieved togetherness with Mrs J in play. Although we know from research (Main & Weston, 1981) that the baby's attachment patterns to mother and to father are virtually independent of each other, the success of psychotherapy depends upon positive developments in one relationship becoming generalized to other relationships. As yet there is no systematic study of when this transfer begins and what facilitates it. In Max' case Mrs J did not know in which relationship "togetherness" began or whether it developed in therapy and home simultaneously.

The development of Max's new attachments was accompanied by a reduction in his defensive behaviour. He became less reckless, less uncooperative, and more popular with his peers, but still sometimes disruptive and still behaving in a disorganized/controlling manner. He developed a kinder attitude to pets and successfully adopted a hamster. At times he made great efforts to be good and expressed the wish to be good enough to marry and have children when he grew up. Instead of projecting all his fears, he could now contain and talk about some of his worries, his failure at school, his dread of attack and of being given away.

Pauline regrettably broke off therapy after only a year. She did not tell Mrs T what changes she had made at home but was proud to tell her of a steady boyfriend—her first "real friend" and, remarkably, a boy of whom her parents approved. Her adoptive mother reported that Pauline had become affectionate and helpful in ways she had never been before, but she still rejected her adoptive father. She also reported that Pauline had recently cried for the first time. While telling her adoptive mother how her cat had been run over, Pauline asked her why her eyes were running. She had surprised herself by the spontaneous expression of her need for comfort from her adoptive mother. Another element of her attachment system was no longer segregated.

Although abused children can make significant changes in therapy, their liability to respond violently to unexpected reminders of trauma may remain. If therapy lasts long enough, they may come to recognize "trauma triggers" and try to counteract their effects. Pauline continued to have unaccountable rages in response to any kind of intrusiveness. Max enacted an involuntary fight response (Perry et al., 1995) to sudden loud noises and to unexpected happenings, such as a new rug in the therapy room. To outsiders it looks as though the children are suddenly being inexplicably impossible. To the children themselves it may feel that they are possessed by sudden uncontrollable impulses that they scarcely recognize as themselves. They are victims of their own segregated systems and are often left deeply confused by their own feelings and behaviour.

Discussion

It is sometimes feared that individual therapy for adopted children may undermine their attachment to their adoptive parents. However, Max and Pauline illustrate the way adopted children can use their therapy to risk new attachments to parents whom they have previously rejected. This positive outcome can be obtained because the disorganized/controlling attachment pattern is unstable. Self-sufficiency can never be achieved. Children with this pattern depend on others to receive their projection of the negative emotions that they cannot tolerate in themselves. Others must bear the rejection, hurt, humiliation, and despair that they have experienced but have been unable to assimilate. The therapist is open to receiving and working with negative enactments and projections. The most crucial contribution to children's willingness to risk further attachments is probably the therapist's capacity to contain all the negative emotions of "fright without solution" as these are gradually externalized. Previous negative attachment models and their associated feelings can then be expressed in a context in which they are tolerated and acknowledged in words, not by enactment. The therapist's training enables her or him, as far as possible, to avoid joining the dance of attack and rejection, helplessness and humiliation. This means that children become able to see beyond their attempts at enactment and to discover that alternative attachment possibilities are less threatening than they had supposed. A new attachment—that is, an attachment responsive to the therapist's actual qualities—can begin. And, importantly, this can happen without the need to reconstruct trauma or consciously to revisit the past. Before the past can be confronted, a sufficient sense of self, a capacity to mentalize, and an attachment secure enough to hold the pain are all needed. Max and Pauline were on the verge of looking back at their negative experiences when therapy ended. At home Max asked angrily about his history, "Why did it have to happen to me?", while Pauline recalled beatings by her birth father and began to consider his influence on her life without attributing every difficulty to "genes".

Although new attachments can develop without need to talk about the past, much effort in therapy is directed towards talking about the "here and now". Current feelings and intentions are put gradually into words. Clinical tact is needed to find acceptable ways to verbalize what needs to be understood. Mrs J found that Max was able to think about his relationship to her if she referred to it obliquely as his feelings about "the therapy", while Mrs T found that Pauline could not tolerate any mention of feelings at all unless they were exclusively ascribed to her imaginary celebrities. Very gradually, fears like those of being trapped, dropped, punished, or rejected can be heard, checked against current realities, held in mind, and contained instead of being enacted. This move to verbalization is easier to achieve in therapy than at home because there is much less at stake. Therapy provides a trial ground where children can integrate painful emotions in small doses. New developments can be explored before they are taken safely home.

Late-adopted children are often a very tough assignment for therapists who wonder how adoptive parents can cope at all. As therapists we endure repeated dread, alarm, anger, betrayal, humiliation, helplessness, and despair. We are supported by our knowledge of theory that enables us to see the frightened, helpless child behind the controlling tyrant—an insight which facilitates both empathy and affection. Theory also assures us that physical and verbal attacks are not personal, are necessary, and can be understood. Even so, we find we need colleagues for support. If therapists need support to cope, then adoptive parents must need immeasurably more. Max' and Pauline's parents recognized this need. A crucial factor in their children's capacity to change was their own determination to win their attachment and, in this pursuit, be willing, if need be, to change themselves. It was their collaboration with clinic staff and their persistent support of the turbulent course of their children's therapy that made a positive outcome possible.

CHAPTER 10

Where do I belong?
Dilemmas for children and adolescents who have been adopted or brought up in long-term foster care

Margaret Rustin

A sense of belonging

The idea of belonging somewhere is an ordinary and fundamental building-block of a sense of personal identity. Everyday
events remind us of this: a lost child wandering around a shop-
ping centre or park gets asked "Who do you belong to?" The assumption is that the answer will be the clue to who the child is—the son, or
daughter, or brother, or sister, or grandchild of particular individuals.
A child's belongings are those objects that characteristically define him
as a recognizable person: his coat, shoes, school bag, and so on. The
somewhere that we belong starts off as our family of origin in which
we are accorded a place defined by relationships. Around this will be
concentric circles in which we belong in some fashion to wider social
groups: extended family, school, local community, city, region, country.
Recall the addresses many primary school-aged children like to create for themselves, which record all the layers of belonging, ending
up with "The World" and "The Universe". In a religious conception
we all belong in God's family and are protected by His all-seeing eye.
Humanly, the sense of belonging also resides in the recognition of
oneself as part of the sentient group by others. Children who cannot
be brought up in their families of origin suffer a basic disruption in this
sense of membership, of knowing where they belong.

In adolescence, every young person has to work out a more person-ally defined sense of identity. This involves an often painful process of separation from the earlier identity, which is given by virtue of one's child status within a family, an unquestioned simplicity and certainty about who one is. The adolescent can no longer define himself satis-factorily as one of, for example, the Brown family. He is exposed to the necessity of a higher degree of individuation, of the expectation within the peer group of his being at least as much a recognizable member of this vital social group, whatever its particular local colour, as of being a member of a family. There is also an expectation at school and later at college or work that the adolescent is responsible for his own behav-iour and is able to make significant decisions, with parents much more in the background than in earlier childhood. The physical and sexual maturity taking shape through the teenage years carries with it a social assumption of a capacity to take responsibility for oneself.

The challenges of development

This normal adolescent pathway is often quite a difficult one for young people to traverse, and, indeed, in recent years concern about adoles-cent mental health has reached a high level. But for adopted adoles-cents a much more complex process is involved, for the push from both inside and outside the individual is towards greater separateness, and many separations loom. By the time they are teenagers, if not in-deed earlier, young people begin to plan their own leisure activities, to think of independent holidays and travelling, to take part-time jobs, to become involved with groups of friends and sexual relationships, and to think of leaving home. These external markers of greater independ-ence all flow from major internal turbulence. This chapter explores the special problems of development through childhood and adolescence when it takes place against the backdrop of earlier often deeply upset-ting changes in a child's life.

Changes in the pattern of adoption discussed elsewhere in this book have particular consequences for the adopted child's experience. In earlier periods, when baby adoption was more the norm and when the facts of the child's origins might be concealed altogether and were certainly very rarely known or spoken about in much detail, the child's awareness of having two sets of parents might be barely conscious. This situation had its own psychological logic. It tended to leave the individual struggling with an unassimilated sense of difference and apartness and unconscious feelings of loss or confusion or disconnectedness. Present–day practice creates quite a different situation. The majority of adoptions are of older children, not babies. A child adopted at 2 or 5 or 10 has a store of conscious memories of earlier families where they lived and belonged in varying degrees. Their history might include periods of being an "at-risk" baby, a child who has had to act as carer for vulnerable parents, a foster child, often in a number of different placements, or perhaps a separated sibling. Ongoing contact with the birth family may be part of the child's current experience. The complexities introduced by the forms of contact sometimes prescribed by the courts can make the patchwork of the child's earlier life even more strongly present and an ongoing source of potential disturbance. All of this is reflected in what we know about the internal world of adopted children (Rustin, 1999).

The attitude to the lost birth parents will, of course, be influenced by how much time the child spent with them, by the nature of their difficulties in caring for him, and by the circumstances in which he came to be removed from family care. Very often there is an unconscious sense of rejection and betrayal in the child. Sometimes there are also anxieties about having betrayed or abandoned a mother who needed her baby's love, or being a child who was so dreadful that he could not inspire affection in his mother. The helplessness to influence events that many such children have felt arises from the experience of being moved from family to family and place to place in what were often bewildering, incomprehensible, or frightening circumstances. Instead of the unconscious family romance fantasy that Freud described (Freud, 1909c), adopted children have the strange experience of this fantasy becoming real: they are not left to dream of "really" belonging to other more desirable parents, but actually find themselves in a new family which is presented to them as a vast improvement on their previous experience.

Where there has been physical, emotional, or sexual abuse in addition to the painful losses that any adopted child has sustained, the situation has further complexities. Characteristic patterns of such children's personalities often include an omnipotent denial of helplessness and loss, identification with the aggressor, confusions about intimacy, idealization of perversity, generational confusion, including sexual precocity, and very uneven development, and—perhaps most troubling of all—marked distrust of parental figures (Boston & Szur, 1983).

These personality features represent a mixture of persecutory and depressive anxieties and defences and have to be thought about with an awareness of the acute, often protracted and repeated psychological wounds such children have suffered. They are very hurt and deeply suspicious of the motives of other people. They have had little chance to develop as individuals in relationships that would support the gradual relinquishing of fantasies of omnipotence. Only relationships can lay the basis for the child's capacity for emotional contact with himself and growth of responsibility for good and bad parts of the self. Children let down by others tend to be mistrustful of their own goodness and terrified of their hatred and destructiveness. When parents adopt children with traumatic histories, they find themselves at different moments idealized, kept at bay, tested to their limits—in particular as to their capacity to hold on to the child, whatever the provocation—and at times seduced. When sexual abuse is part of the story, there is often a powerful unconscious effort to split the parents and to re-enact the abuse in some way. When we encounter these children in therapy, they often make us suffer, raise our hopes only to trample on them, and expose us to horrible worlds of corruption and cruelty. Yet very often they have a capacity to call from us special efforts in tolerance, understanding, and imaginative leaps. Their psychic survival seems striking evidence of the durability of the impulse to search for a good object and the importance of courage in psychic life.

The young people themselves tell the story of their struggle most clearly, and for this reason I turn now to some clinical examples to amplify these introductory comments. What I hope to do is to demonstrate the way in which the pressures of development intersect with the problematic inner constellation of parental figures that are characteristic of adopted children. When puberty is reached, powerful sexual impulses are stirred up and then inevitably linked with the mostly unconscious picture one has of the sexual couple who were one's origin. The adolescent revisiting of psychological tasks first faced in the oedipal period of early childhood is a very tough time for adopted young people. The oedipal child has to place himself in relation to both parents (Freud) and to acknowledge their independent relationship to each other (Britton, 1998) and enter the triangular space that will be the prototype for much later experience and, indeed, serves as a vital cornerstone of our mental health. Not only does an adopted young person have at least two sets of parents to fit into the picture; he also very often has a sense of catastrophe associated with his birth and early years. This overshadows and shapes his beliefs about sexual relationships. It may serve to inhibit sexual exploration or to lead to acting-out in identification with damaged and damaging internal figures and to a repetition of unconscious early traumas. The early adolescent years are likely to be a period of turbulence and much anxiety for adoptive parents faced with the impact within the family of their children's struggles to make sense of unfamiliar feelings.

I should like to address first some examples of inhibition and delayed development, as I think these are less often the focus of attention because they give less overt trouble to the adults in the young person's life—parents and teachers in particular—although they can be important indications that help may be needed to get things moving.

Concepts of lost parents: Winston

Winston was an African–Caribbean boy who had come into care aged 8. His parents had not lived together, although his father was very much around, as well as a number of half-siblings and other relations. His mother seems ultimately to have felt she could not manage and sought help from social services in looking after him. As I did not meet him until he was 14, and, like very many children in care, there had by this time been many changes of social worker, I never had a convincing corroborated account of what had led to his being brought up in long-term foster care. I did, however, ultimately learn what was Winston's own picture of things. He described absolutely without irony or doubt that his mother had one day taken him to the social services office because she had to do something that day, but that she had not collected him because she had forgotten the address. He believed she was still looking for him. He told me this when he was 16, and it greatly added to my understanding of his state of mind, which was dominated by periods of getting completely lost in his thoughts: huge discontinuities and lacunae were the consequence. There was also a pervasive sense of timelessness in his sessions with me. I would perhaps summarize his mental state as being frequently almost totally lost in time and space. Unsurprisingly, this was unfortunately replicated in the frequent failures in the holding environment to sustain a solid connection for him with the work at the clinic. This pattern of repetition of earlier failure within the care system is well known and indeed difficult to resist when faced with a boy like Winston. Neither he nor his foster carer nor his social worker seemed able to hold on to a connection that he was a person with a right to meaningful continuity. The regularity of school was a hugely important antidote to this state of affairs, and I felt encouraged as I got to know him when he could tell me something about school—and later about work experience—that conveyed that he felt he had a recognized place in that context.

Winston had been assessed as a boy with a moderate learning disability, and, of course, it may well be that there was a genetic factor in his mother's difficulties in looking after him. But what struck me in his psychotherapy sessions was how variable his capacity for thinking and feeling alive proved to be. He was a big lad, but when I first met him he moved very slowly as we walked along the corridor together and sat almost immobile in his chair in my room. He also gave the impression of not seeing much with his open eyes, as if there was an absence of focus or a veil between him and what surrounded him: not exactly sightless, but profoundly diminished vision. He said very little to me, and I often had the impression after I had spoken to him that he might not have heard what I said, because there would be a very long pause before any response came. In the special framework of psychotherapy it was possible to wait through these protracted silences, and usually I would then receive a reply, although it might take the discouraging form that he had now forgotten what I had said or what he wanted to say. I could, of course, imagine just how impossible it would be in the everyday context of home or school for anyone to have the time to devote to finding where Winston's mind had gone. He must continuously have been inviting people to overlook his presence. However, I myself felt that there was another element, as I was not bored by the apparently empty spaces in sessions—I felt energized by the need to search for this boy, as if I had perhaps become in a sense the wished-for mother who was still looking for him and had not abandoned him, as his mother had in reality.

I came to understand Winston's slowed-down state, his immobility in mind and body, and his initial out-of-touchness with his own mental and physical capacities as a profound identification with the lost boy he felt himself to be in his parents' minds. So deeply locked within these inner figures was he that he could experience very little. At times I felt disturbed by the thought that this seemed like a kind of enslavement, in which he was tied to lost and impotent parents and thus without access to any life energies of his own, and I would find myself disquieted by thoughts of the impact of generations of slavery among black Caribbean families.

Interestingly, from this point of view, it was when a more lively male social worker was assigned to him after a long period of his being an "unallocated" case that a more effective partnership became possible at last between myself as a therapist and social services. Prior to that, my letters and phone calls to the local authority were literally never acknowledged. This new partnership brought about an agreement that Winston could manage the journey to the clinic on his own rather than being escorted, which had so often meant a lost session through failure of the escort system. Becoming someone who could get from one place to another under his own authority was a vital step in allowing me to investigate with Winston the aspects of his functioning that led to his getting lost and to his being able to take charge of himself. I began to hear about football games at school, including quite a vivid account of a ball kicked so high it went out of the school grounds, and this sounded more like adolescence dawning. Winston was quite keen on cooking and interested in work experience in a kitchen, and here, too, I got glimpses of energy and activity. In these contrasting cameos, I thought there was some evidence of recovering a better picture of parental figures. Whatever his father's faults, he had certainly both fathered a number of children and maintained limited but long-term consistent contact with them. Winston described to me visits to his father's home and a very affectionate relationship with a smaller half-brother and this boy's mother. The football scene seemed something of a symbolic representation of father and his collection of sons and to touch on the potential sexual development and excitement still very much delayed in Winston at this point. The kitchen scene made me think of his link to maternal figures. I had the impression that food was one of the few points of contact with his foster carer. He had once told me about a visit to a fish market in Jamaica when he went there with her on holiday. This conversation evoked very strong images of colour and smell in my mind, which I had taken as evidence of its emotional importance to him. When I had occasion in a later session to refer back to this, he was very surprised at my remembering it and a real smile appeared on his usually immobile features.

For Winston it seemed as if time had stopped at the point of abandonment (Canham, 1999). The intellectual slowness that became a feature after this was perhaps a mixture of some constitutional factors and a deathly depression in which a large part of himself almost stopped living or at any rate engaging with life. He seems to have felt that if he was not worth holding on to as a son he must be worthless, and to have treated himself as without value or relevance in consequence. He was set to become a shadow of a man. Fortunately he had been able (just) to project his desire for life and to protect it from his more destructive impulses in this way. This was how he came to be referred for therapy initially—both a teacher and his father had been worried by his lifelessness—and also how I was sustained in persisting with his therapy despite so little evidence that anything was going on for many many months. The process of projecting good aspects of the self left Winston, of course, terribly denuded, but I think he must have felt it was the only safe way he had to cling on to hope. It can be particularly difficult for those carrying such projections to stick at the task of maintaining optimism when all their efforts seem so little appreciated. Losing hope in any way forward is one of the greatest threats for all those looking after or working with adolescents who have given up on themselves as they can so often appear to have done.

Fear of growing up: Liz

There was a very different basis for the partially arrested development of Liz, a girl of a similar age but quite other in character. Liz had been adopted at the age of 7, after a relatively brief period in foster care. She and her younger sister had been very seriously neglected by drug-abusing parents, and Liz had also been subjected to multiple sexual abuse by her father and others. The children were in an appalling state when taken into care, though Liz's efforts to look after her younger sibling had protected her to some extent. However, an exceptional social worker found them an unusual adoptive home, one where their parents did not shrink from the knowledge of the children's earlier lives and were also willing to support the psychological help the children needed and to put a great deal of themselves into their family. Liz and her sister had a considerable period of play therapy and settled into a home vastly different from their previous experiences. Liz was bright and at first took to school with enthusiasm. Soon to all external appearances the children were well integrated into their rather privileged middle-class setting. However, early adolescence proved a very difficult time for Liz. She could not make friends she could keep, she seemed stuck in her intellectual development, she fought bitterly with everyone in the family, especially mother. Because she had felt helped by her earlier therapy, she was, however, amenable to the idea that someone outside the family might be able to help her get on better with people, and that was the basis for her beginning therapy with me. She came under her own steam after the first session, quite a lengthy journey, and both she and her parents were very clear that she must have me to herself. The parents met from time to time with a colleague at the clinic.

Liz was an odd mixture. She could and would, unless interrupted, talk solidly for 50 minutes at a time, providing endless details, mostly of her life at school and all the ups and downs of her friendships with other girls. She was 14 when we began work, physically very well developed, but she lived in a world absolutely devoid of interest in boys, and for a long time she had a way of dressing and inhabiting her body that hid all her best features. One of the things that upset her small and elegant mother greatly was Liz's indiscriminate over-eating, and, indeed, she was markedly overweight. The two things that she liked most were playing football and visiting a family friend (a single man) who lived in the country and with whom she shared an enthusiasm for horses, dogs, walking in the woods, and so on. The picture of herself that Liz consciously seemed to want to impress on me was one of self-sufficiency, an absence of emotional depth or curiosity, and a complacent conviction that she was perpetually misunderstood and let down by more or less everyone at school and persecuted by entirely unreasonable demands on her at home. I was left out of the loop, possibly like the friend in the country, and any efforts I made to explore ways in which I might be a disappointment to her were politely but firmly resisted. She liked coming to therapy and was sure I would be able to help, she insisted. Of course, I, in contrast, was deeply unsure and often frustrated by the difficulty of making real emotional contact with her. Nevertheless, at a nonverbal level I sensed some different currents. Liz often played with the strands of her hair, pulling out the curls, sometimes in a sensuous way that suggested something quite tender, and at other times tugging harshly in a way that must have been painful to her and made me almost flinch as I watched. She also very occasionally brought entirely different things into her sessions, including recounting extraordinary vivid dreams, which gave me glimpses of the side of herself she worked so hard to conceal. However, my attempts to talk to her about anything painful were consistently blocked. Sometimes the references to her earlier history in what she talked about seemed so blatant that I would have another go at making links, but Liz's responses were a variant on the theme that her mother was dead—which was true—and that she had no feelings at all about her father. She had a new family now. She had got over all that years ago when she had therapy before. It was really nothing to do with anything, she was sure.

Liz's choice of friends told a different story. There was a long sequence of unfortunate girls I heard about whose mother had cancer and died or whose parents split up acrimoniously or who had big problems with their Dads and were scared to go out, and so on. Liz would adopt the position of looking after these depressed or anxious friends, inviting them to come and baby-sit with her or spending a lot of time at their houses trying to cheer them up. The big sister identity she had occupied as a child for her own little sister seemed an important element in these relationships. She was the one with broad shoulders who could cope with all these tragedies. In therapy, where she might be expected to be allowed to be the girl with problems who was to get help from me, I was repeatedly shown that she was the one who helped others, and the only way in which mention could be made of all the misery she described was to explore what it must be like to be these various girls. Alongside this I tried to show her how useless she secretly seemed sure I was, despite her denials.

The point I want to emphasize is that there was a crucial connection between her failure to develop normal adolescent friendships—initially same-sex passionate intimacies and usually thereafter heterosexual explorations within a mixed adolescent group—and her being trapped as a care-taker of the vulnerability she projected into others. Of course the others were not always willing recipients of her projections, and this must have had a lot to do with the frequent breakdown of her friendships. In this identification with the caring role—perhaps a distorted version of social worker, adoptive mother, and therapist—there was no room for sexuality, aggressive feelings, jealousy, envy, or hurt, not really much room for real life, in fact, although Liz could make a good case for becoming a barrister specializing in child cases and dealing with other people's real lives in that way!

After a holiday break in therapy, which seemed to be experienced quite differently from any previous one in that I was felt to have abandoned her to pursue my own pleasures and personal life and no longer to be anyone she wished to communicate with, she became totally silent for many weeks. Instead of being "her" person, I was now contaminated by evidence of otherness. This perception of me as the neglectful sexual mother who multiply betrayed her by having another baby, by preferring her life of sex and drugs to caring for a toddler, by failing to protect her from her father's abuse, at last brought into the room the basis for Liz's anti-sexual relationship to herself. The sexual woman she had in her mind and who she feared she might become was a heartless and corrupt person whom she therefore had to hold at bay. Enough trust in me seemed to have been built up in our first 18 months of work to allow her now to manage to go on coming to see me even when she felt dominated by a dread of what she felt me to be. She watched me like a hawk from behind a curtain of hair and hands during these silent sessions, checking carefully that I had started the session on time and that I did not defraud her of any of the time due to her.

Working through this experience must have been a terrible struggle for Liz, but oddly for me it was a time of relief. Instead of the tedium of fundamentally avoidant communications, I felt the sessions to be full of interest, however tense and however uncertain the outcome. This was her emotional reality, I felt sure, and perhaps together we could help her bear it and thus she could feel free to become a woman in her own right. After months of virtual silence Liz began to talk again, and I learnt then that some more ordinary things were happening with her peers and her family: pop concerts, thoughts about a part-time job, battles about which school to be at in the sixth form and what A level subjects to take, and about how late she would stay out. A few months of dressing as a Goth were succeeded by other experiments in style and in going to parties. We continued work until Liz went off to university, having successfully fought school and parents about what subject she should study and what university she should go to. As for other adopted adolescents I have worked with, history and politics had become an important area of interest.

Omnipotent defences and the projection of vulnerability: Tim

In contrast with these two young people holding back from venturing into adolescence proper was Tim, a boy of 8 when I began work with him, whose solution to not feeling a secure sense of belonging in his adoptive family was to assert that he could manage all anxieties by himself, without adult help, principally by violently projecting all disturbance and unhappiness into those around him.

Tim had been adopted at age 5, after a period in foster care. His prostitute mother had been overwhelmed by attempting to care for her several young children and cope with a violent partner, and a tragedy had taken place in which one of the children had died in a fire. Taken into care at 2½, Tim, who was his mother's favourite child, showed deep upset around her visits to him and a defiant independence the rest of the time. After his adoption, one of the things most distressing to his adoptive parents was his reaction to being ill: he would take himself off to his bedroom and curl up on his own under the covers, conveying his conviction that there was no one to look after him but himself. I came to know well the intense sense of rejection and hurt that they had found so wounding. Their worries about this aspect of him only emerged after considerable work with their social worker at the clinic. Tim's referral for help had been prompted by concerns about his lying, stealing, and sexual acting-out at home and at school: his apparent absence of conscience about any of these activities and his non-responsiveness to ordinary parental discipline were what worried them.

The issue of whether he could afford to experience becoming attached, and thus having a sense of belonging, was rather starkly present in my initial contact with him. He had begun therapy with a colleague who sadly became ill and had to take prolonged sick leave a few months after starting with him. Tim's violence had already become a major problem in the therapy, and it was clear that a replacement therapist must be found so that his probably extreme reaction to the unexpected loss of his therapist could be contained. I quickly found myself the repository of a range of painful emotions in Tim's sessions, and seemingly with few lines of response that could reach him.

In these early months of work there were many sessions that brought me to the edge of my capacities as a therapist. Tim threatened my peace of mind with a bewildering variety of weapons, and I often felt close to hopelessness about being able to find the part of him that might respond to understanding. I would wake up on Thursday mornings, which was the day of his session, feeling very anxious and physically fearful—would I manage to keep the session within some bearable degree of control? My fears ranged from his dangerous behaviour at the high window, with which he thrilled to torment me, to concern for my room and its contents and for my own physical integrity: not so much direct fear of how he would hurt me, although this did happen, but more subtle assaults, which left me feeling abused and exposed. This was sometimes a physical reality, as when he held onto a handful of my hair as if to pull it out by the roots, but more often it was mental cruelty that I felt the force of. I spent large chunks of sessions with nowhere to put myself—he would commandeer all the furniture and I would feel lost and homeless in my room. I experienced shame and helplessness, knowing that he would jeer at whatever I said and feeling huge and foolish. He once spoke of me as one of the smelly vagrants on the Thames embankment, living in a cardboard box, and I certainly felt exposed to the most cruel elements of his personality in an unprotected way. The sense of shame seemed to me an important element in these countertransference sufferings. As he was a child who would frequently bar me out of my room for parts of every session or run out and invite me to a merry and futile chase all over the clinic, I was also aware of the public quality of this shaming and thought how my colleagues might smile at the spectacle of my absurd position. This often seemed more present in my mind than any feeling of being able to rely on support when up against it. Nonetheless, there were more encouraging elements of which I was never totally unaware. In every session, I could see that there had been some moment of warmth or softness, just enough to keep me going.

His capacity for expressive activity was fundamental in sustaining my hopefulness, even though the activity was often difficult to manage. At times he was more playful, for example in joyful water play. He delighted in the beauty of the soap bubbles he made, and it occurred to me that the absolutely innocent omnipotence of the young baby was an important element in this. The ordinarily fortunate baby has times when he can believe that the world was made just for him, in exactly the way that he desired, and this overlaps with the belief that he can make such a world for himself out of mother and all her riches. Winnicott writes about this experience and relates it to the potential for creativity. The normal toddler play that 8-year-old Tim was now engaged in seemed to have a particular meaning for him. His longings and imaginings of a mother there just for him had probably had remarkably little chance to be expressed or worked through in his early years. The feeding breast–mother of early infancy had been too confused with a sexualized picture of mother to which he had been painfully exposed. There were sessions when Tim would display his body in lewd posturings on my desk, with words, sounds, and gestures designed to stir my helpless distress and to inflict an experience of being violated. I became convinced that his experience of his mother's way of life as a prostitute had been totally unbearable to him. The internal sexual couple now dominant in his imagination used their bodies to create confusion, to project envy and deprivation, and to exploit helplessness. Actual sexual abuse by mother's cohabitee, which probably took place, would only have added another layer to this disastrous catalogue of infantile love betrayed.

Adopted children or those who have had disruptions in continuity of care face a particular loss in being able to find a match between the unconscious phantasy of a lovely world of Mummy and Daddy and baby and the actual experience of being part of a functioning family unit in which these elements are given their place and meaning through parental care. This conjunction has not been available. It is hard for a child entering a family which already has its history and is experienced as foreign and "other" by contrast with that which is known to the child to play with illusions of magical potency, to have moments of resting within them and not be catapulted into the disillusioning reality too quickly. Painful reality has intruded too early into the child's experience.

Putting things right. A crucial sequence of sessions took place after one Christmas break. Just before that holiday, Tim had been telling me about his school play about nineteenth-century convicts sent off to Australia. His part was to play one of the convicts. He described the prison ships and the farewell to friends and family on the last morning and sang a poignant story about losing his homeland and all that he loved. When he returned in the New Year, he looked around my room, and suddenly it seemed he had a brain wave. He began to move all the furniture systematically into different positions—not in a jumble, but in order to create a quite new room. The physical labour involved in this was immense, and as I was concerned about the weight of some items, I offered to help him, which he accepted. We were like two furniture removers. He decorated the newly positioned desk with a plant and ornaments and created a little corner for himself, almost completely enclosed, where he could draw on the low table, kneeling on the blanket and pillow, while I sat and watched on a chair placed just by him. Tim clearly felt at home in a quite new way now that he had devised a way of making the room his own so dramatically. He began each of the following sessions by repeating this sequence.

One day we entered the therapy room together for the first time for many months, as Tim had stayed near me on the walk from the waiting-room. Immediately, with a surly expression, he began to move the furniture around. He accepted my help with the desk, negotiating which end to move, and so on, while I talked about his wanting to make the room feel his own. The atmosphere seemed tense and volatile. He bent to scratch at his leg just below the knee, a bit secretively and with his back to me. I wondered aloud if he might have a sore leg but be unsure about showing me. He came closer and told me "It itches—it's a bite." He fetched the rug and lay down on the sofa and wrapped himself up completely inside it. Just as he had been preparing to do this, I had suggested pulling the blind down, as the room was hot. I decided to go ahead, though it involved leaning over him, which felt dangerously close. He remained peaceful. He lay still inside the rug briefly, then seemed to be scratching at something—I wondered what? He replied, but I could hardly hear. It sounded like "shady and cool". I talked to him about his searching for protection from the sun, which felt too hot today, and then went on to speak about last week, when he had also wanted some protection from the painful loose tooth in his mouth. "I got £1 for my tooth", he interrupted in a lively tone. "Did you?" I added: "You were pleased that I remembered about your tooth and feel more friendly when you know I remember you. Perhaps needing to wrap yourself up was linked with feeling hurt." He emerged, and with great seriousness rolled up the pillow inside the rug, using the whole floor to do this as a neat package, then placed this in his table-corner.

He looked round the room appraisingly. He fetched water for the plants in the watering can: first the one on top of the tall cupboard—removing dead leaves and adding, "It's not growing; there aren't any little ones yet", then the plants on the window sill. "Do you water the plants?" he asked me in a friendly tone of voice. I spoke of his questions about whether I keep in mind the things that are important to him from week to week and whether I know how to look after growing things and provide what they need. He said seriously that he wanted the plants taken out of the room when other children come in here . . . a younger child might pull bits off. I spoke about his doubt about allowing his different feelings to be in the room together: the younger wild and angry little Tim, who has often wanted to attack me and my plants and my room, is feared by the more thoughtful Tim who would like the plants and himself to grow.

Tim fetched his drawing book and pencil and settled down to sketch the watering can. After a while I spoke of his uncertainty about how close he wanted me to be today . . . usually he puts a chair for me just by him, but today his mixed feelings make that seem impossible. He looked up as if light was dawning and rearranged the room to put my chair in its usual place. Then he said, "You can sit there if you want." I moved to sit by him and watch. After a few minutes he realized this altered the light and shade and asked me to move again. He then asked if he can show the picture to his father at the end. I said that we could think about that, and I suggested that he was perhaps wanting to find a Father part of me who will see that Tim is learning from me and recognize what he feels is a good and hard-working aspect of himself. As he carried on drawing, I talked about his interest in light and shade. Perhaps he was wondering if his own light and dark feelings towards me might be able to connect up. He responded by looking behind the desk to his right, into a very dark part of the room. I said he was interested in looking into the darker places. He mouthed into the dark space "hello, hello", and asked if I heard the echo. I spoke of his wish that I listen to the Tim that wants to explore inside himself and me, including the dark corners.

Just as he was preoccupied with this game, he became aware of sirens outside. "What's that?" he asked. I wondered what he imagined. "Murder . . . an accident, someone's hurt . . . fire . . . there's a cat on a roof . . . someone's threatening to commit suicide." I said

Tim was thinking that today the emergency services, which he wants me to have ready for many disasters between us, might be getting there in time with the right ideas. Today he felt more hopeful that he could get a message to me about his worries, that he felt I understood how frightened he was, a bit like a cat stranded on the roof, and this made him feel that a rescue might be possible.

What factors support recovery from loss and trauma?

When children like Winston, Liz, and Tim are offered psychotherapy, it is vital that there is a long enough period of time available for the early abandonments of their lives and the distortions in development that have occurred in consequence to enter into the therapeutic relationship and to be understood within it. Short-term interventions are not effective when there has been severe inner psychological damage alongside external breakdown of care. Both child and therapist need the security of knowing that there can be adequate time and privacy for them to do this difficult work.

The therapist requires a secure clinical setting, with reliable space, the support of colleagues, and access to supervision. When the children are pre-adolescent, the family needs very regular and skilled support in their difficult day-to-day task. For the child or young person, alongside the conviction in the family or wider network that therapy is a worthwhile endeavour, there are many internal factors that make a difference. The very different constellations within the three cases discussed in this chapter indicate how varied presenting problems and personality styles can be. The damage may be visible either in difficult and self-destructive behaviour (Liz), in depression and retreat from life (Winston) or in delinquent antisocial impulses that seem impervious to ordinary restraint (Tim). Other examples would reveal further particular individual patterns of response to early deprivation.

It is vital that a careful assessment takes place to explore the appropriateness of psychotherapy for any individual child. While the evidence of the good results of child psychotherapeutic interventions with this group of children has continued to gain weight over the last 30 years (Boston & Szur, 1983; Hunter, 2001), effectiveness depends on the timeliness of the therapy from the child's point of view as well as the skill and staying power of the therapist. The consent of the child to the exploration of his or her internal world probably cannot be conceived of very often as the sort of conscious "consent to treatment" on which medical models depend. However, if the assessment of child and context includes a chance for the child to experience the kind of emotional exploration and enquiry into meaning that is at the heart of psychotherapy, then a wish to continue work with the therapist is based on genuine consent. This is not, of course, to suggest that a child in therapy will always be eager to attend sessions: reluctance and resistance is bound to occur at difficult times in the treatment, when the child will need adult encouragement to go on with things, and the adolescent will need some measure of more adult functioning within himself.

An interesting example of this latter point was what enabled an older adopted adolescent to commit himself to beginning therapy. In the initial assessment, he had described a deeply unhappy state of affairs within himself and between him and his adoptive family, an entrenched sense of being a second-class child, of loneliness and isolation in his peer group, and of failure to deploy his intelligence at school. However, when it came to it, he also stated firmly that he wanted to solve all these problems on his own and thought he could do this. I offered to see him again six months later so that we could see how things were going, and he was pleased with this arrangement. When we met again, a very similar sequence ensued: he again described how miserable and stuck he was in all areas of his life, but ended with the same resolution that it was up to him to work it out. The adolescent urge to independence made it very hard for him to allow himself to accept help. We agreed to review things again in another few months. Only at this point was he able to say that he was not getting anywhere on his own and that he would like to start regular therapy. I think that this protracted process of decision heralded a crucial turning point, as it served to break through his earlier belief that potency lay in a sort of obstinate self-reliance and to start him on a path in which there was room to tolerate his dependence on others as well as to spread his wings. This proved a fertile basis for a period of therapy which he could feel to be freely chosen and not imposed.

Gathering together a secure sense of identity is a large task for all young people, and the fluid social context of the modern world has intensified the pressure of this inescapable adolescent process. For adopted children the earlier losses, disruption, and uncertainties inevitably make for greater difficulties at times of transition. Where there has been a great deal of emotional pain, confusion, or trauma as well as change and loss, there are additional vulnerabilities. In therapeutic work with such children and adolescents, the one ingredient that seems to be an absolute requirement is that the pace of the work should be very carefully judged. Emotional scars are easily opened, and the levels of pain these children have endured are often extreme. They need to feel held with tact, imaginative sympathy, patience, and courage. Opening themselves up to finding out about the fault-lines within their defensive carapace asks a lot of them. The work requires an attitude in the therapist of "tiptoeing" up to the child's pain alongside a clear-sighted focus on the nature of the distress and its underlying sources.

PART III

PSYCHOTHERAPEUTIC WORK
WITH PARENTS AND FAMILIES

The chapters in this section describe a range of ways in which members of the Fostering and Adoption team have worked with parents, families, and carers. As the needs of the families vary, so it has been necessary to provide adoptive, foster, and kinship carers and the families with different and accessible methods of working together. The underlying traumatic experiences that the children bring with them to their new families are a feature of all the chapters in this section—indeed in this book.

Lorraine Tollemache highlights the importance for adoptive parents to have access to professionals who have not been responsible for placing the children, so that they are able to be open to the difficult and uncomfortable feelings that may emerge. Her chapter also shows the value of continuity in the work, something that is difficult to access in many settings. The work may need to take place over a long period, changing in intensity as the needs of the family change over time.

Sara Barratt describes work with different constellations of families that evolves over time. She writes about the systemic framework that underpins her work. She emphasizes that families can be helped to listen to each another and to negotiate changes in their relationships with one another. She addresses the impact of past experiences that can make it hard to resolve problems in the present.

Sara Barratt and Julia Granville describe the problems that may emerge when children are placed with relatives and friends. Kinship carers may receive little ongoing support from placing authorities. This chapter describes the neediness of the carers and the vulnerability of the placements, particularly when there are continuing and often unsupervised contact arrangement with birth parents. Barratt and Granville write about the use of a systemic framework when working with the children in kinship families, which facilitates expression of their fears and anxieties about their birth families, a particularly challenging task.

Julia Granville and Laverne Antrobus describe unique short-term group work in parenting that brought together adoptive, foster, and kinship carers. Although the groups stand alone as a treatment method, Granville and Antrobus draw attention to the importance of linking them to other work provided by the team: some carers already had other ongoing work; some were in need of more. This chapter also shows the need for creating a nurturing context to sustain the carers through intensive work to adapt their ways of parenting this group of children.

Jenny Kenrick

Minding the gap: reconciling the gaps between expectation and reality in work with adoptive families

Lorraine Tollemache

This chapter addresses the gaps between the hopes and expectations of adoption and the often painful realities of the experience, and how we have helped families to bridge them. This is because adoption is a complex process, and the hopes and expectations of each person involved in it are invariably different. Though many remain unvoiced and some are only partially conscious, they are still difficult to relinquish. Most people know that adoption today is a particularly risky enterprise because it sets out to remedy earlier failures and experiences of loss and trauma by putting together children and adults who have only a nominal opportunity of choosing each other and no previous experience of living together. Their reactions to this experience can be explosive and leave everyone shaken, not least the social workers who carry heavy responsibility for the outcome.

There is great need for families and professionals to have access to a team separate from those that make the placements but familiar with the demands of the situation, where there are opportunities to work out what may be going on, the adaptations that are necessary, and where feelings may be expressed and understood. There is frequently little opportunity for the latter because, as Lear has said (1998), "there is a wish to ignore the complexity, depth and darkness of human life . . . there is a wish in everybody to ignore pain". If something as challenging as building a family through adoption is to have any chance of success, families and those who work with them must be open to feelings that are often hidden and emerge in unexpected ways. The defences of denial and pretence do not work.

It can be particularly difficult for adoptive parents to find a place in which their reactions can be expressed because they can realistically feel that conveying unhappiness and dissatisfaction too openly could result in children being removed by social workers who may fear that a mistake has been made at the start of a placement, or, at a later date, that the adoptive parents are the abusers. Children placed for adoption suffer from poignant dilemmas and can carry a huge burden of guilt and responsibility. Social workers also face virtually impossible tasks working as they do within the constraints of targets and tight time frames. I describe work with all three groups—adoptive parents, children, and social workers—though my main concern is with adoptive parents. This is because I believe that most hope is placed in them.

Within this chapter I describe different dilemmas we have encountered and the ways we have addressed them through five fictional families—composites of many we have seen. In each there is such a clash between the hopes and expectations of different individuals that continuing seems difficult. The first family illustrates themes of loss and choice, the second illustrates the impact of traumatic early experiences, the third the plight of a single-parent adopter. The last two describe families where there were both birth and adopted children and where each posed a threat to the other.

Choices and losses: Green family

John and Mary Green decided to adopt a child after years of marriage and many unsuccessful infertility treatments. They had chosen to have two siblings. These children had said they wanted a "forever family", but after two years there was no move by the parents to apply for an adoption order and the social workers who had poured all they could into helping seemed as helpless and despondent as the parents themselves.

This family illustrates the fact that in adoption choices have to be made before anyone knows what is being chosen, or before what is lost is properly acknowledged and grieved. Indeed, there can be little space for grief in the process. Many adopters, like the Greens, have had to cope with the blow of infertility and the invasiveness of failed infertility treatments when hopes are raised and dashed repeatedly while life is put on hold. They are then expected to open themselves to the fresh invasiveness of adoption procedures and to be ready to take on the children who are made available, rather than the babies they may really have wanted.

The Greens had chosen to adopt older children, perhaps to make up for lost time and before they were judged to be too old to be adopters themselves. Despite the preparation they received for the task, they were shocked by the unremitting rejection they were subjected to by the children who were placed with them. The children were still attached to other parents. By the time they were referred to the Fostering and Adoption team at the Tavistock, the Greens' confidence in their capacity to be good parents had been severely shaken.

A colleague and I saw them in various combinations—as a family, as a couple, or with one or both of the children. Later we were joined by another colleague who assessed the older child in his own right. We wanted to provide them with opportunities to communicate both separately and together, so that we could work out with them what might be happening and set about bridging the gaps between what they had all hoped for and the undeniably increasing misery of their daily lives. We discovered that different levels and pockets of unhappiness existed. First, the couple seemed flat, though the mother was the more distressed. She was gaining least from the two children, their rejection repeating the rejection she had suffered at the hands of her own mother. Next, it was clearly difficult having two children at once. They were never all right at the same time, taking it in turns to be "the problem", testing out their belief, based on their experience, that no birth parent or foster carer could cope with them both. With our help one of the children grew closer to her new parents. As the couple learned to understand her and to claim her more confidently, she began to settle.

The older child remained a problem, stirring up his sister if he sensed she was happy. His dilemma was poignant. He simply could not forget his birth mother and continually wondered if she had now "grown up enough" to be able to look after him. He had been told that his birth mother was too young and that was why they had been removed. He had blotted out earlier abusive experiences, and his memories were confused; but he also realized that he had been offered something good by the adoptive parents, and he was frightened to throw this away. What could he do about the birth mother he had tried to look after as if he were her parent and who now existed in a childless state, unable to say goodbye to her children or to release them to start afresh?

Over weeks we noted improvements, yet the family remained in a powerful state of tension. There was no move towards adoption, and the social workers grew worried and impatient. This worsening of the situation before things can improve is something we frequently experience in adoptive families. It highlights a normal yet anxiety-provoking phase in the adoption process, but through this process these parents really chose to adopt the children, though they risked nearly losing them.

The change was set in motion when they told us—the first time they had divulged it to anyone—how desperately unhappy they were, and of their sense of depletion, failure, and isolation. They did not like the people they had become, or the parents they were turning into. Disappointed, flat, and flattened, they felt they functioned by rote. They had hoped to feel love for the children. As they could not, they felt fraudulent. No amount of praise or reassuring them of the good job they really were doing made any difference. They had decided they could not go on, the children must go back. Voicing these feelings had a powerful effect on us. We felt profoundly bleak, but we knew they must be taken seriously. At this point parents and children can be at greatest risk. Sudden moves can be made, often unnecessarily, because anger and disappointment are being acted out.

We subsequently learned from the children's social worker that he had decided that the children should be moved speedily. This provoked extreme shock, but with our help the parents began to think how they might make the children's last weeks with them happier. Then, at the prospect of actual loss, they were galvanized. Thoughts of what might have been were driven from their minds; they appreciated the real children and the strides they had all made. They knew there would be no second chances of having children and discovered they could not bear to return to the emptiness of their lives without them. They really *chose* them for the first time, and the children, predictably, responded. They had in fact become increasingly anxious to be claimed. Being more certain of their own feelings, the Greens could then withstand the fluctuations of the children's. It was a relief to everyone.

We were able to regulate a harrowing situation by establishing a framework of meetings in which legitimate but powerful feelings could be shared and contained without a replay of previous loss. There was, instead, a chance for second thoughts. The *Oxford Dictionary* defines grief as "deep or violent sorrow", and in this situation a great deal of grief was being expressed: first, the grief of the parents at their infertility, exacerbated by the many failed infertility treatments. Their feelings of anger and distress, which had been repressed and denied until the placement, were triggered then for the first time, and mourning began. Second the grief of the children, who realized at the same point that they, too, were not like others, living with birth parents or with foster carers who had not set out to replace their birth parents. They could not understand whose fault this was. Was it the fault of one of them who had been too much for their birth parents, or the fault of the judge who had made the decision that they should be moved, or the fault of the prospective adopters who had "stolen" them, or of their birth mother who had not really wanted them, despite her protestations of the opposite? The social worker's reaction was also linked to grief and the anger that accompanies this. He had worked tirelessly on the children's behalf, yet this had come to nothing.

Because there were two of us working constantly together, joined by a colleague and backed by our team, and because we were from a separate institution and had perhaps the least to lose, we could be open to what was going on. We had established the trust of the family and the social workers and could contain and digest the powerful feelings projected into us. We could think in a situation where the capacity for thought is endangered. It was clear to us all that a couple like this could parent and love the children, though they had to discover this for themselves. Here, imminent separation triggered attachment behaviour: these parents, unlike the birth parents, *could* claim the children. Without the containment we had been able to offer, many adoptive families may break up needlessly. An adoptive parent's belief that they can be a parent needs nurturing. It is often fragile and shaken by difficult experiences. An adopted child's belief that he can be good enough, that he will not be rejected again, is equally fragile. Both need the help of others to keep the hope alive. We know that grief is a recurring theme in adoption. The experience of grief visits those in adoptive families again and again, but once it is recognized it is more easily overcome.

The impact of early trauma: Julia

Some families reach us many years after children have been adopted, when there is a more acute sense of crisis and they feel they cannot continue together much longer. Indeed, the cost of their remaining together thus far soon becomes clear to us as we see how deeply traumatized they all are. The burden these parents carry must be better shared. In these situations we gather together a team, first within the specialist team and then outside it. These are teams that fully grasp the depth of the damage inflicted on the children and the impact of this on all with whom they have contact. We become an extended family that can support and contain the adoptive family.

Julia was a deeply traumatized child who before the age of 3 had been subjected to situations of extreme and prolonged terror at the hands of her violent and mentally unstable birth parents. Though her mother had been in care herself and her father was a known paedophile, the couple moved frequently so that social services could not intervene until the next child, a boy, was born. The experienced foster carer with whom both children then were placed found Julia the most difficult toddler she had ever cared for. Despite this, both children were adopted rapidly by a couple with whom, on the surface, they seemed well matched.

At first Julia monopolized her inexperienced new mother with single-minded intensity, allowing no one else near her. Then she rejected her just as vehemently. The degree of hurt and shock this mother experienced paralleled the hurt sustained by Julia originally. It was profoundly destabilizing for this new and vulnerable parent to be made to feel as if she were deliberately setting out to harm the child she had fought so hard to secure. Julia had learnt to defend herself from being flooded by psychic and physical pain by dissociation, instantaneously cutting herself off from her disturbing responses to closeness, projecting these into others. She set out to control anyone caring for her and so avoid the risks of dependency. The violence and unpredictability of her behaviour was intensely wearing and traumatized her new mother, who closed down. She became cold and rejecting in turn, though inside she felt upset, ashamed, and disorientated. The fact that Julia's brother did respond to her provided little comfort, as Julia envied and attacked this relationship. Her behaviour organized and dominated the whole family, so that nobody in it could be themselves.

Establishing proximity was a major problem in the family, as we found when we met them when Julia was 8. She played out her internal scenario repeatedly with small animals: she seemed preoccupied by a mother-and-baby pair (the kangaroos) and a crocodile. These animals can epitomize dangerous and cruel or close relationships and are seized on by many children; but in Julia's play the crocodile and kangaroo identities switched suddenly and unpredictably. It was not clear what triggered the change. She clearly identified with the crocodile, which took delight in biting and hurting others. This reflected her relish at other people's fear of her and the sense of power this gave her. Though she craved the closeness of the kangaroo pair, she did not know how to be close or what others expected of her. She would suddenly invite sexual closeness, profoundly disconcerting to those with her, demonstrating an intrusion she had undoubtedly experienced.

Hodges and Steele (2000) have described how one of the story stems they use diagnostically, which involves a toy elephant, is repeatedly chosen by sexually abused children to demonstrate a sudden bad/good shift. At one moment the elephant is kind, giving smaller animals rides on its back, the next it stamps on them or sticks its tail into them. It may then switch back. The child cannot reconcile these contrary experiences of an adult and hold both in mind at the same time. These children are highly watchful in case good people turn bad or bad people good.

I have found that the adoptive parents of such children need to be treated with great delicacy: proximity has become risky for them too. They may also be acutely aware of the reactions of others. Some feel judged as unsympathetic, critical, unloving, or too keen to get rid of a child they have adopted. After years of difficulty, they certainly feel exposed as inadequate parents. They may feel pitied; they often feel trapped, particularly if they are attached to an adopted sibling. Repeated interactions with a child who feels trapped himself may trigger memories of his own previous trauma, intensifying the current experience. The presence of a steady and confirming partner may be reassuring, but it cannot prevent the profound sense of breakdown, the disintegration of the self experienced by the parent on the receiving end of a traumatized child's behaviour.

Herman (1992) has written of work with traumatized adults and the need to establish first a sense of safety and next a sense of control. She notes:

> Though the single most common therapeutic error is avoidance of the traumatic material, probably the second most common error is premature or precipitate engagement in exploratory work, without sufficient attention to the tasks of establishing safety and securing a therapeutic alliance.

If it took time for Julia to be able to trust her therapist enough literally to remain in a room with her, it took time for this mother, who felt done over by professionals and children alike, to feel safe enough to be herself with me. The feeling of safety grew when she realized I would not blame or pity her or suddenly intrude with pointed questions. I would go at her pace into regions into which she led the way. I was familiar with the experiences she described through working with many adopters and could put them in a context without dismissing them.

Achieving a sense of control over Julia needed a panoply of interventions. The psychotherapy we could provide for her gave us an insight into her inner world and helped her to feel less alone. Her parents, however, needed respite from her, a breathing space in which to regain their sense of equilibrium before they could be interested in her again themselves. They had been relieved to see that Julia's therapist, who was subjected to attacks similar to those inflicted on them, could tolerate these and begin to understand her. They needed additional practical help. An experienced foster carer was found. She helped them to develop a clearer, more predictable, more detached model of parenting. It was counterintuitive. It was a model they could not have known, but they practised it with increasing skill, gradually overriding Julia's rigid defences so that, like a recovering anorexic, she could allow herself the "food" of emotional and physical experience that she had craved but of which she had starved herself.

With such children, school usually presents a problem. They cannot learn because they cannot risk thinking and not knowing. As they are humiliated by the growing gap between themselves and others, their tantrums intensify. Harassed teachers cannot cope. Few schools can manage without the extra resources a Statement of Educational Needs provides, but securing such a statement involves prolonged and intense negotiation with another department with its own exacting criteria.

The detailed assessments that the teams inside and outside the Tavistock provided eventually secured the precise resources this family needed, but there were also numerous meetings—for example, with social services. Their initial impulse had been to remove Julia from the family. They assumed that these parents had caused her problems, rather than realizing that they were provoked by the earlier maltreatment. Having located the respite care and appropriate schooling, however, we had then to fight for them to be provided for long enough to make a difference. The cost of each resource inevitably drives a wedge between agencies, compelled as they are to repeatedly justify each expense. Then problems may be forced back onto the adopters. "After all" the agencies may argue, "the parents chose to have the child in the first place". This provides CAMHS professionals with a crucial role. We must clearly identify the symptoms of severe neglect and abuse before adoption, particularly when it has occurred early in a child's life. These are frequently overlooked or minimized, but, as Gerhardt (2004) demonstrates, they can be devastating. Adoptive families are given relatively little help or time within which to remedy the problems of children from the care system but with enough help we find that they have some chance of succeeding.

Single adopters: Tracey

Single adopters are increasingly chosen to adopt children as it is recognized that many successful parents are single. There can, however, be a false expectation that they will be able to manage the impact of any child without the help and support of a partner. Where adoptive children have previously been physically, sexually, or emotionally abused, this places a special strain on them and there is often a desperate need for a third person to intervene to protect the mental health of both.

Tracey was 8 when she was placed with her prospective adopter. The referral to us was made almost immediately because the new mother felt invaded and confused. What belonged to her and what to the child? Her experience was like that of a birth mother with a first-born child, but magnified. How could she work out how much of this was "normal" when she had no experience of birth or adoption? She had, however, chosen Tracey with care. Tracey had no wish for contact with her birth family, where a great deal of sexual abuse had taken place. She was relieved to be rescued. However, having been invaded herself, like Julia, she now attempted to invade and control everyone else. Her new mother was filled with panic.

We set about disentangling things and setting up boundaries, embarking on separate work with both the mother and the child. Tracey could only make limited use of psychotherapy, but the contribution I could make was to become the mother's partner, helping her to re-establish herself in a more secure way until the unknown became more familiar. For example, the help she had counted on soon melted away. Some friends, resenting Tracey's intrusiveness, kept away. Others were uneasy at leaving her with their children. The new school made endless complaints about her behaviour with both teachers and pupils alike. This mother felt angry and upset, as the problems were not of her making but ones she had bravely hoped to put right. On top of all this, she faced returning to a taxing job once the adoption leave ran out. Overwhelmed by the impact of what she had, perhaps too naively, taken on, she postponed seeking an adoption order to avoid being left to fend for herself. This annoyed the hard-pressed social workers. The local authority had already paid for a therapeutic community for Tracey before she was placed for adoption and were keen to see her settled, with the emotional, financial, and practical burdens assumed by someone else.

In the light of our assessments of Tracey we could represent her very real difficulties to other professionals, so that this mother was given some of the additional help she needed through the turbulent stages of Tracey's development. We worked steadily together over a number of years. Tracey's progress was spectacularly difficult, particularly during adolescence, when she repeatedly put herself at risk, expecting to be rescued. The internalized presence of her abusive birth family manifested itself frequently—for example, when she began to bully and abuse other children. Like many adopted children, she increasingly gravitated towards the very environment from which she had been removed. She was, in effect, doing her own "life-story" work, living out the stories she had played out in her psychotherapy. She was finding out for herself whether she had been thrown away or stolen, whether her birth family really cared for her. She was setting out to bridge the gaps, finding out where her identifications lay and where she felt most "at home".

It is during this period that adoptive parents can feel most alone and may again need help. They often feel an emptiness and grief like that experienced by a birth mother first of all: a sense that they are invisible, that parenthood was a sham, and that they have no part to play in the lives they see "their" children setting out on. A CAMHS team can help at this point, particularly if they have known the family for some time. We become a reference point for the parent, for the child, and for the new professionals who may have become involved. Sometimes we find we can validate a separation between adoptive parents and children so that they can resume their relationships on a different footing.

Though some adolescent adopted children leave their adoptive families prematurely, they need to come and go. This mother managed to keep the door open. Tracey lived for a time in a number of other families and residential institutions. Her identifications were complex, spanning as they did extremes of experience, of social class and culture. Later, as new friends and families let her down, she began to freshly appreciate the adoptive mother who fought so tirelessly on her behalf.

Combined families: the Brown family

In order to encompass the complexity of adoptive families today, I want to touch on families where birth and adopted children are combined—an experience that can extend and enrich everyone but one that carries risks, especially for children.

The Browns already had three children, but the mother had long dreamt of adopting. She persuaded her husband and their children that new brothers or sisters would complete the family and help others less fortunate than themselves. The children, being considerate, agreed. As the parents were successful and experienced, they were welcomed by social workers, who, like them, underestimated the impact of a small "gang" of siblings with allegiances to other families and little wish to belong to theirs. The birth children, raised more tenderly, were directly exposed to the ruthlessness of these children and simultaneously found themselves cut off from the parents, who had nurtured them lovingly but now seemed oblivious to their plight. Indeed, the whole family was drawn in to control and contain the new comers. A distorted family structure soon developed, one that it seemed impossible to change.

As has been clear, adoptive families can lose sight of what is "normal" as they attempt to help and integrate the children they have taken on. Indeed, the abnormality of some behaviours may only emerge when there is a change—for example, a change of school. New teachers may then draw attention to the disturbing behaviour parents may have denied because it is directed at other children in the school. At this point parents may seek our help, shocked by what is emerging and uncertain of what they should do.

Again we provide a framework that allows parents to address the gap between their expectations and the painful realities that are emerging, and to feel grief. For example, some parents may have to face the fact that their birth children have been abused by the adopted children, that their sense of security has been shaken, and that they were abandoned by them when they most needed help. They may learn that the adopted children had also been placed in an impossible situation and struggled with divided loyalties and an acute sense of loss. Marital relationships may have been damaged by the experience of adoption. Any naive attitudes that adopters may have held are certainly exposed. Sometimes a range of therapeutic interventions is needed. However, we have found that many parents can and do adjust to the realities they face. They reorder their priorities and learn to cater for the differing needs of each child while caring for each other. Remarkable integrations are then achieved, and the lives of individuals are enriched.

Eddie

A less happy outcome was possible for the family who adopted Eddie. His parents were not able to make these adaptations for a number of reasons. He was 5 and had been adopted for two years when a birth child, a little sister, arrived unexpectedly. This pointed up very painful differences between the two children and put a great strain on everyone in the family. At the first family meeting the dilemma was evident: Eddie was not brought; he seemed to live on the edge of the family. We wondered why, and whether he could belong to it. Much had been tried already. Eddie had been in psychotherapy. We started to work with the whole family, but though there were moments of hope after some of our interventions, nothing could be sustained.

Eddie was undoubtedly an odd child, with a stilted, unreal air, unlike his sister, who communicated with others naturally and confidently. Eddie mimicked people instead. First he mimicked my colleague, whom he obviously admired and wanted to be like. We learned he also wanted to be exactly like his sister. When he didn't get exactly the same treatment as she did, his tantrums were volcanic. As his sister grew and developed a mind of her own, Eddie attacked her; the parents flew to protect the younger child, and this increased his resentment. It also gave his sister an intoxicating sense of power.

Mimicry is a way by which many abused children try to manage living. Eddie had been profoundly damaged by his birth parents who had, together, sexually, physically, and emotionally abused him. He could not develop. For example, he had no means of knowing what stimulus came from outside or inside himself, when he was hot or cold or hungry or tired or hurt. Though 9 when we met him, he would, like a 2-year-old, endlessly ask "why"? He could not remember the answers he was given because he was so busy gathering up bits and pieces: scraps of information or food or miscellaneous objects. Rustin (1997) has said of children like Eddie "only by holding on to all the bits and pieces of experience can they safeguard a sense of the 'continuity of being'" though "these fragments exist in a jumble, they are not located in a past present or future". This is because the categories of past and present have not developed. Instead, "they are in a world of continuous present . . . this creates an atmosphere of suspended animation" She goes on to explain how the compulsive activity sets up a wall that frustrates those trying to reach the child and how living by mimicry is also profoundly unsatisfying for the child, leaving him "empty and desperate". All this made sense of Eddie's stilted manner and of his increasingly relentless tantrums. However, we noticed that he was not the only person in the family who was in trouble.

We noticed that his father was also living on the edge in a different way. He was often ill, none of our interventions were of any lasting use to him, he seemed unreachable, he, too, had an unreal quality. We began to see that he was profoundly affected by Eddie's presence and by our attempts to reintegrate him into the family. We learned that, like Eddie, he had been traumatized in the past. Eddie's behaviour reactivated these experiences for him, and he coped by exploding or withdrawing. His wife was worn out trying to hold the family together. She had to choose between continuing in an increasingly distressing situation or preserving him, her marriage, and their birth child and abandoning Eddie. Both parents were ridden with guilt and needed our help to facilitate a separation and dismantle a damaging situation, salvaging enough to counteract the sense of ruin that a failed adoption can induce.

Eddie needed particular care delivered by an adult solely responsible for his needs in an environment adapted to his needs. This is available in some therapeutic communities or a family that cares therapeutically for children such as the one Cairns (2002) describes. Eddie could not be expected to adapt to the needs of a family. His path would, inevitably, be a difficult one. We find we have an important role to play working with a local authority when children re-enter the care system. It is then that they can be in the greatest danger of being lost. Every placement breakdown leaves them feeling more desperate, abandoned, and murderously envious of those who have the good experiences they crave. They become more damaging. An agency that knows a child and its history can help to identify what can be realistically expected of them and of subsequent carers and to see that the relationships they have achieved, however partial, are not lost. Eddie's adoptive parents remained loyal to him, they continued to see him even if they could not live with him. In this way the unrelated fragments that characterized his inner world were not entirely replicated in his external environment. Some narrative could be developed by those who cared for him to help to link his experiences together. Elizabeth Bishop's wry poem "One Art" (1983) states:

The art of losing isn't hard to master
So many things seem filled with the intent
To be lost, that their loss is no disaster.

We know that the opposite is true. Accumulated losses are disastrous for everyone. The art of remembering and holding in mind is the one we need to cultivate.

Conclusion

This chapter describes the way we have worked with some adoptive families to link distressing and fragmented experiences together in a way that is meaningful for them, helping them to move forward more hopefully. All were bruised by painful experiences. They had all hoped that adoption could remedy previous ills. Having exhausted their own resources, they felt helpless and isolated; some felt humiliated and an overwhelming sense of failure. It was not easy for them to open themselves afresh to us.

The response to the help we can offer is, of course, varied. Many parents, though clearly at their wits' end, are nonetheless desperate to learn about the children they have taken on and welcome any information we can give them. They also welcome being seen separately from the child and sometimes from each other, and, though distressed at what may emerge in thinking about the present situation in the light of the past, both in relation to their own lives and those of the children, they adjust, moving on to changing their lives in ways they may not have imagined. They have the reflective capacity defining those designated as "secure" in Main's Adult Attachment interview. This may have been lost in the confusing early months or years of the adoption, but when their own experiences can be validated and those of the children better understood, they move on, even though their children may be no easier to care for.

Another group of parents are more ambivalent by the time they reach us. Less interested in the child causing them grief, they may exhibit symptoms of secondary trauma themselves. We have found that with enough help over time and opportunities to regulate the degree of intimacy they can sustain with a troubled child, adoption can prove satisfying. Their own attachment patterns may be deemed "insecure avoidant" or "insecure ambivalent", but current research by Coram Family (described by Steele in chapter 3) suggests parents designated as "avoidant" may be less worn down by an adopted child's behaviour than are those who are too responsive to them; a less intense atmosphere may better suit the child. A small group of parents (illustrated in Eddie's story) have one partner who is suffering from acute and unresolved experiences of loss and trauma. They are clearly very vulnerable. The Coram research shows that these adoptions are prone to disruption. Parents and children need help to find an alternative that leaves them as intact as possible while preserving the links that can be sustained.

We have found that, as professionals, it is essential to be therapeutically eclectic, finding the intervention that feels relevant for a family itself and remaining committed to them for long enough to make a difference. We expect adoptive families to take on, extend, and adapt themselves to unexpectedly painful situations for life. Like them, we must open ourselves to others with disparate ways of reading the world, developing our own skills while retaining a sense of our own integrity. It is a not easy to maintain the curiosity, energy, and imagination this requires, yet we expect this of adopters. When we succeed, the work is intensely rewarding.

This is true of adoption itself. It offers unique opportunities. It offers adults the opportunity to be parents, to have a link to the world and to the future. For many, life without children seems empty. It offers children an opportunity to have good experiences of parents and perhaps a chance to make more positive links with birth families. It can give them a sense of hope. Though adoptive parents cannot replace birth parents and adopted children cannot replace birth children, adoption provides opportunities for different kinds of creativity. Because there are risks attached to this kind of family building, adoptive families need others who can help them to bridge the gaps between expectation and reality, who can keep hope alive within the parameters of the possible.

CHAPTER 12

Systemic work with families after adoption

Sara Barratt

C hildren are often described as "belonging" to their families. We talk about "our" children and like to think that they will become the people we want them to be. Adoptive families struggle to find a way to "belong" to one another within a context of other belongings. This chapter discusses work with families after adoption and the dilemmas they encounter in finding a way to "belong".

During my professional life I have worked with adoptive families and children through the process of assessment, placement, and breakdown, with adopted adults referred by their GP and, as a family therapist at the Tavistock Clinic, with families after adoption. I draw on these experiences and in particular the work undertaken to help families develop a way of living together that fits well enough for each member of the family.

Much of our work is with families who have adopted children removed from their birth families following concerns about parenting, or with families who have adopted children from overseas. In our multidisciplinary team we work initially with all parts of the system: the family together, the parents on their own, the young person and/ or siblings and involved professionals, such as social workers and teachers, where appropriate. The most common themes in our work are the influence of the past on the present family predicament, of loss and of children's loyalty to their family of origin, all of which may never previously have been discussed, even with a professional.

It is important to remember that not everything should be talked about within the family; all members may need the opportunity to talk alone with the therapist, in order to understand and think about some feelings and experiences that are affecting them, which may not be usefully discussed in the family context. For example, it may be difficult and inappropriate to talk about past tensions around infertility and the decision to adopt in the presence of adopted children. These issues influence the dynamics of a family and need to be discussed and understood, at least initially, separately from the children. Frequently, addressing the question of infertility may begin to change the problem behaviour that is leading to family difficulties. Providing a flexible approach to family work ensures that everyone feels that their needs are being met. It enables the family to use its own resources to change relationships.

Sometimes the guilt and desperation are so intense—for example, concerning the feeling of hatred that may arise between adults and children—that it is necessary to talk in a setting where they will not feel blamed. This also provides the opportunity to consider what can and cannot be talked about openly. Sharing shameful emotions often provides a sense of relief. The new understanding gained from talking with therapists and receiving feedback can help adults and children separately to move on: either to feel differently about their relationship or to attribute new meanings to the feelings they have about one another.

We work with families to unravel their past experiences and to think about the way it resonates with their present. By drawing family trees, children and adults are able to talk together about their family. It gives them the opportunity to think about the previous experience of family life that they hold within them. We create family trees with great care, always checking with children whether and where they want to include their current and original families. Through the use of the family tree we provide an opportunity for family members to understand the impact of past experience, by focusing on a drawing on a piece of paper rather than being in eye contact. This enables the adults to listen to often painful accounts from their children, which they may prefer not to hear. Through these explorations, we try to find a way forward for the family so that they can create a new family story, which is acceptable to all.

Working as a team of therapists with different professional and personal backgrounds has led to conversations about our cultural beliefs about families. This challenges us to be more flexible in our work. Some are naturally more allied to the child's perspective and others to the adult's. Work with a colleague either in the room or behind a one-way screen is helpful to keep us aware of our assumptions and prejudices and to ensure that we find a way to understand the perspective of all family members without imposing our understanding or beliefs on them.

Children moving to adoptive families may have had many hopes and disappointments prior to the placement. They may have experienced several changes of social worker and of carer, each of whom has different cultural experiences and beliefs about children. These beliefs may come from professional experience, from the stories that have been passed down over generations, from the experience of migration or of lived experience, which all contribute to their ideas about the needs of children. There are many people who have a role in the lives of the children, however briefly, and who play a part in creating a story of their life, which the children have little opportunity to confirm or refute. We have received referrals for children giving details of their family background and structure drawn from minutes of case conferences in which professionals had provided inaccurate information. Other referrals detail non-existent half-siblings or extended family members, giving hearsay accounts of events that have not been substantiated by family members. A carer has described her concern that only the misdemeanours of the child she looks after are recorded. She has found caring for the 12-year-old boy a rewarding experience: she says that the case notes do not describe his warmth, enthusiasm, or sense of humour, and the recorded catalogue of psychopathology and misbehaviour means that he would now be difficult to place in a family. In particular, the emphasis on negative behaviour does not support the child in thinking positively about himself.

Children in a busy foster family or from a chaotic birth family may never have been the focus of attention. The move to an adoptive family, where there may be no other children and where every aspect of their life and behaviour is noticed, provides no space to hide. The child, unused to being the focus of attention, may experience the adoptive parents' efforts to form a bond as too intense. For adoptive parents and adopted children the idea of being a family has been a dream. Each has an idea of what it will mean. The intense wish for this family to be like a birth family and be able to find intimacy and affection are difficult to talk about, as are the disappointments that accompany the lived experience of family life. There may not be the opportunity for the child to think or talk about the way previous experience of distress and loss influences their feelings about this new family. For both adults and children struggling to form attachments to one another, the yearned-for family can easily turn into a disappointment, leading to a feeling of failure.

The adoption process

Prospective adopters require considerable determination and resilience to pursue their application. Would-be adopters usually come to adoption following treatment for infertility, which has made them feel investigated and exposed. The decision to apply to adopt takes them again into a situation where they are investigated, this time to demonstrate that they can provide safe and consistent parenting to troubled children. The process can further undermine their self-confidence and lead to them feeling that they should be able to cope with any distress or challenging behaviour that a child may bring. Adopters tend to come from articulate middle-class families who have the language to communicate with professionals. In order to recruit adoptive parents from a more diverse group that reflects the racial and ethnic mix of children seeking homes, agencies provide parenting groups and parent training programmes and ensure ongoing support for adoptive parents.

The adoption application form includes questions about applicants' willingness to accept children who have experienced parental mental illness or sexual abuse. While some may have an understanding of the impact of such experiences on children, others can only think hypothetically about what this may mean. Priel, Melamed-Hass, Besser, and Kantor (2000) describe the importance of the adoptive mother's capacity for self-reflectiveness and stress that the ability of adoptive parents to think of themselves as parents is an important factor in the adjustment to family life. This reflects our experience as therapists that adoptive parents need to feel entitled to parent. Adoptive parents may ask the social worker about the possible effect of the past on their adopted children. They will not know the actual impact until after the placement, when they are struggling to manage and cope with the child's and their own emotions and the accompanying rage that a challenging child can evoke.

Lucy

In talking about her experience of Lucy, who hit and kicked her when she was diverted from an activity, Myra told me that she bit her to show her how much it hurt. Myra felt ashamed that she had behaved in such a way and said that, in that moment, it was not possible for her to calm the situation. Both she and Lucy would come to our sessions reporting that each had been "abused" by the other. We worked on changing behaviour and helping Myra to understand the complex and contradictory feelings that Lucy evoked in her.

Having been exposed to investigations, often over several years, adoptive parents want to close the doors and establish themselves and their child/ren as a family. It is, therefore, more difficult to seek help. They often feel near to breakdown by the time they reach our service. It takes time to develop a therapeutic relationship and for parents and children to have the confidence that they can find ways of relating to one another. This needs work with parents on the emotional resonances from the past that can create a gulf between them and their children. Children need help to give voice to their past experiences that influence their feelings about and responses to their new family.

The child in context

From a systemic perspective, our ideas about ourselves are developed from a sense of cultural history and from the feedback we receive in the different contexts that we inhabit. The traditional system of closed adoption leads to adopted children feeling that they have no access to a part of themselves. The theory of social constructionism (Burr, 1995) provides a useful framework to understand the difficulties that can arise in adoptive families. It proposes the idea that "reality" is created between people and that those with power are in a position to define the truth for those over whom they have power. In the field of adoption, adults, whether professionals, carers, or adopters, are in a position to describe the experiences of children, to which the children have little opportunity to contribute.

The adult, dominant discourse about the children created between birth families, carers, and different professionals can lead to contradictions in the children's understanding of their lives and their identity. It also means that the experiences of adopted children are not validated and become subjugated to the adults' story. Thus, over time, a child's recollections are taken over by the adoptive parents' accounts of the child's past. The memories that they may retain about their family of origin are forgotten or dismissed, resulting in a loss of part of their identity. Thus, in accepting the discourses of the adoptive family, children may lose aspects of themselves to which they did have access in their memory but in which they have lost confidence. A related issue of physical identity arises when there is no contact and there are no pictures of the birth family, so that adopted children may not know where their physical characteristics or skin colouring originate, seeing themselves only as "different" from other family members.

The shadow of the birth family may hang over adoptive families. For some adopters, ongoing contact with a birth family is seen as important in enabling the child to develop an integrated sense of self. For others, whose idea of an adoptive family is that it will become similar to a birth family, contact may be threatening. Some young people seek out their birth families and are supported in this by their adoptive parents before they are 18. Others need to have some distance, possibly having children of their own, before they can start to think further about their identity. Buchanan (2000) talks about the strength of her feelings when her birth mother, whom she met when she was 41, refused to disclose any information about her birth father: "I feel strongly that I have been denied part of my history. This has to do with paternity, inherited characteristics, and how I came to be here, rather than fathering." It has been my experience that, for many adopted adults, it is the deepening of the knowledge about themselves that is more important than making a relationship with their birth families.

Sandra

Sandra, aged 32, married with a baby son, was referred because she was feeling depressed and suicidal, with a strong compulsion to run away. She had been adopted as a baby and brought up in a religious family; her adoptive brother was seen by her as the favourite in the family. Sandra had felt criticized and intruded upon by her mother during her teenage years, both for her lack of academic success and her appearance. There were many rows, from which her father distanced himself.

When we started to work together, Sandra used the sessions to strive to improve her relationship with her adoptive parents and modify her responses in order to avoid arguments with them. Since she did not want to invite them to our sessions, I worked mostly with her and, occasionally, with her husband, William. When their son was 2, Sandra felt that she had to seek her birth mother. This was kept a secret from her adoptive family. She was unable to see them during that time, as she felt she was being disloyal. She worried that they would criticize or reject her if they found out and also that she would be unable to cope with the emotional repercussions if her birth mother refused contact.

Sandra's investigations took her via Southern Ireland to North London, near to her present home. When she located her birth mother, June, the latter immediately responded and wanted to meet Sandra. Sandra needed time to adjust to the idea that she would meet her mother and to think about the implications of this on her relationship with her adoptive family. After a short time she arranged to meet, carefully negotiating the support she would need from her husband.

Sandra learnt that it had been impossible for June to parent her and that she gave her up for adoption to ensure that she was well cared for. June had continued to work in a very low-paid occupation and did not have the emotional or physical resources to look after a child. It was important for Sandra to understand the origin of some of her characteristics and to find answers to questions about her mother that she had held throughout her life. The opportunity to identify a missing part was more important than maintaining an ongoing relationship with her birth mother. She also learnt that her birth father, who had died some years previously, had retained a friendly relationship with her mother. Sandra has maintained spasmodic contact with June but is more emotionally connected with her adoptive family. They are still unaware that she has found her birth mother, but she is now able to have a less hostile relationship with them. Sandra and I have continued to work together occasionally to help her reach an understanding of herself as child, adult, partner, parent, and daughter in three different families. It has been a struggle to maintain her relationship with her husband while trying to develop a new sense of herself. He has at times joined our sessions to work on the impact of Sandra's personal explorations on their relationship. This work has taken place over several years, with Sandra returning for sessions with me when confronted with different issues, such as the criticism and anger she received from her family for having a third child. The opportunity to reflect on the impact of infertility on her adoptive mother helped her to manage her own emotional responses. She is now at ease with the emotional distance from her birth and adoptive family. The work we undertook combined the support to research her origins while managing changes in her current family relationships.

As family therapists we work to help adults and children listen to one another's experiences so that the adults can become aware of aspects of their own behaviour, which resonate with the child's previous, often negative experiences. We try to help the parents and the children find a way of being together, which takes account of the children's and adults' experiences from the past and present. Parents may reject aspects of children that do not fit their own expectations. These may be seen as the part of the children which belongs to the "other" family, who were unable to nurture them. For adoption to succeed, adopters need to find a way to accept the whole child and to help children talk about their experiences in an accepting way.

Referral to an agency such as ours implies that something is "wrong" in the family. As family therapists, we believe that change can best be achieved by enhancing the positive aspects of relationships. While we advise family members on what they could do differently, we also discover and emphasize what is working well and promote the use of more positive language between them. This becomes even more important in families where members are distinguished as "good" and "bad". Such descriptions need to change so that there is, instead, an understanding that the child is not inherently bad but that their more challenging behaviours have been created in particular contexts.

We talk to families about distinguishing between behaviours that need to be attended to with consistency and those that can be ignored. We emphasize that the need for good relationships is often more important than the need for good behaviour, and the experience of constant criticism, however justified, can lead children to give up the idea that they can ever get it right. We try to help parents find more positive ways to encourage new behaviour.

Working with young people and their families

Many of the families we work with have been well prepared during the assessment process and seek help appropriately when difficulties arise. Grotevant (1994) conducted research into levels of openness in adoption; they conclude that an important factor for adoptive parents is their feeling of permanence and entitlement or, as they put it, connectedness with their adopted children. They suggest that adopters will always have a sense of the wider systems in their family, whether or not they are in contact with birth parents. While this chapter does not enter the debate about open and closed adoptions, it is interesting to note that the above research shows that there is little difference between the experience of parents in confidential and those in open adoptions: those who have confidential adoptions feel protected from reclamation by birth parents and those who have open adoptions feel protected by having a relationship with and knowledge of the birth parents. Whether or not adoptive children know what is happening in the lives of their birth families, they usually hold them in mind, sometimes worrying about what may be happening to siblings or how their parents may be coping without them. Our experience is that siblings have different relationships with their adoptive parents. One child may be referred as "being" the problem, while the sibling fits in easily with family expectations, perhaps having had a different relationship while within the birth family than the referred child.

Adoptive parents seek advice about talking to children about their birth families. They feel that to talk about birth families may be experienced by their adopted children as rejection, while not to talk about them may lead the children to feel that they are a forbidden subject.

Jean

Jean was worried that she had not shared aspects of her 11-year-old son's life-story book with him. There was no information available for her 15-year-old adopted daughter, and her son's book contained the names and addresses of his birth family. She was worried, not only about how much information to share with her son, but also about the effect of this disclosure on her daughter. Jean came to the sessions alone, saying that she was under pressure from the social worker to give her son all the information that was available. She felt that this could be harmful, but that their relationship could be jeopardized if he knew that she was withholding information from him. We spoke about her concerns about her son's birth family, the effect of this on his view of himself, and also how to manage the process of this disclosure. Parents often feel that the issues they are worried about disclosing to their children should be imparted in a serious "meeting" format. Jean was tempted to give her son the life-story book to read on his own but appreciated that this might leave him distressed and isolated. We talked about ways in which she could be more comfortable "with" him, so that she could feel that she had done her best to support him in coping with this new information while ensuring that other family members played a part in the process.

Adopted children can be worried about discussing positive memories and feelings for their birth families because this may be experienced as disloyalty to the adoptive parent. The dominant family/professional story about the birth family may be that they are harmful. However, the child may wish to incorporate good memories with bad. We enable families to talk about these preoccupations and reassure them that there is not a "right" way to talk to children about their birth families, particularly when the history is one of abuse and cruelty. Adults can fall into the trap of believing that the child has no recollection, because the child's history can be so abusive and distressing. Creating a context in which children feel that they can ask questions and receive honest answers can be hard. The anxiety about "getting it right" gets in the way. Parents are often surprised at how easy such a conversation has been in reality. We then work to encourage them to keep the door open so that the child feels that they can ask further questions.

Families often consult our service when children are struggling with adolescence. They wish to explore their ideas and dilemmas about their identity separately from their adoptive parents.

Susan

One 13-year-old girl, who had been living with her adoptive parents for two years, asked to see me alone. She was adamant that she did not want long-term individual psychotherapy but that she needed to talk by herself. Her parents found this difficult to accept, as they felt, at the time, that they were forming attachments as a family and that individual therapy would interfere with the daughter's attachment to them. However, it was agreed that I would see Susan individually for two sessions and that these would be confidential; Susan would decide what could be fed back to the next family session. When we met, Susan said she was worried about her birth family and felt disloyal when talking about them with her adoptive parents. She was also struggling with her feelings of betrayal if she started to feel part of her adoptive family. She used the sessions to think about how to manage the complex dilemmas of working on her identity, coping with the difficulties in friendship groups that come with adolescence and finding a way to live in her new family.

Attachment and the family

Those who are adopted from overseas have often spent time alone and under-stimulated in orphanages or have suffered abuse in families. Archer (1996) suggests that when children have suffered traumatic disturbance to the attachment process in the first two or three years of life, it is important, when trying to sustain placements, to validate the pain that families are going through.

When difficulties emerge in the adopted family, there is a danger that both family and professionals will intervene in a way that singles out the child as the one with the problem. While there is no doubt that children who have not experienced secure attachments will find sustained intimate relationships difficult, adoptive parents also have an attachment history that affects their response to the child. Thus, the attachment difficulty emerges between people.

Elspeth and James, Philip and Lisa

We worked with Elspeth, James, and their adopted children, Philip and Lisa. Elspeth came from a poor white family; her parents had separated when she was 8, and her mother had quickly re-part-nered. James was brought up in an affluent two-parent family. Elspeth and James came to parenting after several years of infertility treatment. Philip and Lisa had been physically and sexually abused by their father and had experienced several changes of foster home since leaving their mother. While Lisa settled well at school and was able to show affection to her new parents, Philip engendered a feeling of hopelessness and disappointment in his mother, who felt that he was always critical of her parenting. She felt she could never properly please him. The family was at the point of breakdown, with James working long hours and Philip spending an increasing amount of time alone in his room. Lisa occupied the space of the "good" child. Our work was to help the family to make connections between their past experience and the present while focusing on small patterns of interaction between Philip and his mother to encourage them to look at one another and respond to one another rather than avoiding contact. Philip's behaviour, which was seen as stubborn, could be interpreted as depressed, and we tried to help Elspeth and James understand Philip's behaviour as sad rather than as bad and goading them into anger.

Working with families who are at the point of breakdown can be very painful for parents, children, and professionals. It can be difficult to listen to the strength of antagonism between parents and children. They often come to therapy because the dreams they each brought to the adoptive family, their hopes and ideals, can be very easily shattered. It is important to hold onto the family tensions and help the family to reconsider the expectations they have of one another in order to have a workable relationship.

Overseas adoption

The shortage of white British babies from 1980 onwards led couples with sufficient resources to adopt children from overseas. Having completed home study reports for such couples wanting to adopt children in the late 1980s, I found that individuals and couples were dissatisfied with the UK adoption system or had a personal connection with the country of origin of the child they wished to adopt. The quality of their preparation and assessment was variable. Many adopters were not given the opportunity to explore their reasons for adopting a child, nor to consider the emotional impact of adoption. The new adoption legislation gives a greater responsibility to adoption agencies to provide a thorough assessment and preparation for overseas adopters, thus providing more protection for both children and parents.

Parents who have adopted children from overseas may have a greater sense of autonomy because they have felt less controlled or judged by an adoption agency and because geographical distance provides physical safety from birth parents. In my experience, they are usually comfortable about talking to children about the past, since this openness does not give rise to the fear that the birth family can still "take" the child.

In Rutter's study 165 adopted children from Romania (O'Connor, Rutter, and the English and Romanian Adoptee Study Team, 2000; Rutter et al., 2000), one remarkable finding is the degree of satisfaction expressed by the adoptive parents. Perhaps this can be explained by the fact that they may have felt like pioneers in that, for some, a particular political ideology had determined the children's separation from their birth families.

Jacob

Jacob and his family referred themselves when he was 11 and at the point of secondary-school transfer. Following a special needs assessment, his parents and school were concerned that he would not survive in secondary education. Jacob had lived in a Romanian orphanage until the age of 4. His adoptive parents, Barbara and Martin, worked hard to form a close bond with him through talking and close physical contact. They made friends with Romanian people in the United Kingdom to ensure that he had connections with the country of his birth. Barbara and Martin said that they had been introduced to several children before meeting Jacob, with whom they felt an instant rapport. Perhaps the feeling that there is a choice and that their child is selected from a number of potential adoptees gives this group of adopters a strong sense of entitlement.

While adoptive parents are usually able to tell their children the story of the day they first met them and the reason they were chosen, children may have a different memory, often one of confusion that they do not have the opportunity to talk about openly because the parents' story dominates the conversations.

Barbara described in detail the day she first met Jacob, while he has a memory of being surrounded by many adults. He was told that one was to be his mother but could not understand how to recognize her. After several visits, he realized that he could recognize her by her watch. This has continued to have some importance in our work, because Jacob, as an adolescent, is more interested in "things", such as electronic goods, than in forming relationships with his peers, with whom he has little confidence. An example of this arose when discussing this chapter with the family: Barbara remembered that the children in the orphanage did not have face-to-face contact with their carers. The carers stood behind the rows of children in order to feed them, thus enabling two children to be fed at the same time. We thought that this could account for Jacob's inability to recognize his mother's face and would explain why he initially recognized her from her watch, and why he continues to be more absorbed by gadgets than people.

During our early sessions, Jacob leaned across his mother's lap and always maintained physical contact with her. Martin seemed to be an observer to this intense relationship. Initially, the sessions focused on closeness and distance, whether Jacob could be allowed to travel to school without an adult, and how he could cope with bullying. Jacob has given his account of his experience in the family, which is often different from that of his parents. He has welcomed our sessions to provide a forum in which he can talk about his successes at school and in his relationships, while his parents tend to focus on the negative aspects of his life. We have also been helped by O'Connor and Rutter's research (2000) in our understanding and promotion of his success in managing his life in the context of the early deprivation that he suffered. We have worked separately with the parents to help them support one another in allowing Jacob more independence and to be less intrusive in every aspect of his life.

In many families, the negotiation around autonomy usually causes tensions. For adoptive families, as in the case of Susan (above) the parents may not feel that they have had their fair share of parenting before the child finds relationships with peers more important. The children are often struggling to manage peer relationships and cannot confide in their parents, for fear that they will become too intrusive. For only children there is no other child to divert the focus of attention, and this pressure, while negotiating a life-cycle transition, may lead to dangerous family arguments or silent avoidance.

For Jacob and his parents, the process is painful; he is not managing school or peer relationships in a way that they would like but is adamant that he is happy at school and with other young people. Now aged 14, the emotional differences between him and his peers are more obvious. However, he says that he has found a satisfactory way to make friends and manage bullying at school. Martin, also an only child, was bullied at school and finds it difficult to understand how Jacob can cope without seeking protection from his parents. Barbara and Martin are also concerned that he is still rocking as he did when they first adopted him; that he is not completing his homework tasks, nor achieving the educational results that they hope for.

Rutter (2000) and O'Connor (2000) describe the difficulties the Romanian children experienced in learning and note that the lack of stimulation during the early period of their lives leads to long-term cognitive impairments.

I have shared this information with Barbara and Martin to try to normalize Jacob's response to learning, but it has been difficult for them to conceive that Jacob is not simply lazy; there are frequent arguments that deny the extraordinary progress that this boy, with such a bleak early history, has made in actively participating in life. Our work with this family is to help them to listen to one another openly rather than defensively. Now the parents seem to be feeling more encouraged by their capacities to parent.

The expectation of educational achievement is a common dilemma for adoptive families. This may be because adoptive parents have achieved academically and because they cannot understand the extent of the impairment to the capacity to think and learn that come from early deprivation. The educational system tends to judge parents for their children's lack of achievement. In addition, the parents have difficulty in coping with their children's failure to learn, and this makes school and homework the focus of many family sessions. As a therapist I work to help parents become reconciled to what it is possible for their children to achieve.

Rituals

We have found that open acknowledgement of the past has been important for adopted children. Many children maintain contact with birth siblings and letter-box contact with their birth family for birthdays and Christmas. The marking of these important events can be difficult for adoptive parents but maintains the children's link with the past, helping to create a developing sense of identity, which includes their origins. Celia Falicov (2002) described the loss and pain that is experienced by migrants. She says that being uprooted from their country leaves them with a strong feeling of loss, with no cultural collective to mark their transition. She describes the loss of ritual or familiar patterns as an ambiguous loss, saying that the "uprooting" leaves dirt and soil behind. Professionals and carers of adopted and looked-after children will be more concerned about children's experiences of abuse. They may privilege these over the positive aspects of identity that have been lost through the transitions within the care system into adoption. Adopted children have had several "uprootings" and parts of their cultural and lived experience have been left behind each time. Helping to maintain a sense of connection with the past and with the origins of self by telling stories and creating rituals is important for adopted children and is an important factor in developing a new family identity.

Rituals are markers that bring pleasure and pain. Many adoptive families celebrate adoption day each year. For families with children who have ongoing links with siblings adopted in different families, gatherings to acknowledge a birthday or at a school holiday are important. They can also be painful times when adoptive parents make an effort to ensure a happy celebration, which is then ruined by a child who may "spoil" the occasion. It can be helpful through exploration in family sessions to acknowledge the impact of resonances of the past for children. That the past is so important to the children can leave adoptive parents feeling that all they have offered is rejected. Where possible, we encourage them to predict possible difficulties and plan ways of avoiding pitfalls on future occasions. As children develop, there are times when they welcome this connection with the past and times when they reject it. But there is a sense that they appreciate their parents' concern to value all of their experience.

Living in the present

Professionals working with adoptive families can be so seduced by the effect of the past on the present that they ignore the problems that arise in everyday life. For example, food plays an important part in the lives of children in transition.

Stephen

Stephen, with whom I worked for several years, had left his family home because of neglect. He and his younger brother had survived by scavenging food from dustbins. He moved from foster carers, where he developed an interest in cooking, to a Jewish prospective adoptive mother, where he ate kosher food, and then to a vegetarian foster carer. By this time he was overweight, so when he moved to new prospective adopters, they put him on a diet. I became aware of the radical transitions that Stephen had made, which could be tangibly described through different cultural beliefs focused on food.

The family's culture influences all aspects of day-to-day life. We often see our way of life as "obvious", unspoken, and considered universal.

Families want to talk about the arguments that take place about the "stuff" of everyday life, such as sitting at a table to eat, tidying bedrooms, and washing. These difficulties arise in most families, but birth children already have a "map" that helps them to manage parental demands. Adopted children struggle to meet the requirements of intimate family life. We work with family members, both together and in subsystems, to diffuse the symmetrical behaviour that arises from these tensions. Since almost all adopted children have experienced several changes of home, therapists should enable the child to describe the changes they have encountered, whether about food, washing, or expressing anger. It is sometimes difficult for adults to recognize the degree of accommodation that children are required to make in changing families.

Conclusion

Life in a nuclear family requires constant negotiation between parents and children. For adoptive families, the points of transition bring tensions that cannot be foreseen: trigger points may arise from resonances from the past for both parents and children. We help family members to talk and listen differently to one another by offering an "outside ear" that gives them the opportunity to change. Family therapists try to help families to translate understanding into action. The description and understanding of a child's past experience and effect on the child within the family can lead to suggestions from both children and adults about new ways of behaving that can make daily life more tolerable.

Work with adoptive families often needs to take place over a long time, because past experiences of intimacy profoundly affect the ability to trust in a close relationship. Our sessions often focus on ways of managing closeness and rejection. The needs of adults and children also change over time. Our multidisciplinary team provides the opportunity to work flexibly in the context of a familiar environment to meet those needs.

CHAPTER 13

Kinship care:
family stories, loyalties, and binds

Sara Barratt & Julia Granville

There has been a marked change over the last few years in the number of referrals to our team for children placed with relatives and friends. These have come to represent between 12.5% and 26% of our total referrals over the three years to 2005. In most of the kinship cases we see, the major issue that has led to the children needing an alternative placement has been parental drug and/or alcohol misuse. There are often accompanying issues of adult mental health difficulties, domestic violence, child abuse, and neglect. Some kinship arrangements have come about because of forced migration due to war, conflicts, and persecution that have split families apart. The families who come to our service are drawn from a wide ethnic, racial, and class background. This picture reflects the American experience (McFadden, 1998). There is a body of research into kinship care from both the United States and the United Kingdom confirming that kinship carers overall are older, less well off, have poorer health, and are less supported than other foster carers (Broad, 2001; McFadden, 1998; Sykes, Sinclair, Gibbs, & Wilson, 2002).

The carers are a diverse group, including grandparents, aunts and uncles, sisters, step relatives, and family friends. This reflects the definition of kinship care described in the study by Broad, Hayes, and Rushforth (2001):

A child living away from the parental home with a relative or friend, with the knowledge of the social service department, who would otherwise be with stranger foster carers, in residential care, independent living or adopted. The kinship care placement is either initiated by the social services department or via a relative or friend, and involves some sort of assistance or arrangement, including making decisions about legal orders, financial and social work support.

The experience of the carers with whom we work is that local authority support, both financial and emotional, is variable, and, for many social workers with heavy caseloads, the knowledge that children may be physically safe means that they are no longer held in mind because of the pressure of other work and the need to respond to more vulnerable families. This often leaves kinship carers with inadequate financial support and feeling resentful of the lack of recognition by the social worker of what they do.

Over a number of years, we have developed a particular interest in working with this particular group as systemic family therapists. We have found that working as a small team enables one therapist to take the lead with the family, while the other can be freed to take a more "meta" position. The second therapist may identify themes and dilemmas, pick up on the process between the family members and with the therapist, and can offer reflections on these and the sometimes unspoken areas that may be clamouring for attention.

History of formalization of kinship care

The care of children by their relatives or extended family networks has always existed across cultures and societies. In more recent years it has become an increasingly used placement choice in the United Kingdom for children where there has been a breakdown in parenting and where social services have become involved. The national figure for 31 March 2001 was that 6,600 children were being looked after by friends or family in foster placements supported by the local authority (Hunt, 2003). In the second half of the twentieth century there was increasing intervention by the state in the realm of childcare and child abuse. "Abusive families" were often pathologized and not seen as a potential resource for children needing alternative care. The family dynamics that might be understood as having given rise to the parents' deficits were seen as excluding the wider family from having the capacity to care. In a context where a parent or family was seen as harmful or incapable of meeting a child's needs, it could seem best and perhaps simpler to make placement decisions for children where contact with their birth family had ceased. Professionals often overlooked the need or possibility of initiating or continuing contact with or care by members of the extended family. A child was seen perhaps as a tender or damaged shoot that needed to be transplanted to new and better soil and growing conditions. It was easier to make placement decisions about a child if you did not have to consider their relationships with their birth family. The Children Act 1989 brought into legislative focus the presumption that children should be brought up in their families of origin wherever possible. The Act formalized the duty to support contact and give consideration to the child's extended family relationships and racial and cultural identity in decision making. In social work there has been an increasing influence from developments in New Zealand, Australia, and the United States arguing for the placement of children with extended families and communities. This particularly related to children from indigenous and minority ethnic groups, whose children had been commonly placed "cross-culturally" and were "lost" to family and community. These developments led to a growth of interest in kinship placements.

Discourses about attachment

Kinship care is often rightly promoted as providing greater continuity of attachments and relationships for children who cannot be cared for by parents. Kinship carers may well have pre-existing relationships with children and will, at any rate, have knowledge of and connection with the family, even if they have not known the children well. They will hold family stories, including some about the birth parents, complicated though these may be. We discuss this further below.

As therapists, we believe in the importance of attachment within families. Additionally, for looked-after children and young people, relationships with professionals such as social workers and foster carers should not be underestimated. The discourse of attachment is frequently used within social services to support the use of kinship carers. However, social service departments are structured in a way that in effect mitigates against attachment. There are duty teams, short-term teams, long-term teams. The high turnover of staff and frequent re-structuring means that children and families will almost always have worked with a series of different professionals. In a video of care leavers' stories, young people talked time and again about both the significance for them of their social workers and the frustration of the numerous changes they experienced and having to tell their stories repeatedly to new people (Tavistock Training Publications, 2006). For children whose social worker may have a highly significant place in their lives, this can mean that there may be no one who holds the full story in relation to that child's lived experience.

This compartmentalization is similarly reflected in the demarcation of different types of carers with whom a child may be placed, again ensuring that attachments will be disrupted. The assessments that short-term, long-term, kinship, and adoptive carers may undergo and the payments they receive are likely to be different. In some authorities kinship carers, unlike foster carers, will not receive the support of link workers. Their main point of contact with a local authority can be through negotiating payments. The level of support, both financial and other, is also often affected by the legal context for the placement, which will generally move from a care order to a residence order. The pressure to close cases and reduce costs is perhaps inevitably a factor in both placement choice and the push to change legal status and the consequent level of support provided. We are not arguing here against the well-founded desire to minimize the involvement of statutory services in children's lives. Children's attachment and identity needs can indeed be enhanced by placement with family members and friends. However, such plans need to be made with an appropriate level of consideration and support, as with other placements, if they are to remain stable and secure and able to meet children's often complex needs. It is important that they are not used as a cheaper or easier solution justified by a superficial recourse to ideas about attachment.

Presenting problems

Most of the families we see are referred by social workers. Presenting difficulties include: problems for the child in school, disturbed or challenging behaviour at home, uncertainties about how to talk to children about their history, covert concerns about the viability of a placement, and differences of view within the network. What often emerges in the course of the work are issues about the relationship with the birth parent(s) and changes in the relationships within the family, often as a consequence of the placement.

The kinship family is a place where different generations and family relationships coincide in unanticipated combinations. The kinship family is often constructed quickly in response to a crisis. Because the carers are often family members, they may have the idea that they should be able to "look after their own" and that they should not need to consult outsiders, which may be seen as a betrayal of the family or as a failure to cope. Through meeting with as many family members as possible, we seek to provide a neutral space for talking and try to provide a "safe" environment where different perspectives may be discussed and the children's experiences with their birth parents explored and understood in a way that helps family members manage the current relationship problems they are encountering with the children. This is an important factor in our work. As with many families, the talking may only take place in the therapy room. When asked whether they have talked about the previous session, families often say "no". There have been times when we have been irritated by this. However, we have come to believe that it is the more secure and containing space in the therapy room that is important and the talking cannot happen outside. As with violent families, the triggers may be too dangerous without the therapist being there to provide a safe environment or to be blamed for asking the wrong questions.

The birth parents, *in absentia*, take up a lot of space in the minds of a kinship family. Carers may feel angry that their son, daughter, or sibling has abandoned or mistreated their child. This is often a more acceptable reason to be upset than for themselves, whose life has been radically changed by the arrival of the children. The focus of our sessions is frequently on the child's behaviour rather than on the reason for the work. As therapists, we often find ourselves in the position of talking about and thus bringing the parent into the session.

David and Simon

In the following example David, aged 7, lived with his younger brother, aged 5, and their maternal grandparents. He was referred because the school could not contain his behaviour in class.

Therapist: Does Mummy get to hear about school?

David: Sometimes.

Therapist: How often do you see her?

David/family [mumbles]

Therapist: When did she last come round?

Grandfather: A couple of weeks ago.

Therapist: Oh, so since we last met.

Grandmother: And she took the boys out for a couple of hours.

Therapist: Where did you go?

David/Simon: Dunno.

Grandmother: To David's school.

Therapist: Did you go, Simon, as well?

Simon: Yes.

Therapist: Is that the kind of thing you do with Mummy?

David: I like going out with Mummy.

Therapist: How often do you go out with Mummy?

David [mumbling reply]

Therapist: Does she tell you when she's coming, or is it a surprise?

David: We don't know.

Therapist: What does she do when she's not seeing you?

David: Goes out with friends.

Therapist: Do you worry about her?

Simon and David [reply simultaneously]:

Simon: No.

David: Yes. She's dumb anyway—that's what Granny says . . .

Therapist [to grandmother]:   Do you think Mummy is trying to encourage David to manage at school?

Grandmother: I don't know what she says when I'm not there. I do try to tell her what's going on, and she seems to be pleased.

Therapist: Do you think it makes a difference to David?

Grandmother: It encourages him.

Therapist: Do you think he is more keen to please Mummy, or you, or Granddad?

Grandmother: It might be confusing.

The children are very aware of their grandparents' disapproval of their mother. The emphasis in the sessions is on the boys' behaviour at school, and we try to relate this to the children's relationship with their mother. The grandparents prefer (as is illustrated later in this chapter) not to talk about their daughter and convey the message that talking about her to the children makes things worse.

One of the important themes in the literature is the relationship between professionals and kinship carers. Laws' (2001) study of kinship carers in Wandsworth illustrates the difficulties carers have in receiving adequate financial support for parenting children, and the local authorities' pressure on carers to apply for residence orders, which frees them of financial obligations. This reflects some of the distress expressed by the carers we see, who feel embarrassed to ask for payment for the children they care for, but who at the same time resent the failure of the social services departments to provide adequate financial support. Kinship carers are often on very low incomes, and there is ambivalence on the part of social workers and carers about entitlement to payment. While grandparents seem to take on the feeling of "entitlement" to care more easily, it is different for other family members, who may have given up work to care for children of their extended family. It is complicated for them to ask to be paid for the care of children in their family, and yet they feel exploited by social services departments who are sometimes reluctant to pay what is due. Kinship carers are left feeling in the wilderness, with little support, either financial or emotional. This can also reflect their position in their extended families. Several carers have talked about the lack of support, either through respite care or emotional support, from family members after they have committed to caring for children of their kin. This, in turn, connects with their relationship to attending our service, as it is difficult to feel as if they are a "client" of a service with the prejudices that referral to CAMHS teams can attract. They would not usually see themselves as people who would consult with a CAMHS service, and we find that they may struggle to engage for a long period of time.

Themes from clinical work

Engagement

Kinship families referred to our service may experience the referral as a criticism of their care; there may be ambivalent relationships between the family members and the social services department around the way each intervened with the children and their parents. The meaning of the referral to the different parties can profoundly affect how we are seen and how carers are willing or able to engage. Referral or asking for help can be feared as signifying that carers are not managing and may raise the possibility that children could be removed. In a situation where the child is a family member, it is difficult to clarify who has the overall responsibility for the care of the child. The local authority may have legal parental responsibility, while the family, who may have a strong belief in the child belonging to them, may have no legal rights.

To clarify the work that is expected of us and the relationships within the network, we always meet first with the referring professional—usually the social worker—and the carers. In order to agree a mandate for the work, the different understandings need to be explored and clarified. We can also establish the basis and structure for the work: for example, whether the social worker will attend future meetings, how the carers want the social worker to be involved, and how they define the problem. We spend time understanding the carers' underlying worries, which may not be discussed in front of the social worker because of a concern that, for example, the child may be removed, or because carers need the space to think about the decision they have taken, or which has been made for them, to take on a child.

The first stage of engagement is to give the carers the opportunity to talk about their feelings about taking on the care of a child in the family, interrupting their life plans, or the support to and from extended family members.

Sophie

Sophie was newly married, and her husband and his siblings took on the care of his deceased sister's three children. The initial part of the work focused on helping them to negotiate finance and support from the social services and to discuss the management of the children's behaviour. Only after several months of work was Sophie able to talk about her personal distress that the care of these children had interrupted and perhaps prevented the possibility of her having children of her own.

Entitlement

The sense of commitment that carers have shown to the children they look after has been immensely impressive. All have given up personal aspirations in order to care for children of friends or relations. The warmth, resilience, and determination shown by carers aged from 17 to 75 have been remarkable.

Kinship care often starts as a crisis response, for example, to the disappearance, death, or hospitalization of the birth parent/s. When, over time, it becomes clear that the children cannot return to the parents, the carers may want and/or feel obliged to commit themselves to caring for the children. We find that it takes time for carers to voice their anger and resentment, particularly when the birth parents are leading self-destructive lives. Then carers may feel that they are re-visiting the patterns of their childhood by being expected, and allowing themselves, to take on responsibility that belongs elsewhere.

The position of the kinship carer in the structure of the family influences their sense of entitlement to parent the child/ren. On the other hand, their generational position and the way they are seen by other family members will affect the way they take up the role. It has been our experience that grandparents are mindful of the failure of their own parenting when they take on the care of grandchildren. Their generational position means that they are at ease with taking on parental responsibility and the authority of that role. They may be motivated by a need for reparation of the past, and their motivation may be driven at least in part by guilt. They may have the feeling that their child's failure as a parent may reflect their own failure to adequately parent him or her. In this light, there may be an impulse to expiate the past, or to redeem it, by showing that they can do the job of parenting in the present. Conversely, feelings of guilt or anger may be pushed away, and a determined reliance on external explanations for the parent's (their own child's) failure in parenting may be constructed. There can also be a sense of resignation in grandparents who have given up plans for their future in order to parent their grandchildren. However, the arrival of grandchildren may also fill the space between couples that has been vacated by their children. The grandchildren may bring new life to their relationship. Grandparents have described their grandchildren as keeping them young, but they also have times when they feel exhausted. As with many kinship carers, it is difficult to ask for or feel entitled to respite.

Uncles and aunts parenting the children of their siblings, taking up the task, often in crisis, have an expectation that they will receive support from other family members.

Maya

Maya, who was caring for the son of her brother in an overcrowded flat, anticipated that other family members would provide support and respite. This happened at the beginning, but as time went on, she found that her sisters and parents were giving financial and emotional support to her drug-addict brother, often providing a home for him. Their support was then no longer available to her, and she felt excluded from family life. Maya was left feeling uncertain about whether the family were giving her the right to parent. She was then caught in the middle between her family and social services in terms of loyalty, but she needed to use social services and ourselves to support and reinforce her authority to parent and to make decisions about the appropriateness of contact, which she felt could be harmful.

Aunts and uncles who are carers describe feeling that the expectations placed on them when they were children—for example, as the one who can manage independently or who does not need to ask for help—continue, and they are ascribed this role as adults. Several carers describe their anger at their drug-dependent sibling who, once again, is "picked up and wiped down" by members of the extended family while they are left to get on with the care of a distressed and demanding child. Rage with the failing parent (their sibling) is fuelled by the experience of a grandparent still giving support and succour to that parent while the carer is expected to pick up the pieces. This pattern links with old and familiar relational patterns with the grandparents and other aunts or uncles. Parenting a niece or nephew could seem like a route to recognition from the grandparents. However, taking on this role in the family can prevent them from establishing their own lives and relationships. They remain stuck in old family patterns.

The parent may come to represent all the weaknesses or deficits in the family. For carers, differentiating themselves from the parent who has failed may allow them to distance themselves from their own feelings of vulnerability and disappointment. This can have a profound impact on the child's sense of self when asking questions such as: "What have I got from my parents?" "Is there anything good that comes from my Mum or my Dad?" The accounts from different family members may be confusing for a child, where one family member may deny or minimize a parent's failings and another may maximize them. If families can draw on more complex stories of the parents, their difficulties and deficits can be situated in a context that makes these more understandable, if not excusable or forgivable. Children then have access to richer descriptions and explanations.

Our experience with a number of older sisters caring for a younger sibling has been that they have had to be very determined to persuade the authorities that they are capable of parenting. Sibling carers may

172 PSYCHOTHERAPEUTIC WORK WITH PARENTS AND FAMILIES

have suffered themselves at the hands of their own parent, and there may be rage at the absent or failed parent on their own as well as their sibling's behalf. It may be easier to be angry on account of a younger sibling than for themselves. Parenting a sibling can often lead to the older sibling's experiences and feelings becoming confused with those of the younger. The motivation to care is complicated by anger or rivalry with the lost or absent parent. While anger at the parent can be energizing, it may also make it harder to see a younger sibling's different feelings or experiences. There can also be a conscious or unconscious wish to do better than their parent. There is something particularly confusing in terms of generational position and the issue of entitlement for a sister or brother to parent a sibling. Holding on to anger with the parent may have the effect of energizing and bolstering their authority to parent. This can leave both carer and child with unhelpful, stuck stories about the history.

Peter and Olive

We received a referral from a social services department for 5-year-old Peter, who was an unaccompanied minor. He had been difficult to contain and had changed foster families several times. His 17-year-old sister Olive had come forward to care for him, but there were serious concerns, which to some extent we shared, about whether this was viable. Olive was wary about officialdom, which is common and understandable in people fleeing their country and when their position in the United Kingdom and their future is so uncertain. The whereabouts of their parents was unknown. It had not been possible to ascertain how or why the two siblings had arrived, about a year apart, in the United Kingdom. We worked with Peter's new foster carer, the social worker, and Peter and Olive. The foster carer provided a very important bridge in helping and supporting Olive in building and developing her relationship with and parenting of Peter. The carer, from a neighbouring country, took up the position of a quasi-family member, providing backup when Olive requested it. We helped the siblings to think about how they might live together, and to develop a coherent story about the rest of their family whom they had left behind. They were able to begin to share memories of the traumatic events that had led to their parents sending them off into the unknown to protect them. They began to remember the loving bonds with their mother, father, siblings, and kin. Olive began the work with serious concerns about the wisdom of revisiting the past. Peter was showing a disturbing level of confusion about who he was. Olive gradually came to recognize the importance for them both of recreating their shared story. This cemented their relationship and allowed Peter to settle, despite the painfulness of the process at times. They began spontaneously to work on the issues between sessions, bringing drawings of the family members, which brought them to life in the sessions.

Trauma, death, and loss

Most children whom we see have a history of neglectful and chaotic parenting from adults who have major problems with drug and/or alcohol abuse. Their parents were often physically or psychologically absent. Children have described feeling worried and helpless with parents who, they feared, might die or whom they experienced in an unresponsive, almost deathly state. These experiences seem to become re-enacted in the current family, where carers describe children who cannot let them out of their sight and who cannot be re-assured that they will not be left alone at night. It seems that because these children have very early experiences of abandonment, they have developed a heightened anxiety about being left. Our experience is that, at the time when a child may begin to feel safe and life becomes more predictable, the fears of abandonment are heightened; it feels as if it is too dangerous to relax; while you are tense and worried, you have some control.

Jan

Jan, now aged 10, who has lived in his kinship family for 18 months, described how, in the past, feeling very alone, he had walked in the street at night to see if his mother would notice. He remembers being scared. He looks back at himself, as a little boy, recalling these fears—for example, of feeling so alone that he would go into the street at two or three in the morning to find cats to play with. There are now times when he says he thinks about taking himself off on his own, perhaps because he can never trust that there will be someone there for him. He can only depend on his familiar patterns of self-reliance, which lead him to re-live the lonely isolation of his early life. He still finds it hard to sleep and, for many months, would call out at night if he heard the front door close because the fear that he was alone was always with him.

For children whose parents have led chaotic lives, either through substance misuse or mental health difficulties, actual death or the fear of death may feel very close at hand. Some children will have lost one or indeed both parents. Fantasies, rumours, or knowledge of what a parent may be doing, their current state, and, indeed, whether they are still alive may be present for carers and children alike. For some children these fears may become generalized to other significant adults or to themselves. This is often unspoken between the child and carer. It may emerge in the course of sessions, sometimes obliquely referred to by carers or children.

Children who have lived with a parent who is self-harming through drugs or alcohol or who has been in a violent relationship have a close relationship with death; a parent may have been barely conscious or threatened self harm on many occasions. Even expressions such as "you will be the death of me" have a particular meaning for children brought up with danger. However, as adults, we often find it difficult to talk about or imagine the child's lived experience and therapists and carers may prefer to believe that the child is ignorant of the danger that the parent may be in. With careful preparation and permission the children are easily able and relieved to talk about their concerns that their parent may die. Jo, aged 10 years, said, "I don't like it before coming, but after I've been I feel better."

Fredman (1997) describes ways of creating new stories with different family members in her work with families in which a member is dying. The children we work with are separated from their birth parent. Just as, when living with someone who is dying, we can usually only relate to the " living" part of them, children and carers who are getting through the strain of living together day to day cannot bear to add the distress of worrying about the absent parent to their conversations. Thus, our sessions at the Tavistock Clinic can become a "safe-enough" environment to talk about the absent parent. When a parent has died, sometimes in ways the carers feel are too unspeakable to be named directly, it can be a relief to all when the truth can be acknowledged.

David and Simon

An example of confusion for the children was shown when June and Leonard, Simon and David's grandparents (see above), told us in a jokey matter-of-fact tone that their daughter had been seen by a friend and that she was, therefore, still alive. They felt that their two grandchildren did not worry about their mother because they did not ask about her often. David then interjected that he thought Mummy might be dead and they would not know. In a later session with the grandparents, they talked with profound feeling about their incomprehension about what had happened to their daughter. Leonard admitted that it would have been easier if she had been dead.

Therapist: Thinking about grief and loss, if you are grieving, people in very close families don't talk because they want to protect the other person. If I say that I am upset now, it will upset them. I don't know if it fits for you and the children that you are mindful that if you talk about it, will make things worse and be more upsetting?

Grandmother to Grandfather: It is just avoidance, isn't it?

Therapist: Do you get upset when you talk about it?

Grandfather: I do get upset. I was talking to my nephew, and I said, "I wish she [mother] was dead", and he said, "Don't say that again." He wasn't even born when I left home [referring to expected level of respect for an elder], but I felt sad saying that. . . . [Tears] . . . But the older sister [aunt] is very good with the kids.

Therapist: But in a way for you it would be simpler if she just wasn't around.

Grandfather: Mmmmm

[Both grandparents very tearful . . . pause.]

Therapist: It's hard for you to talk about together because you haven't got a story about what's happening to her.

[Long pause]

Grandmother: Anyway, you don't want to say to them, "Your mother's just gone and left you." That would just make it even worse.

Grandfather: That's the reason why . . . That's why I thought, out of sight, out of mind.

Therapist: But while she is out of your sight, she isn't out of your mind. . . . There is something very important about what you have just talked about. . . . You don't want to say to a child that your Mum's left you. But it is still there and part of their experience—whether you say it or don't say it, it is still part of their experience, and when you don't say it, it leaves them on their own to manage it for themselves. We, as therapists, have an idea that if you, the people who care for them and love them, are able to talk to them about this painful stuff, it will help them to manage these feelings.

Being able to have this conversation allowed them and us to connect with the emotional resonances in a more direct way. It enabled grandparents as well as children to open up the conversation about mother's absence, sporadic appearances, their fears, anger, loyalties, and disappointments. It loosened what had felt like a desperate blocking of discussion in an attempt to protect themselves and each other from the pain, guilt, and shame of the situation.

Many of the children in kinship families have talked to us about their fear of being on their own and of being abandoned by their current carers. Neither Jan (described above) nor Sabina, another child living with her grandparents, could bear their carers being out of sight at night or in the day. This seemed to us to mirror experiences these children had probably had very early on of being abandoned. They shared the experience of having parents who were drug- or alcohol-dependent and were consequently unresponsive at times. This experience of being in the presence of someone but unable to rouse them, not held in mind, has made them feel as if their existence depended on eliciting a response. This can become an entrenched pattern, which is then experienced as a behaviour problem.

There is a difficulty in talking about someone as dying. When this is something that is self-inflicted—for example by drugs or alcohol—there is the anger and frustration of knowing that a family member is "choosing" to live a self-destructive life, together with the feeling of guilt and helplessness, and an unsaid feeling that the family is to blame. The idea that the parent could choose to save him or herself means that it is particularly difficult to identify and talk about the continuing worry about death. This also makes it difficult for us to help carers provide a coherent story for children. Unlike unrelated carers, personal distress and guilt are caught up in the attempt to name the concern that the parent is living a dangerous life, the future of which cannot be predicted. The imperative to manage the tasks of everyday life has to take precedence. Talking about someone as possibly dying raises the anxiety that one is wishing them dead. In these circumstances, it is often easier not to know how the parent is living his/her life. We provide a space to talk about painful topics. Grandparents may voice unspoken fears about the death of their child, children may be left with the potential total loss of their parents, which resonates with their actual early experiences of their parents. Families then leave a session having to manage all that this may raise.

We need to pay attention to pacing, to getting the balance right, based on feedback, between discussions of practical issues and advice and a delicate entering into exploration of the painful unspoken stories. We often direct our questioning on behalf of others in the room, in particular the children, who may not be able to articulate the question themselves. In this we draw on our own responses (countertransference), which may contribute to forming hypotheses, which will influence the direction of subsequent questions (Flaskas, 1996). We might amplify certain aspects of conversations that can become themes in the work. We explore the influences on and connections between relationships and the wider contexts in which the families are embedded.

Life-cycle interruption

The huge change in the lives of kinship carers when they take on the care of children from the family features prominently in both the American and the British literature (Broad, 2001; Crumbley & Little, 1997; Pitcher, 2002). The families we see often talk about these changes in their lives and expectations. As placements almost always occur in a crisis, the decision about taking on the permanent care of the children is usually made *post hoc*. Choice for kinship carers is inevitably a complex issue. Carers often express a sense of commitment and ownership in relation to their children, but it may also often be tinged with a feeling of burden. Their lives are turned upside down. For older carers, plans for retirement, travel, and perhaps a period of focusing on their own interests and relationships are suddenly interrupted. They have to return to parenting. Younger carers may have to make adjustments in their career, work, and study, with plans and ambitions put on hold to take up the role. They may find themselves parenting a sibling at a time when they were not yet planning families of their own. Others may end up with much larger families than they had intended through kin and birth children, with the consequent stretching of personal, financial, and environmental resources.

In our work we draw on a life-cycle perspective to explore some of these effects. We create a context in which to consider the carers' expectations of this phase of their lives and the process of choosing to care for the children, examining the different strands that made up that decision. Carers often talk about the stresses and strains of the changes in their role in relation to the children and the other family members. Joseph Crumbley (Crumbley & Little, 1997) gives a rich overview of the adjustments in roles and relationships that are involved in kinship placements.

David and Simon

June and Leonard, the grandparents of David and Simon, above, talked about the expectations they had for retirement, spending time at the family home in a Southern African country, having time to relax and take it a bit easier after a long working life. Instead, June was working night shifts in order to care for her grandchildren before school, and Leonard looked after them in the school holidays, finding the demands of two boisterous youngsters stressful and exhausting at times. Both, however, also talked about the positives, feeling that the children kept them active, making them walk to school. They said that they enjoyed having them and getting to see *Harry Potter*!

When a sister or a grandparent becomes a parent, there is a considerable adjustment for both child and carer of accepting or taking a position of authority and an entitlement to parent (Ziminski, 2004). Children challenge them with "You're not my Mum", and carers, particularly siblings who may also have been abused or neglected by the birth parents themselves, are painfully aware of this. In sharing the parents who failed, a sibling carer may find it difficult to find authority to contain the behaviour and distress of the child. Authority can become confused with abuse under the shadow of the history. The carer may feel quite overwhelmed, both by identifying with the child's experience and in trying to act like the parent s/he never had. The multiple voices that support or threaten the new relationships or the stability of the placements can be teased out in our therapeutic conversations.

We try to enable carers to find a way to value aspects of the children's relationship (sometimes idealized by the child) with the birth parent. This can be a difficult position to take, as carers are often very critical of the children's care at the hands of parents. Due to the past history of family relationships and complex webs of loyalties, it is often hard for carers to help children construct a coherent account of their lived experience. Our position and work as "outsiders" provides the opportunity to work with the different subsystems in the family in order to allow family members to give voice to their distress and concerns. These are then more able to be brought back into the conversations of the family sessions.

Finally, it is important that alongside our therapeutic work, we become advocates for kinship carers in the social care arena. We may be needed to negotiate with housing, social services, and education departments or to contribute to appeals to the immigration department. This aspect of the work may be essential for creating the bedrock necessary for any therapeutic work to be undertaken, but also in engaging with the family's pressing needs in their social and economic contexts.

We have described the particular difficulties faced by kinship carers taking on the parenting of the children of relatives and friends. There can be no doubt about the value of enabling the children to remain rooted in their families of origin in this way for the sake of their identity and connectedness to significant others. Kinship care involves a complexity of relationships, history and memories, trauma and loss. A powerful web of changing roles and relationships forms the backdrop to the care of a child. Kinship care is not a simple solution. The provision of therapeutic support has been crucial for many to enable them to explore the inevitable conflicts that arise from children's loyalties and experiences of previous poor parenting, which are even more salient when the placement is within the same family or network.

CHAPTER 14

From tired and emotional to praise and pleasure: parenting groups for adoptive, foster, and kinship carers

Julia Granville & Laverne Antrobus

In this chapter we describe parenting training groups that we have offered alongside other clinical work to families referred to the specialist Fostering, Adoption and Kinship Care team at the Tavistock Clinic. We consider what is special about these groups and the various additional issues that needed to be addressed because of the particular needs and demands of adoptive, foster, and kinship families. We explore some of our ideas about the cognitive–behavioural approaches of the group programme we have followed and how these fit with other core theoretical models and trainings.

Many of the families we work with come to us in a state of exhaustion and despair. Some of their struggles are undoubtedly shared by parents in more ordinary circumstances. However, for adoptive, foster, and kinship families, the difficulties in managing the daily tasks of parenting and the levels of challenging, disturbing, and oppositional behaviour in the children for whom they care may be extreme. Parents and carers may be feeling defeated and in touch with sides of themselves they just did not know existed, which can be very disturbing for them. As in many fields, offering groups to people who have a common presenting difficulty may be a helpful experience that enables them to begin to feel less isolated and more empowered to deal with problems and to connect with their strengths. For this reason, and in response to a growing body of research into the effectiveness of some parenting programmes, we decided to train in and then offer some groups to parents seen by our service. The aim was to offer a structured parenting programme and an opportunity for parents and carers to come together with others in similar circumstances.

In our clinical practice we had heard from a number of parents who had attended community-based programmes that they had found this experience less than helpful. Their experience was that they had to explain themselves and their family and that others might not understand the particular issues in fostering and adoption or raising the children of relatives in kinship placements. They also felt that the difficulties their children presented and the experiences that their children might have had previously were of a completely different order to those of other children and that others' reactions to this just added to their sense of isolation and difference. For this reason we felt strongly that it would be important to offer a group for these particular carers linked to the specialist service offered by the Tavistock Clinic.

The other factor we considered important was for parents/carers to work with group leaders experienced in the particular processes, challenges, and joys of caring for this group of children with their huge levels of need. There is an interplay between children's previous experiences in their families of origin, parents' experiences of becoming adoptive, foster, or kinship carers and the current parenting and relationship dilemmas that are particular to these families. Parenting can feel a very different experience for these carers. Their care of their children starts from a different base, and this affects the sense of entitlement to parent and the meaning of the relationships they are building in the family. Offering group-based parenting training provides an opportunity for parents and carers to share their experiences, strengths, and concerns with others and to work on developing their skills alongside others in a supportive environment. The approach is an empowering one for parents who are likely to have felt rejected, angry, defeated, exhausted, blamed, and blaming. It may offer a different experience of the relationship with their child in the here and now and become a part of a "virtuous cycle" for both parents and carers and their children.

Aim of the groups

The Incredible Years training programme was developed in the United States by Carolyn Webster-Stratton (1992). It uses group discussion, videotape clips, modelling, and role-play rehearsal to help parents and carers with children aged 2–10 years. The programme aims to prevent, reduce, and treat conduct problems in children, to develop social competence in children, and to strengthen parenting competence and use of non-violent disciplinary approaches. It has been used successfully in clinical as well as community-based settings.

The overall approach is based on a behavioural/cognitive model. It was influenced by the work of Patterson (1982) and Forehand and McMahon (1981) on understanding and treating non-compliance and oppositional behaviour in children. The approach has been widely used in both the United Kingdom and the United States, and there are particular adaptations of it being developed. An example of this is the adapted programme developed and run for groups of adoptive parents by Coram Family (Henderson & Sargent, 2005) and that with foster carers (Pallett, Blackby, Yule, Weissman, & Scott, 2005).

The Webster-Stratton approach has been well researched in both the United States and the United Kingdom (Scott, Spender, Doolan, Jacobs, & Aspland, 2001; Webster-Stratton & Hancock, 1998; Webster-Stratton & Herbert, 1993). Interestingly, from Scott and colleagues' research it appeared that the children showed improvement in behaviour problems, including attention and hyperactivity. The positive effects were maintained at follow-up.

This is a well-evidenced approach that is likely to bring a significant benefit to the children presenting as particularly challenging in terms of their relationships with their parents and carers, and to their parents' confidence in addressing behavioural difficulties. In addition, there is a potential gain in relation to prevention of difficulties with other children in the family, who may currently be seen as unproblematic. This way of working is very much in line with current government policy. For example the children's *National Service Framework* (DoH, 2004, p. 16), Part 1, Standard 2, promotes the provision of targeted and specialist support for parents and specifically addresses the importance for adoptive parents and those who care for looked-after children to have easy access to high-quality multidisciplinary support. This acknowledges the high levels of need among these children and young people and their families. The recent legislative changes in the Children and Adoption Act 2002 are intended to ensure that assessments and services for post-adoption support should be offered more systematically. Overall, there has been a political push to offer parenting programmes more widely for children and young people and for those most at risk of exclusion and of criminal or antisocial behaviour.

There are a number of programmes available. The basic programme focuses on training in parenting skills and strategies; the advanced programme for parents focuses on communication and problem-solving strategies; the school-age programme supports children's education alongside promoting positive behaviour and reducing inappropriate behaviours. There are also teachers' and children's programmes. The approach has been used in schools to promote parents' support of their children's literacy. We used the basic programme, but in the future would very much like to offer a children's group alongside the parents' group.

The basic programme starts with building positive interaction through play between parents/carers and children. It then moves on to strategies for limit-setting and boundaries. It is a highly structured programme, and from our experience and from the research it appears that a high level of engagement can be built up. In addition to the group time, there are home visits prior to the group and telephone contact between groups. The research suggests that all the elements—group process, video, role-play, homework, and telephone contact—are integral to the success of the programme.

Our groups are run by two staff members and require a substantial commitment of time. It is not a cheap option. There is considerable complexity in running such groups. Facilitators need to "teach" the material, model, and encourage/train parents and carers in trying things out. We need to attend to group process and to create a therapeutic "temporary secure base" (Byng-Hall, 1995) in which members feel safe enough to try out new ways to be with their children, to feel able to make mistakes and to learn. The facilitators need to hold the group through painful and upsetting times as carers share experiences they have had with their children, sometimes with difficult personal resonances. Operating at these different levels, moving in and out of teaching and therapeutic positions is a complex and demanding experience. Contrary to financially constrained managerial views, in our opinion this is not a way of working that should be delegated to the least trained or experienced workers. These are labour-intensive groups, though this is offset by numbers involved and the potential long-term benefits.

As well as time together to prepare materials, set up, and clear away for the actual groups, we made time each week to review contact with carers during the week, to debrief from the group, and to talk about our co-working relationship. This felt essential for us to deal

with the inevitable resonances with our own experiences and to manage the impact of the emotional content of the groups.

Our experience is that other conceptual frames—systemic, attachment, and psychoanalytic—are not contradictory to this structured
approach and indeed can be complementary to it. For those of us who
undertook the training, it seemed that, while the approach was different in theoretical orientation from some of our own trainings and current ways of working, it could be a complementary addition to work
already being done.

Our initial hope, borne out by subsequent experience, has been
that the work in the group was supported by the family and individual work that might also be being offered. It was helpful that there
was some general communication with individual or family therapists
working with the families and that other therapists understood the approach being offered in the group. Assessment about the suitability of
a group approach was both by the referring clinician or professional
and then by us in initial conversation and following the home visit. As
the majority of the families were known, this was relatively straightforward. Apart from the basic age criteria for a child in the family and
that carers were either adopters, foster, or kinship carers, the kinds of
issues we considered were ability to attend a group reasonably consistently and capacity to manage the give and take of a group context. We
were looking for parents who showed some signs of being willing to
make some changes and to give things a go. Within that there was a
lot of room for a range of feelings and responses to the approach. The
boundaries between the different aspects of work offered to the family had to be discussed clearly with the group members to ensure appropriate confidentiality and transparency. We had positive feedback
from clinicians, and indeed from fostering link workers, about the
changes and improvements that they were seeing.

Clearly the level of commitment and attendance required of those
coming to the group is considerable. There was a question about what
should happen to parents' and carers' other sessions, if any, during the
period of the group. Options were for the other work to carry on as
usual or for parents/carers to attend less frequently. Some families did
not attend other appointments for the duration of the group but then
reviewed and/or restarted on completion of the programme. Parents
and carers negotiated the options with the therapists working with
their family.

Initial costs for the groups included purchase of materials, but
subsequent costs were mainly for staff time. Ongoing costs included

providing folders for handouts, books, or photocopies of reading materials. We gave fridge magnets for parents to stick up reminders, memory joggers, and positive statements. Each week there was a light healthy lunch and refreshments as well as (not so healthy!) chocolate—aptly named "Heroes" and "Celebrations"—to hand out to mark achievements, contributions, and hard work. This was all very much part of creating an environment and atmosphere of positive valuing of each person and the efforts and commitment involved in attending. For us this was an essential ingredient in the mix that led to the high level of engagement that enabled change to take place.

We offered daytime groups and were not in a position to offer a crèche. This clearly had implications for who would be able to attend. Despite this, we had working parents who came, having made flexible arrangements with their workplaces. Many parents and carers had a long history of having to negotiate with employers because of the frequent demands made on them in relation to their children due to difficulties at school and frequent specialist appointments. In the clinic context running a crèche would be an expensive option, while provision of costs for childcare would probably be a more practicable option. However, we would like to run a parallel children's group in the future.

The parents and carers who were invited and joined the groups were in themselves a diverse group, caring for children in different contexts. Foster carers are employed by the local authority and may have children on a short- or long-term basis and will therefore have a different relationship and identity as carers to an adoptive parent. Indeed, it is significant to consider the extent to which they experience themselves as "parenting" as opposed to "caring", the meaning of these for them, and what this signifies in terms of the personal and professional identities and relationships that are thereby constructed. Foster carers may have a very different sense of responsibility or engagement with the children's difficulties. They are, on the whole, less likely to feel personally implicated in these. However, there can be a common desire to help with difficulties and manage them as well as possible. Kinship carers will be either blood-related or will have a relational connection to the child and birth parent, and so are very different again in terms of identity and history as carers. We thought long and hard about how this might be in a group, with some parents, for example, having no birth children and/or having struggled with infertility issues. Others would perhaps have adopted children from overseas, and still others had come to caring because of the failure of their own children or siblings to parent adequately. In the end we felt that we would work with the group around these different experiences and routes to parenting the children in their care. We hoped that talking about those differences and identifying the perhaps more significant commonalties of caring for children who had early disrupted and often adverse experiences would be part of the process of developing enough trust to work together to make changes. It was necessary to consider how the strategies developed in the group worked for particular children. We needed to be aware of how previous experiences, possibly including traumatic or abusive ones, might influence the application of ideas and strategies from the programme. We had to consider both the severity of some of the behavioural difficulties the children showed and the potential for re-traumatizing.

We wanted to be mindful of the diversity in the group and included ourselves in some specific exploration and acknowledgement of this. We began the group session by talking about names. We asked where group members' names came from, who had chosen them, and what their meaning was. This brought forth rich stories of family, culture, and language. The talk was personal, linked to histories, and opened up interest and respect for all of our differences. On another week we asked people to bring something that was meaningful and important in what it said about them. Someone brought a Bible, many brought photos or a piece of material or a picture from home. Someone brought a library card, someone else a football club membership. All had stories and significance attached. For some the focus was on themselves, for some on their family, for some on faith, for others on culture and heritage.

Bringing out these histories created a context where difference in other things—background, family expectations, and experiences—became more possible. Each topic we covered had resonances for group members in different ways. So, for instance, when in the first weeks we focused on play and improving the relationship with children through play, this was something that felt very different for different group members. This was a prime example where an overarching systemic frame seemed helpful. For instance, people's beliefs about adult–child relationships, their thoughts and feelings about gender, and their experiences as children of play and the presence or absence of siblings, or toys in the Western sense, all played a powerful role in shaping what they felt they could and could not do comfortably with their children. Exploring these in an accepting context, thinking about what was comfortable for group members to push themselves on, how couples might share things between them, were all fundamental to making the programme work for everyone.

Another example was when we looked at praise to reinforce desired behaviours. One of the exercises in the programme asks group members to recall the most recent time they were praised. This can be a highly emotional experience for people, and for some of them this may therefore be hard to do. Again we found it important to explore family of origin experiences and beliefs about praise. Someone from an African–Caribbean background talked of the saying from her childhood that "self-praise was no compliment". This reverberated for several others who talked about attitudes to praise and encouragement versus criticism in their families of origin and in the present. This discussion of the context made the debate about the helpfulness of praise for desired behaviour more meaningful and allowed for the exploration of a range of attitudes. Our experience was that it was necessary to explore the emotional connections to experiences of giving and receiving praise in order to enable parents to use praise effectively and to understand what their struggles or reluctance were about.

Another area where scripts for family relationships and behaviour seemed an important element to address in relation to the programme was that of authority and discipline in families and the intersection with gender. Many parents in these groups were struggling with parenting in the ways they had absorbed through their own families and through the cultures in which they were embedded. Differences in ethnicity and cultural backgrounds in the families—between couples and with the children—complicated this experience. Simply following the programme without some deconstruction of attitudes, beliefs, and well-known ways of doing things was not going to work. Doing this was a first step in making some different choices. Without an acknowledgement and understanding of the importance of the different ways families had developed their parenting, we would have been imposing the techniques in a directive way without the psychological fluidity needed for new ideas or ways to be absorbed and adapted in their particular family constellations. We were aiming to create what family therapist, Barry Mason (1993) has called "safe uncertainty", a situation where the known ways can be questioned and there is enough safety and security to try out something a bit, but not too, different.

Evaluation

What is in it for the parents?

The groups of about six included a mix of parents and carers from white/UK and black and minority ethnic backgrounds. There were two male–female couples who attended throughout and another father who attended when he was able. The attendance was very good, only one carer stopped coming, and that was because of illness. The men's contributions were appreciated, and the group were able to "bring in" some absent partners through the home-based tasks and discussion. Issues relating to gender as well as the intersection with culture came up in discussion, and also how couples negotiated parenting and their differences and commonalities. As the facilitators we needed to ensure that different voices could be given space.

In order to evaluate the impact of the programme, we asked for written and verbal feedback from group members throughout. In addition, a colleague undertook a group discussion and individual feedback interviews with our second group.

The parents' commentary throughout the groups showed that this had been an experience that had allowed them to grow and develop. Many of the comments highlighted the supportive aspects of the group. Parents clearly valued this way of coming together. The weekly feedback forms provided us as facilitators with instant responses to the session and allowed parents to give their immediate reflections with regard to what they had learned or valued.

Comments included:

"Thanks for listening to my problems."
"I had an opportunity to practise (role-play) what I needed to do."
"It was helpful to hear other people's views."
"It is good to meet other people with similar problems."

Parents particularly appreciated the presentation of ideas and strategies and despite many groans and much hilarity found the role-play practice helpful and effective in enabling them to try something at home. Watching video vignettes was a less valued aspect of the programme. It may be that parents found it harder to relate to vignettes where the parents shown were from a different cultural background or that watching others in role-play sometimes gave them the feeling that the children's behaviours being shown were not like those they were dealing with, leading to a reaction of dismissal.

As facilitators, we noticed that some parents' self-confidence grew. Others felt able to share their anxieties with the group and with us. We aimed to draw on strength-based models, emphasizing and noting the exceptions to problems and successes. Part of our job as facilitators was undoubtedly to work on containing the anxiety of the group members and modelling appreciation and praise for their efforts.

The 12 weekly sessions each introduced a different concept for parents/carers to consider. Each week a new task was set, and parents, often after a role-play, went away to "have a go" with their own children. We found it particularly helpful to start each session with questions about how things were going—this "trouble-shooting" seemed extremely helpful, and as facilitators we increasingly found ourselves taking a different position—that is, allowing the parents to help each other to problem-solve. It was heartening to see the group exploring their different approaches and solutions together, seemingly oblivious of us.

The pacing of the sessions was an important component of the success of this approach. We felt that it was central to make time to take care of the parents'/carers' needs. Tea, coffee, and lunch were essential ingredients, and parents/carers felt that their efforts had been noted and said that the gesture of offering lunch was much appreciated.

Our experience of running these groups is that there is a skill in balancing the pressure to get through the material in the programme and to provide time for more free-ranging discussion. Particular issues arise in the time between groups that parents will need and want to talk about. There are always connections with others that can be drawn. Building on ideas from other parents or carers can be particularly helpful. We have often felt—and this is an experience shared anecdotally with other group facilitators—that having some additional sessions over and above those set out in the programme would be helpful. This would give parents more space to talk rather than just pushing through the material. We have also looked at doing some home-based work alongside or following the group to help reinforce and generalize changes.

As part of our role as facilitators we telephoned each parent/carer to hear how things were at home, how they were managing the homework, and so forth. Parents/carers told us that they welcomed these calls, which kept them on track or gave them an opportunity to express their upset, especially if things were not going to plan. It was also a time when issues could be raised individually, perhaps before bringing them to the group. The telephone calls gave us (facilitators) another opportunity to acknowledge how tough it is to be parenting children who have had such difficult backgrounds. These midweek calls provided some individual opportunity to talk with carers as well as a chance to reinforce the efforts that were being made at home. The calls were an important ingredient in the success of the work. The use of phone calls in this way as part of the engagement might indeed be helpful in the context of other modalities of therapeutic work.

An outstanding feature of the group were reports of the observable changes in each of the children. Parents experienced different degrees of success, but all commented on feeling differently about their children and feeling that they were moving in the right direction. For example, one mother had felt overwhelmed by the difficulties and conflict with her daughter at times. In the group she developed a clear strategy for the mornings before school and practised in the group. She worked on her tone of voice, simplified her requests to her daughter, made clear statements about the consequences for non-compliance, and thought through what this would really mean in practice with a series of "what ifs". The following week the mother had the experience of her daughter seeming to realize that she would follow through her clear commands with consequences. Her daughter's tantrums subsided and they got to school on time and without the distress and upset that had accompanied most mornings. The mother had a glimpse of a possibility of change and a different relationship with her daughter.

A foster carer found that the most effective way to change things with her angry and rivalrous foster children was to give both of them structured separate individual "special time". She gave praise when they helped in the home and asked for things politely. Slowly but surely things improved, and she was delighted. Among her realizations was that the things that had worked so easily with her own children were not so simple with her foster children, who could not trust—at least initially—her care and appreciation of them.

Of course there were setbacks and struggles. We talked about children upping the stakes when parents become firmer or clearer. One mother described sitting in floods of tears behind her magazine while trying to "ignore" (the technique of the week) her child's tantrums. Another carer talked about holding her son to stop him kicking and head-butting and the fear that she would soon not be strong enough to do this. Another family came back from a homework task with a list of "house rules" that had been devised by the children alone and laid out the children's expectations of the adults, with nothing at all in the other direction. Constant re-working of these kinds of examples with some humour and sympathy in role-play expanded the range and confidence of parents in responding, so that limit-setting could be both firmer and, crucially, safer for all. We predicted the ups and downs that parents would experience, and this helped contain the group members through their struggles with change.

A major difference between this group and perhaps many community-based groups is that all the children in the families had suffered disrupted attachments, at the least. Many had also experienced highly adverse and sometimes abusive early care. We needed to acknowledge this, giving time to talk about attachment and recent research about brain development from both a psycho-educational stance and in thinking about the emotional realities and development of the children described to the group by their carers. Thinking together in the group about the impact of early trauma on aspects of development offered a chance to help make sense of behaviour the children were showing alongside "managing" that behaviour more effectively. Thinking a little about how they might work with children on emotional recognition and language within the aspects of the programme also developed. Children's previous experience of rejection and loss, the unavailability of reliable, responsive, sensitive parenting in the past, was alive in the struggles in the present. While it was undoubtedly important and helpful to develop strategies to manage and change behavioural and interactional patterns, it was also crucial to think about the experiences and meaning of these for the children in parallel.

We thought with parents about their expectations of children, what was realistic or not, and what change they might hope for. We talked a lot in the group about how common it can be for children in foster, adoptive, and kinship situations to show regression and what parents might make of this and how they could respond. This was an issue that Norma Sargent from Coram Family had highlighted in her groups of adopters and one that also seemed to be borne out with foster and kinship carers.

Particular techniques in the programme needed to be thought about carefully in relation to particular children's experiences. For example "time out" can be used very effectively as a consistent response to violent or destructive behaviour. It provides a structured response when both adults and children can calm down and a situation is stopped from escalating. However, with some of these children it might have the potential to spark a traumatic flashback of past abuse. It should therefore be used with careful preparation, thought, and caution and with the adults in a calm and controlled state of mind themselves.

As we needed to keep in mind the past attachments, losses, and experiences of the children, so we also needed to be mindful of the interrelationship with those of the parents and carers as re-expressed in the present in their parenting and other relationships. Fraiberg's notion of the "ghosts in the nursery" (Fraiberg, 1980) was helpful to us in this.

For the two parental couples within the group, both were able to observe and praise each other for the subtle changes that they noticed in each other's parenting behaviour and relationships. Both couples gradually mixed with the other parents, making alliances to some extent with others across gender and culture. At times group members allied with same-gender parents. At times they gained support from common cultural experiences and expectations. Sometimes similarities and differences around comfort with play, with being firm, with commonly felt upset about their children's early years or empathy with similar experiences as children themselves, or with the powerful desire to parent, meant that all at times drew succour from shared experiences with others in the groups.

Areas of difficulty

At times both the parents/carers and we felt that a link with their children's school would have been helpful. There was a need to liaise with school about the changes parents were trying to make, so that schools could support and reinforce this. Talking to teachers and supporting children's learning is an important feature of the programme, and some contact with school, perhaps from us as well as the carers, would have been helpful. This would inevitably introduce higher cost implications, both of facilitators' time and funding.

The link with ongoing therapeutic work at the clinic was important. For both facilitators there were some multiple relationships with a number of the families, as we were involved in other aspects of the services they received. This meant a careful negotiation about these dual relationships and thinking between us about our roles with each family in the group. The intensity of the work in the parent group highlighted gaps in the continuity of the intervention. For some of the parents there was a need for something more and the risk of a sense of being abandoned with their struggles at the end of the group that the less intense ongoing work could not fill.

Time continues to be a significant issue. The preparation and running of the group requires large amounts of time, which needs to be adequately resourced.

The importance of supervision should not be underestimated in order to keep us aware of group process, to be mindful of our own responses to the work, to ensure the quality of the work and maintain our sensitivity to the issues raised, and to support our co-working relationship. We have been able to develop a working style that accommodates our other responsibilities in the clinic setting. However, "self-management" does not feel like an effective way of monitoring progress, and regular supervision needs to be built into the running of groups to support the facilitators.

Thoughts for future groups

Our thoughts at present are guided by the success of the groups run so far. Feedback from the parents/carers shows that the groups were highly valued.

In the future we would like to offer a regular cycle of parent/carers groups using this approach that would enable parents/carers to join at a time that feels right for them. This could be as a first intervention, alongside other therapeutic work, or as a follow-on, depending on parents' and clinicians' discussions.

Our experience has been that the 12-week programme requires opportunities for review, to meet up with the parents/carers to hear how they are progressing and to "top up" their self-confidence to keep going. We think this should be built in. It would also offer opportunities for follow-up evaluation of the effectiveness of the programme.

There were direct requests from some parents/carers for a more formal series of workshop events to hear about subjects such as attachment, loss, and relationships to give them a firm foundation for their continuing parenting. We feel this would be a helpful adjunct to the work offered by the group and would build on the occasional workshops that are already offered.

Based on our experience of running these groups so far, we have made some plans for the future. We would like to run a children's group alongside the parents' group. We would also like to offer more home-based work for those who need more or cannot manage the group context. We think some follow-up sessions with observation-based interventions at home would be a useful adjunct to the group work. We believe this would allow parents to fully embrace the concepts and skills that are introduced at each session and enable on-the-spot "trouble-shooting" opportunities to maximize success.

In conclusion, our experience has been that a group-based parent training approach has valuable things to offer adoptive, foster, and kinship parents and carers. The gains in confidence, in making connections with others, and in developing closer and more satisfying, less conflictual relationships with their children have been considerable. Further work on combining parents' groups with group work with the children would be a fruitful future development. This would be an area for possible research in relation to effectiveness with this particular group. Using a cognitive–behavioural approach was effective in making changes. A wider family systems or psychoanalytic and attachment perspective added a depth of understanding of these particular children's difficulties and enabled parents and carers to unpack the meanings in both the children's and their own responses. This, in our view, worked well alongside offering the Webster-Stratton programme. Working in conjunction with other parts of the system—either with other clinicians working with the families or with schools—is an important part of embedding and solidifying changes.

PART IV

CONSULTATIVE WORK WITH PARENTS, FAMILIES, AND PROFESSIONALS

The chapters in this section describe different aspects of the consultative work of the Fostering and Adoption team. Each stresses the paramount importance of addressing all members of the complex networks surrounding looked-after and adopted children and those in kinship care.

In the first of these chapters, Caroline Lindsey clearly states the need to help professionals to explore the individual issues and professional agendas that may profoundly influence their thinking and decision making.

Lorraine Tollemache, writing from a combined systemic and psychodynamic viewpoint, gives examples of consultations to families and professionals.

In the third chapter, Caroline Lindsey writes about consultations addressing the specific topic of contact. She suggests ways in which decisions may be made that focus primarily on the needs of the child, while keeping in mind the wishes of the adults.

Jenny Kenrick

CHAPTER 15

Consultative work with professionals

Caroline Lindsey

Throughout this book, it has been made clear by many authors that work in fostering, adoption, and kinship care, in common with many aspects of mental health care, is essentially of a multi-systemic nature. In chapter 17 I paraphrase Winnicott by saying that "there is no such thing as a looked-after or adopted child", meaning that whether or not contact with the birth family is enacted in practice, the original family is always an integral part of the child's existence and is looked after or adopted along with the child. In addition, however, a significant number of professionals are also involved in the lives of these children, young people, and their carers, with differing responsibilities and for varying periods of time. The practitioners belong to a range of agencies, including health, social care, education, youth justice, police, and the legal system, each with their own ethos and beliefs about their role, preferred outcome, and authority for decision making on behalf of the children and their families. It is rarely possible to work with a child or family effectively without involving their network. Furthermore, it is often the case that the problems being presented are most appropriately addressed by working with the professionals, both with and sometimes without the members of the family. This is because the difficulties may be located in the wider system as much as they are being enacted within the family (see Emanuel, chapter 18).

Using the idea of the problem-determined system (Anderson, Goolishian, & Windermere, 1986), it is helpful to conceptualize problems being created or brought into reality through the conversations that take place between people and therefore to realize that in order to address the issues, it is necessary to bring them all together to find a solution. Anderson calls this group a "problem-dissolving system". It is often the case that some families find symptoms or behaviours in children they are looking after intolerable, while others live with them with little or no difficulty. This may depend on the story or explanation they give for the behaviour, which may be one that creates it as a problem or one that fits with their life experiences. For example, many children who have been abused and neglected have issues with eating. They may refuse to eat or may want to eat too much; they may store food or "steal" it from the cupboard. In one family, the adopted child's greed was accepted as a manifestation of his difficulty in believing that there was going to be another meal, based on his experiences of near-starvation in his birth family. They worked with him towards a time when it would again be possible for the family to go out to a meal in a restaurant without being embarrassed—something that they had always previously enjoyed together—but they were happy for this to take as long as it did. In another family, the child's "stealing" of food was experienced as an attack on their parenting, which meant either that they were failing as parents or that he was delinquent or disturbed in some way. The story that the second family told about the eating resulted in the creation of a problem, while the first family told a story of survival and recovery.

Similarly, the ways in which these stories are then re-told in conversations with social workers and other professionals, and how they are received and told again in case conferences, supervisions, consultations, and so on, may bring forth a problem-determined or problem-saturated system. For example, it is a frequent experience that a birth parent visiting at a foster-carer's house may bring clothes and food with her for her young child. She may proceed to change her clothes and feed her daughter and brush and comb her hair. This behaviour may be construed as an act of love and concern, signalling her ongoing commitment for her child, but it may also be seen as critical and undermining of the carer and the placement and as evidence of a failure to accept the reality of the child's removal from her care. The broader context needs to be taken into account in order to address fully the meanings of this behaviour for all the parties. In the context of a placement with a view to possible rehabilitation, the failure of a mother to act in a parental way on contact might be a matter of concern to the social worker. On the other hand, in a situation where the decision has been made that the child is to be permanently removed, the mother's actions might carry a less positive meaning for the future carer. There may be cultural beliefs affecting the mother's behaviour too, which need to be taken into account from her perspective. The ways in which the foster carer and social worker perceive the meaning of this episode and how they speak about it together, with the mother, and with others may then determine whether or not a problem-determined system is created between them.

The context of consultation

With these ideas in mind, consultation may be offered under a number of circumstances. Workers may approach us specifically for help to resolve an issue where there is disagreement or when they want the chance to talk over a dilemma with someone from outside their system; we may ask to see all the professionals involved when we receive a referral for an assessment or treatment of a child where the contextual issues seem to need clarifying. We almost always ask to see a referring social worker and her senior for an initial consultation to agree the task, to clarify the lines of authority and responsibility for decision making and their expectations. We may invite the social worker or another professional identified as a key person to continue to participate in the work with the family. We often re-convene the consultation after doing some work with the child and family, in order to feed back our views and to re-connect with the system around the child, as described by Tollemache in chapter 19. There are many variations and no hard-and-fast rules.

Many agencies have practitioners working within the organization who are available for consultation and supervision. Internal consultation, while helpful, poses challenges to those offering it and to those participating. As an NHS-based team, we are in a position to offer external as opposed to internal consultation, with the advantage that we are neither employed by nor managed by those in the organization whose workers are seeking help. While we are responsible for the quality of our clinical work and for any opinions we may offer or recommendations made, it is the social workers or courts who are authorized to make decisions. This gives us the chance to explore freely the issues raised, offering the professionals a space away from the workplace to address their concerns. This conversation by itself may sometimes be all that is required to clarify their thinking and give them a chance to go on in their often challenging work. On the other hand, being a service local to a number of social services departments gives us a chance to build up familiarity with workers and the chance to identify when there seems to be a recurring issue in one of the teams. It may then be appropriate to take this up by offering a team consultation or discussion with senior members of staff to reflect on what may be going on.

It is inevitable with such complex family–professional systems that differences of opinion—sometimes of a conflictual nature—arise, whether between carers or adopters and social workers or court-appointed child and family workers, between different members of the social work system, with birth families, sometimes involving the young people themselves.

Interprofessional differences do not leave the children untouched. It is a not infrequent experience to find that young people's difficulties in a family placement with a carer, particularly those of a challenging nature, may be greatly ameliorated when the adults resolve their disagreements. This is, of course, familiar to parents who know that when they do not agree, their children may play up. It may not be so obvious when the conflict exists, for example, between the social worker and the carer.

Beliefs, assumptions, and meaning

These differences of individual perspective between professionals may often arise from the beliefs which they hold and the meanings that they consequently attribute to the situations in which they are involved. I have referred in chapter 1 to the model "the Coordinated Management of Meaning" (Pearce & Cronen, 1980; see Figure 1.1), which creates a hierarchical organization of levels of context, to elucidate the complexity of socially constructed meanings inherent in our personal and professional lives. Contradictions may arise between the different levels of context, giving rise to confused messages. For example, the belief that children should live with their birth parents and that every effort should be made to maintain continuity of relationship and parenthood—a socio-cultural norm—may sometimes be experienced as in contradiction to the belief that children should be securely placed outside the home as soon as it is clear that rehabilitation is not possible: a belief based on professional understanding of a child's developmental needs and underpinned by research that shows the potentially negative impact of delay (see Music, chapter 4). A mother may tell us that that she believes that her child's safety comes first—a sociocultural norm—but at the same time convey that she is not prepared to give up her relationship with her abusive partner—her life script.

This model may be helpful in understanding how the disagreements and conflicts between professionals and with families arise. This can be particularly emotionally charged in the field of fostering, adoption, and kinship care because we all come from families, and the very words involved—parents, children, birth, care, and so on—arouse strong feelings. On the one hand, there are the professional contexts in which they operate, which give meaning to their understanding as they relate to the stories that families and colleagues bring to them. These include their professional relationship to sociocultural norms, encompassing the legal framework, which may be experienced as constraining or facilitating; the values and responsibilities of the agency which employs them and the practice of the team of which they are a member; the knowledge, skills base, and ethical standards arising from their professional training; and the specific practitioner–family relationship that has arisen in each case. These levels of professional context are closely interwoven with the personal life of the practitioner and relate to their membership of a community, race, culture, and religion, and also to the beliefs and experiences in the families in which they have grown up and in the families they have themselves created (see Table 15.1). All of these, too, profoundly affect the way in which they understand, act, and make decisions about the children who are their patients, their clients, or for whom they are caring.

Table 15.1. Levels of context

Professional	Personal
Socio-cultural norms	Socio-cultural norms
Agency ethos	
Team ethic	Family beliefs
Professional life script	Personal life script
Professional–family relationship	Family–professional relationship
Conversations over time in different professional settings	Conversations over time in different professional settings
Stories	Stories

In one case, a social worker and her senior came for a consultation to discuss the options for placement of a young girl aged 5 years who was unlikely to be able to return to her birth family. They wanted to resolve a difference of view concerning adoption or foster care before taking the case to the panel for further discussion. As the story unfolded, it became clear that the social worker was becoming emotionally distressed by the conversation. She explained that her motivation for being a social worker had been the desire to rescue children from abusive situations (personal/professional life script). With her permission, we learnt that she had been fostered as a young child when her parents were unable to care for her, but she had remained in contact with them. There were several features in common with the story of the little girl, who was happy with her foster carer and had expressed a wish to stay there. It seemed that the social worker's own experience was making it hard for her to consider the benefits of adoption and the possible necessity for less regular contact, alongside her conviction about the advantages of fostering for this child. Her personal belief was that fostering was always the placement of choice, although she recognized that social work practice did not accord with this. Once she and her senior identified the meaning that this particular case was having for her, it became more possible for all the options to be considered from the perspective of the child's needs.

However, in many cases it is not appropriate or possible to address in a consultation the professionals' beliefs and assumptions that affect their relationships with each other and with clients or patients. Other ways have to be found by the consultant to address the dilemmas brought for discussion. It is, therefore, very important that there are opportunities for professionals to consider how their personal life and professional experiences influence day-to-day practice. In psychoanalytic training this is achieved through the training analysis. In systemic family therapy training, personal–professional development seminars take place throughout the training, dedicated to addressing the connections between personal beliefs and clinical practice and making use of personal and professional genograms (Hildebrand, 1998; Lindsey, 1993). These include issues such as race, culture, and spirituality, for which the cultural genogram may be helpful (Hardy & Lasloffy, 1995), as well as beliefs about parenting, authority, and gender. The training for social workers in fostering and adoption at the Tavistock Clinic— the "Children in Transition" course—offers an opportunity for the participants to consider how they came to be involved in working in the field and where their key beliefs about family and parenting originate. They are encouraged to find a way to continue the conversations they had started in the group in their team or agency with trusted colleagues, with the idea that deconstructing their beliefs in this way would facilitate reflective practice and be protective both to them and to their clients.

Methods of consultation

In thinking about the complex systems around the child, it is helpful to map the relationships that all the parties have with each other, perhaps with the use of an eco-map, in addition to identifying the family relationships, by drawing up a genogram. In training social workers and other professionals, it has also been useful to draw an eye in the corner of the whiteboard, taking up Humberto Maturana's idea of "objectivity in parentheses" (1988), to remind ourselves that we "cannot not" see things from our own perspective. It also signals how important it is to take up an observing position. When we are involved in a conflict or dilemma, it is very easy, as described above, to lose the ability to see alternative viewpoints and to behave—as Maturana puts it—from a "universa" rather than from a "multiversa" position.

This is why it is helpful to work in a team, since we can offer differing views, reflect aloud on each other's thoughts, address a feeling of being stuck when it arises, and ask questions of each other, as well as of the consultees. We have to bear in mind that a team can also "fall in love with its ideas" to the exclusion of others, and that may sometimes result in a lack of difference. In other words, the team may tend to come up with the same ideas, almost irrespective of the family that is being seen. We address this by working with different members of the team, usually in pairs. It is also the reason why being curious and having a questioning stance (see chapter 1) are valuable in consultations, to enable the challenging of firmly held positions in a non-instructive way (Campbell & Grønbæk, 2006). Developing ideas about how the situation has come about by attempting to bring all the information into a systemic hypothesis provides material for questions to further understanding of the dilemmas. Especially in the field of child protection, it is very easy to slip into a position of mutual blame and criticism. The practice of positive connotation and of reframing ideas positively plays an important part in making each participant feel that their contribution is valued and valuable, even when some ideas are seen to be more useful than others. As is apparent from the case examples below, it is possible to appreciate how someone may come to take up a particular position, even when other ways of seeing the issue may seem more helpful.

Case examples

Work with the professional network, alongside therapeutic work with children, where there was disagreement

A consultation with the network, consisting of the children's social workers, foster carers, link workers, and the school, was requested in relation to difficulties over contact issues. Therapeutic sessions were being provided jointly to two teenage children in transition, for whom, although it was clear that they would not be returning to their parents, plans for long-term placement were uncertain. Alongside the sessions for the siblings there had been regular consultations with the network. At one stage concerns were raised about the increasing number of unscheduled and, at times, frightening—to the children and to the foster carers—contact taking place with one of the birth parents. There was some mutual criticism and concern expressed between the carer and social workers about how this was being managed.

During the consultation, the ideas held by the foster carers, school, and social workers about what it meant to each to agree or to refuse contact were explored. Each member was invited to articulate the beliefs that they held about the value and risks entailed in contact for the children. The carers had strong feelings about depriving the birth parent, who was unwell, and the children of a relationship with each other, believing that this was cruel and that it would give rise to feelings of guilt in the children. This was strongly influenced by the importance for the carers of their own tightly knit community and supportive family. This had led to them taking an accommodating position to the parent, believing that their presence would be sufficiently protective of the children's emotional well-being. The school's view was organized by their previous experience of this parent, with whom they had had numerous difficult and abusive confrontations, which had been threatening to staff. The social worker was organized in her views by the history of unreliable parenting, child protection concerns, and the responsibilities arising from a care order. Her professional duties included an expectation that she would work with written agreements and supervision of contact with this parent. The parent had been extremely difficult to engage in a partnership around this work. The unscheduled contacts were undermining the social worker's authority and broke the written agreements expected by her seniors and the court. The link worker was particularly concerned about the stability of the placement, seeing this as being threatened both by the effect of the contact visits and by the social worker's criticism of the carers. She also questioned the carers' personal/professional boundaries and the impact of this unscheduled contact on the carers if it were to continue.

Exploring these differing ideas, beliefs, and influences on the positions taken by the members of the children's network enabled a different sort of conversation to take place—one that was less than had been the case previously about blame, criticism, or making demands on one another about how each should behave in the situation. It allowed for the emergence of a more shared understanding of the dilemmas that each one experienced with the contact arrangements. In a context of appreciation of everyone's position, it was possible to develop mutually acceptable plans that could be agreed and which clarified the expectations of both carers and social workers as to how future contact visits would be managed.

A consultation where there was a dilemma to be resolved,
for which an outside opinion was sought

Following a brief assessment of an 8-year-old girl, who had had a previous placement failure, a consultation was requested jointly by the potential long-term carer (currently a short-term carer) for the child and the child's social worker. They were not in disagreement with each other or the agency. They wanted help in facilitating their thinking together about how and when to talk to the child about the plan for the placement to become permanent. Both had a strong desire to tell the child as soon as possible. The child was expressing, through play, drawings, and indeed directly in words, a desperate wish to be claimed by the carer and to stay in the placement. They believed that knowing that this was the plan would, after her previous experience, help her to feel more settled and secure. It would relieve her of the burden of the uncertainty as to her future. They thought that being told would have a beneficial effect on her behaviour, which was particularly difficult at school, and which they attributed to her preoccupation with where she was going to live. However, they were constrained by the bureaucratic processes of which they were a part: the need for the completion of the assessment of the carer as a permanent foster carer and ratification of the care plan by the local authority. The carer was very reluctant to say anything to the girl that could feel like a promise and that she could not absolutely guarantee. The social worker felt that his professional ethos also meant that he could not say anything that was not finalized, even though both he and the social services department were fully supportive of the plan.

Deconstructing the different aspects of their dilemma in conversation with them, without giving advice or instruction, enabled them to think for themselves of ways that they could recognize the little girl's wishes without transgressing their ethical positions. They agreed to say to her that it had been helpful for them to hear what she wanted. They would say that they needed to know this, so that all the adults who were thinking about what was best for her and making the decisions would know her feelings. They agreed also that it would be acceptable to tell her, in response to the wishes she had expressed, that they agreed that her idea of wanting to stay with her carer was a good one. They would let her know as soon as they could when it had been finalized.

A consultation following a referral for therapy where disagreement in the network arose at the outset, needing to be addressed before any further work was undertaken

A referral was made asking for the assessment of the therapeutic needs of a young sibling group, placed for adoption, with a history of severe abuse and neglect in their birth family. In the telephone calls before the consultation, a difference of view emerged about whether the placement was meeting the children's needs. This allowed the team to consider how to conduct the consultation with the children's social worker, the family link worker, and the birth family's social worker and to develop some hypotheses about the differences, given the short time the children had been in the placement and the complexity of caring for a group of siblings who had each been abused. The team agreed that it was going to be important for the differences of view about the placement to be talked about openly in the initial meeting, so that they did not get drawn into a position of joining one side or the other in this split.

In the first consultation meeting, the children's social worker was concerned about the reported level of behavioural difficulties in school, the poor relationships that the siblings had with each other, and the slow progress of settling at home. He communicated a strong sense of duty towards the children. He felt uncertain that the carers were offering enough to the children in terms of individual time and attention, stimulation, and firm boundaries. He had expressed this view to the carers directly. They had felt very undermined. Both they and the family social worker, who had been through the process of obtaining the care order and knew at first hand what the children had experienced, felt that the difficulties resulting from the children's early experiences of neglect and abuse were not being taken into account sufficiently by the newly appointed social worker. They thought that it was not realistic to expect that the children's difficulties would diminish to the extent that he seemed to expect, within such a relatively short space of time. The link worker was concerned about the pressure on the potential adopters, who were already being challenged by the children's neediness. The children's social worker expressed his sense of responsibility to get the placement right for the children and about the target time for achieving the adoption order. In the session, the team took a position of neutrality, using their curiosity to explore the ways that each member of the network perceived the children and what explanations and understandings they had for their behaviour. This began to enable less polarized and defensive positions to be taken. The team was aware of the need not to define their task in a way that could be constructed as assessing the placement. They offered a multidisciplinary assessment to think about the children's psychological, educational, emotional, and therapeutic needs and to enable everyone to consider what would be helpful to ensure placement stability.

Afterword

What all these cases have in common is to demonstrate the potential effect of a consultation to facilitate professionals in their ongoing tasks. It is not the role of the consultant to make decisions or give advice, although this is often sought. But it is possible to reflect the thinking in the group and to feed back the dilemmas that have been described, which, in turn, allows new ideas and conversations to emerge. It is important to distinguish the different roles of the members of the team for everyone in the network, so that it is clear when they are acting as consultants, when they are speaking as therapists to the child and family, and when they take on the role of expert to offer opinion to the court. Members of the team also facilitate the consultative process by regularly clarifying for themselves as part of their self-reflection how they are defining their role. This ensures that they remain in a position of curiosity, able to open up opportunities for thought and reflection rather than closing down conversation with certainty and opinion.

CHAPTER 16

Therapeutic consultations about the transition into care and children in transition

Lorraine Tollemache

This chapter sets out to describe how the containment provided by the consultation process can help professionals to develop a coherent narrative about the experience of families for whom they are responsible. These children and their parents are often psychically disabled by the traumatic experiences they have endured, and they have only a fragmented, partial, or distorted sense of what has happened to them or what is happening in their day-to-day lives—indeed, in all of their relationships. They and the professionals who work with them can become blind to and defended against knowing what is going on because it is so painful. Consultation can provide a mental space in which they can begin to allow themselves to see the damage that has been done and continues to be done, so that they can work together more realistically to counteract this and towards achieving change.

Consultation forms a substantial part of the work done by the Fostering and Adoption team at the Tavistock. It is generally sought when professionals disagree about decisions that have to be made. In this chapter I illustrate two situations and the consultation we provided by describing aspects of work with families who are amalgamations of many we have seen. I first explore the dilemmas that arise when there are disagreements over whether children should remain in worrying birth families or should be removed from them, and the role that consultation can play in these circumstances. I then look at the role consultation can play when there are difficulties with finding permanent placements for children who have been removed from abusive families and have become increasingly abusive themselves. Other consultations are described in this book, for example consultations about contact. Most consultations are brief. The situations I describe in this chapter, however, have required us to provide consultation over prolonged periods of time. This is perhaps because of the sheer difficulty of the tasks expected of social workers, and also because of the rapidly changing nature of the care system, described by Lindsey in the introduction to this book.

A tenet of our consultative work is that all the relevant parties in each situation must be present at an initial meeting: indeed, identifying and involving them in this meeting is the first work we do. We find that being from a different organization allows us to remain neutral when we meet and that working in pairs helps us to maintain this stance. Though the latter is not always possible, we make it a priority in complex cases where it is difficult to make a judgement. At this initial meeting, working within a systemic framework, we ask numerous questions to clarify what must be achieved, each person's agenda, their professional responsibilities, and the dilemmas each faces, as well as the ideas and beliefs behind these and the conflicts that have emerged between them. There is seldom an opportunity for all these things to be freshly explored away from the workplace. Intervening as we do at the interface between the professional system and the family, and being familiar with many of the issues, we are able to ask questions that help to re-examine many assumptions. This process can help people to redefine the priorities and re-order them within a time frame. Together we then draw up a plan to which everyone can agree, allowing work to be undertaken in a collaborative way. We begin to create a common narrative, a frame of reference about the case, which can be returned to and updated, guiding the work. Most importantly, it can sustain and bind together a group of professionals who may then become the only people who hold a child's or family's history in a world characterized by rapid loss and change. This working group is collectively responsible for the outcome, counteracting the tendency to thrust responsibility on one or two beleaguered individuals. As well as working systemically, we also draw on psychoanalytic and attachment theory. The poet Yeats memorably said "Things fall apart, the centre cannot hold" (Yeats, 1921). We see this tendency all too frequently, particularly where children—and often their parents before them—have been subjected to experiences that have overwhelmed their capacity to function. We believe it is necessary to have a range of frames of reference available to us in order to understand and intervene in the most helpful way.

The transition into care

Removing children from their birth families is a painful experience, both for the members of the family and for the professionals who work with them. Professionals come from families too, and they may have very strong feelings about splitting up another family or, alternatively, leaving children unprotected in an intensely vulnerable position. Many are understandably plagued by doubt, and there can be acute differences of opinion among them about the action that should be taken. However, the way this decision is reached can profoundly influence what happens next.

We find that there are recurring themes that emerge when we work with families where children are believed to be at risk but it is unclear whether removing them from their birth families will do more harm than good. Often there is concern about parental alcoholism or drug misuse; there may be domestic violence or mental illness in these families, with corresponding neglect of the children. Many such families have been known to social services for years: their cases are opened and closed regularly, a great deal of work may have been done with them. Such families are often very mobile, moving between numbers of local authorities and taking off when the focus on them becomes uncomfortable. They often seem to be "closed" to outsiders, to form a clan of their own, though this clan may span a number of generations and a mother may have multiple partners who move in and out of it. Lastly, the level of concern about the families inevitably fluctuates. If it escalates sufficiently for social services to instigate care proceedings, fresh difficulties can arise. As more people become involved, differences of opinion proliferate. The basis on which a decision is finally made may be questionable and based on very flimsy evidence.

For example, in one family referred to us and known to social services for years, a worrying parental relationship had improved over time, and the younger children seemed to be less neglected than the older ones had been. Then it was suddenly discovered that a number of children were involved in sexually abusive behaviour towards each other. The parents were upset by this revelation, but although they castigated all the children vociferously, they appeared to do little else.

The social workers, shocked and concerned that they had previously underestimated the seriousness of the state of affairs, instigated care proceedings and planned to remove the youngest children. The children's guardian *ad litem* disagreed with this plan, as did the expert witness. Their disagreements highlighted real uncertainties. It was by no means clear that removing the children would be constructive, and no clear care plan had been made for them.

Each professional's view reflected both the complexity of the issues and the experiences each had had in working with the parents. For example, the social workers, who had had the longest involvement and carried statutory responsibility for the children, were treated as the "enemy". The guardian who opposed their plan was treated by the parents as their "saviour". She keenly appreciated how bereft they would be at the loss of the younger children when their lives apparently revolved around them. The expert witness noted that the parents undoubtedly minimized the seriousness of the abuse, but he also noted that the children themselves did not seem overtly disturbed by it. He believed that splitting the family up was not justified.

Cases like this are the bread and butter of a social work Child and Family team. The buck stops at their door. The complexity of the issues involved and absence of conclusive evidence mean that differing professional opinions can seem equally valid. We believe that in situations like these consultation can foster a more collaborative working together, so that a sound decision can be reached—one that neither minimizes nor overreacts to what is going on. We also believe that as consultants we may need to remain involved for some time rather than dipping in and out of a situation that is fragmented enough already.

Our interventions and the theoretical frameworks that underpinned them

In such cases, after an initial meeting with the key professionals involved and meetings with the parents and the children, we meet the professional group again and jointly formulate a plan by which, through a series of interventions and assessments by ourselves and others both from the Fostering and Adoption team and the community, fresh recommendations might be arrived at. The court often welcomes such an intervention, because it gives families a second chance. However, the process of reassessment linked to new initiatives, and the formulation of fresh recommendations, inevitably takes time. The increased pressure on parents may be passed directly on to the children. Becoming directly involved lays us open to the same conflicts and anguish that other professionals have experienced. We find that we are moved by parents and children and worried by the possible results of splitting them up. We may be tempted to overlook parental shortcomings and can understand why copious social work files remain unread. Our own experiences of loss inevitably affect our reactions. However, the presence of a co-worker, the structure provided by the framework of meetings with the working group we have established, and our discussions with colleagues in the Fostering and Adoption team all provide places in which we can make sense of our reactions, many of which provide important clues to the family dynamics. This helps to re-orientate us, and, as we look at what has happened in a family in the past and what is happening in response to new initiatives, a new sense of direction may emerge.

For example, in some families we see that in spite of fresh interventions and the second chances they have been given, there is a lack of any real change. We may become aware of the paucity of parenting, the continuing neglect of the children, and above all a parent's refusal to work with professionals, despite their good intentions. More worryingly still, we may see how cruelly they treat any child who rocks the boat and how terrified their children are of letting anything slip, of betraying anything at all to outsiders. We may notice how some children effectively give up and close down, seeming to have minimal expectations for themselves but a blind loyalty to the family. Many can fear that any change might lead to the actual death of a parent and the end of the family itself—a fear that is frequently exacerbated by a parent's threats of suicide. In short, sometimes it can become clear that children do need to be taken into care. Although we may be able to provide clear evidence to support this, unless we have collaborated to make detailed care plans for each child, the situation remains no further forward.

Psychoanalytic theory helps us to understand how some parents are unable to perceive their own neglectful or destructive behaviour. Instead, they instantly cut themselves off from any awareness of this and blame others. Klein's concept of the paranoid–schizoid position is particularly illuminating. It is described more fully by Kenrick (in chapter 2) and is a mode of functioning arising from an early phase of development. It makes extensive use of the defence mechanisms of

splitting, projection, and projective identification. A person functioning in this way sees the world in highly polarized terms, and people
or events as being good or bad—not a mixture of the two, as someone operating from a more developmentally mature position realizes.
Unwanted aspects and emotions belonging to the self are projected
into the other, who then becomes the one who has the unwanted feelings—for example, anger—and is reacted to accordingly. Projective
identification, a more powerful form of projection, can create even
greater problems. A person consistently operating in this way inevitably experiences massive confusion and has great difficulty understanding what is going on in relationships, what belongs to them and
what to another.

We are treated by parents such as these in many of the contradictory and disconcerting ways that others have experienced previously. At one moment we are seen as "good" because we are on
their side, and they therefore cooperate with us. The next moment
we are seen as "bad" and threatened or avoided. The switch in their
behaviour can be triggered by something almost imperceptible. They
cannot accept help from us unless our thoughts exactly match their
own—indeed, they cannot deal with anyone who is beyond their direct control. Parents like these may be suffering from an unresolved
traumatic experience that triggers such highly unpredictable behaviour. They cannot trust anyone. Instead, they may fuse together and
fiercely and rigidly defend themselves against a world they experience as unpredictable and damaging. Their union makes them even
less accessible to help.

Some parents can feel a measure of relief when evidence is presented to them clearly and not unsympathetically. They may then
accept that their children need levels of care they cannot sustain themselves. They can become the non-parental parents Lindsey describes
in chapter 17 and give them up. With others the imminent prospect
of separation unlocks other responses. Because they are just surviving psychically, these parents cannot think about their children or see
them as separate from themselves. Instead, they reject all evidence of
maltreatment, maintaining the fiction that "home" is the only safe and
good place—a fiction that is held on to by the children who remain
with them. Such families collectively make it their mission to retrieve
all those placed in foster or adoptive families. There is often only a
small window of opportunity in which something might be achieved
for the children who need, and are able to use, the compensatory care
another family can offer.

Moving children on, if only temporarily, from families such as these is indeed difficult. The very process of removing them can be dramatic and fraught with difficulty. For these reasons every detail of the next placements has to be planned in detail and managed by a tightly coordinated team focused on each child. The hierarchies of abuse that we identify in birth families are difficult to counteract even when children are placed elsewhere. Hierarchies of abuse are also played out and mirrored in the professional groups surrounding a family. For example, we have witnessed how the splitting and scapegoating that goes on in a family can be inflicted on social workers, who may be first blamed and abused by the parents and then dismissed by the professional network, who may devalue their opinions and their long experience of working with a family. Their responses become fragmented and disorganized as a result of this. Cairns proposes that such reactions in professionals can be the result of what she calls "secondary trauma" (Cairns, 2002; see also Emanuel, chapter 18). They may be further disabled by the lack of containment provided within their own overstretched and fragmented departments. This is partially remedied through consultation where sustained thinking becomes possible within the professional groups we form. However, the professional group is also vulnerable because of the rapid turnover of staff. This means that children are left vulnerable again.

Children in transition

When children reach care, their situation may be no less precarious, for a number of reasons: First, children's disturbance and distress is not necessarily obvious, and the level of the damage they have sustained is frequently underestimated. This, heightened by their distress and bewilderment at a move, often surfaces once they are placed and has a considerable impact on their new carers. Second, matching children with families is notoriously difficult when, inevitably, much is unknown about either. Often children cannot forget their birth families, and sometimes a birth parent's efforts to reclaim them increases greatly once a care order has been made. Lastly, the social workers who hold parental responsibility for a child often change or move on.

It is during this precarious transitional period that consultation is most needed to ensure that the lengthy time it can take to achieve a degree of stability and permanence is used thoughtfully rather than being filled by re-enactments of the earlier abusive patterns, this time played out in the new systems. As consultants we have often found it necessary to build ourselves into the system for a time as children easily get "lost": social workers may have other priorities, plans may fall through, and parents' needs can dominate.

The composite case described next highlights some of the complexities of finding a permanent-enough placement for two children when care proceedings had been preceded by years of neglect and abuse. It addresses the aftermath of traumatic experiences and its effect on sibling placements, and how much or how little can realistically be achieved for children whose early years have been blighted and whose development is circumscribed in ways that we often blind ourselves to because it is too painful to see. The case I describe was again referred to us by social services. It concerns two small boys. Through the consultation process we evolved a small team who remained dedicated to them despite their many moves. The work falls into two phases, during the second of which we had to re-examine the evidence we were presented with.

In this family the plan to place two children together in an adoptive family had stalled. Two years into their short-term foster placement no adoptive family had been found. Prospective parents were put off by the mental health problems of the birth parents and their use of drugs and alcohol. Paul and Jimmy were aged 6 and 4 when we first met them. Because they had been together through so much adversity it was hoped that adoption might offer them some stability and counteract the pull of their birth parents. However, during the two-year wait Jimmy, the younger boy, became attached to his foster carer, who was prepared to keep him. She was an experienced foster carer and her busy home, full of grandchildren and foster children, reflected the boys' earlier family, though its order was quite unlike the birth family's chaos. She did not want Paul, for whom she could feel little affection and with whom she felt she had made little progress. Paul still lied, he was also very destructive. He seemed empty and unreal beside the livelier Jimmy.

Because the plan was to place the boys together, and because we recognized the level of Paul's disturbance, we recommended that he should be placed in a therapeutic boarding school, returning to the adoptive family, where Jimmy would be at weekends and in the holidays. He would thus be able to get the additional help he clearly needed and also would have a home. Not unusually, the local authority deemed this plan too expensive. Soon afterwards both children were placed with inexperienced, unprepared adopters. We elected to remain involved on a consultative basis, realizing the problems were far from over—a decision that was welcomed by the social workers dealing with the case.

Splits can happen in relationships as well as within individuals. While Paul was seen as the difficult one, Jimmy could be felt to be less problematic. The good/bad split between the boys played out in the foster family was repeated with the potential adopters, and when this placement broke down because of Paul's behaviour, both children were returned to the original foster carer. By now it was believed that Paul had proved himself to be un-adoptable and could only be contained in a specialist foster placement. Jimmy was returned to the same prospective adopters who, like the foster carer, had warmed to him and wanted a second chance.

By this point many children in care have had a series of social workers who have had little time or opportunity to begin to understand them or develop any relationship with them. First, it is hard to piece together what they may have been through by reading the copious files that have accumulated, or to visit them because they are placed far away. Often there is no time to get to know their current carers and schools, the actual context of their daily lives. Above all, it can be extremely difficult for social workers to set up the conditions within which to meet a child regularly and then begin to make sense of their own experiences of working with the child. Child psychotherapists bear witness to the difficulties of working with children such as these in this book. Social workers require many theoretical frameworks to guide them in what they do and help them to put together the evidence they gather in their attempts to hold parental responsibility for children. The highly complex tasks they must undertake require training, opportunities to consult with others, and time. These two children were fortunate in that they had a very experienced and competent social worker. She was also allowed enough time to be able to do all this. She was a central member of the team.

Despite the dedicated and skilled work that went into this case, evident at the many consultations we had with key individuals in the children's lives, the foster carers and adoptive parents, the managers, the schools, further deterioration and breakdown could not be prevented. The level of trauma experienced by both boys was extreme. Jimmy was unable to settle in his adoptive family, and Paul had problems with his specialist foster carer. One reason for this was that neither child was able to understand why he could not return to his birth family. The birth family made it very clear that they had not relinquished them during contact visits. The difficulties broke the nerve of Jimmy's prospective adopters. They gave up this plan and offered to foster him instead. He had desperately needed them to claim him decisively. Finding that he was no longer "good" beside a "bad" Paul, he had begun to show them that he could be equally damaging. The split between the boys had ended. Meanwhile Paul's even more extreme needs could not be met in his specialist placement either. He required dedicated care exactly tailored to meet his needs, delivered in a form he could accept as a 10-year-old, the "provision of primary experience" that both Dockar-Drysdale and Cairns describe (Cairns, 2002; Dockar-Drysdale, 1993). Instead, his foster carer gave up on him too, re-placing him with a far more rewarding baby. He was moved first into a remote room in the foster home and then into a small children's home, one that could not do the job either. By now time was running out for both boys.

They began to ricochet around foster families and children's homes, separately but in tandem, in frequent contact with each other. As part of the team assembled around the case, we decided that we must re-examine the choices and some of our own assumptions as well as those of others working with us. We found that one of these had concerned foster carers and that a possible solution had been staring us in the face, though it carried many risks. We realized that the original foster carer's obvious commitment to Jimmy should be taken seriously. She *had* claimed him and kept in touch with him through many placements. Foster carers are often experienced as the first people really able to parent, and often no work is done to help them or the children to cope with their sense of loss when parted. Good matches may be made quite spontaneously in foster families. Though a reunion is not always advisable, we believed that a placement with this foster carer should be reconsidered.

Such reunions are not achieved easily. There are many risks in-volved. Children, in their anxiety at their capacity to destroy re-lationships, may sabotage them themselves. This means that they can continue to hold on to a foster carer as an "ideal"—some-thing adopted children may do to a birth parent. Fortunately, both

Jimmy and his foster carer had the courage to test the reality. This time they were supported by us and the local authority. Paul remained in a children's home nearby, on the outskirts of the family. He seemed insufficiently integrated to achieve anything more. This position, half in half out, was one that he could tolerate and perhaps the only one he could manage, rather like the "doorstep" life Canham (1998) describes.

In cases such as these through the process of regular consultations we are sometimes able to free ourselves and others from the grip of prejudice and to make fresh plans. The early years of these children had been full of extreme experiences of danger, abandonment, and constant movement, so that as their social worker observed they had no sense of an internalized good nurturing experience and therefore almost no sense of self. Indeed, any a sense of something stable and good, whether inside or outside, was constantly threatened, if it was present at all. Instead, there was the sense of an inner state that was irretrievably ruined, and one that was intent on reducing the outside world to an equally devastated condition.

In chapter 18 Emanuel describes how the primary deprivation a child experiences at the hand of its parents can lead to secondary deprivation. She goes on to describe the triple deprivation arising from similar institutional dynamics. The defences Jimmy and Paul developed to deal with their earlier abuse certainly prevented them from opening themselves to the love and care new parents offered, leaving each of them even more deprived and empty. It also left them highly envious of any good experience they witnessed one another having. They each did their best to attack and ruin this; it was a reason for separating them and monitoring their contact with each other.

Conclusion

Both cases illustrate situations where, through a lengthy consultation, we could recognize the full implications of the traumatic experiences of the birth parents and see how they impinged on and distorted their own functioning and severely affected the development of their children. This was particularly clear in the second family. Though, despite the consultation, we were not able to prevent the disasters and disintegrations that the two boys experienced, through it an all important sense of continuity was maintained. We could steadfastly hold each child in mind through the regular meetings with the network. We could fight to keep their exceptional social worker in place for them and for the reassessment of the foster carer.

Neuroscientists such as Perry and Gerhardt have defined the effect of trauma on the development of the brain (Gerhardt, 2004; Perry et al., 1995). Music describes neurological changes as a result of trauma in chapter 4. Psychoanalytic literature highlights the different manifestations of traumatic experience in the consulting-room. Laub and Auerhahn have delineated nine forms of traumatic memory they encountered in their work with adult victims of trauma on a scale of nine "forms of knowing", each representing a "consciously deeper and more integrated level of knowing" (Laub & Auerhahn, 1993). For example:

> The least integrated level is "not knowing," a splitting off of reality which creates a fragmentation of the self. In this form of traumatic memory the centre of the experience is no longer in the experiencing "I". Events happen somewhere, but are no longer connected with the conscious subject.

Many of their descriptions illuminate the behaviours we come across. They also point out that we all hover at different distances between knowing and not knowing about trauma, that the knowledge of trauma is fiercely defended against because knowing can present us with

> a momentous, threatening cognitive and affective task, involving an un-jaundiced appraisal of events and our own injuries, failures and losses.

In this chapter I have described moments when we defended ourselves against knowing what was going on. However, because we were working both with others in the network and with our colleagues in the Fostering and Adoption team at the Tavistock, we were able to allow ourselves to know the scale of the damage that had been done to the parents and what was happening to the children. We could reappraise the situation and work out together what should happen next. We could also grasp the limitations of what might be achieved and how important it was not to give up on these children when they had lost so much already.

CHAPTER 17

Contact with birth families: implications for assessment and integration in new families

Caroline Lindsey

Working with questions relating to the issue of contact with birth families is an integral part of therapeutic work with children who are fostered, adopted, or in kinship care. The distinctions between the different forms of care are not always the most relevant factors for the child, birth family, and substitute carers, despite the differences in the legal framework that play a part in determining how much and whether contact occurs. The concept of openness is more important here, regarding both open communication and structural openness to actual contact. Therefore, in this chapter, the material relates to contact in all these different contexts. It is self-evident that the meaning and purpose of contact varies depending on the type of care episode, with whom the contact takes place, and its form. Contact is not an all-or-nothing concept. The infinite variations reflect the unique pattern formed by each family constellation. Hence, there are no hard and fast rules for determining what is appropriate in any one situation, and as relationships develop over time, there are changes in the need and abilities of those involved to participate in contact arrangements. Contact can be defined as the symbolic representation of the young person's relationship with, at least, two sets of families. The type of contact, whether it is face-to-face or letter-box and all the many variations, carries a message about the nature of the relationship. This varies from conveying contact as a step in the process to rehabilitation with the birth family to a loving and lifelong concern and interest in the child who is being brought up by others. It is a socially constructed event in which each in the triad of child, birth family, and substitute carers plays a crucial part, and success depends on the ability of each party to contribute positively to the process. Furthermore, since most of the children and young people with whom a service like ours is involved are placed from care, the ongoing attitude, role, and availability of social work services can be pivotal in ensuring the safety and success of contact arrangements.

The significance of the birth family

It may be helpful for professionals and carers to appreciate the parallel with the statement of Winnicott (1952), "there's no such thing as a baby", which, in this context, can be re-phrased as "there's no such thing as a looked-after child/adopted child"—meaning that whether or not contact with the birth family is enacted in practice, the original family is always an integral part of the child's existence and is looked after or adopted along with the child. The birth family remains alive, consciously or unconsciously, in the mind of the child and his carers, affecting the dynamics in their lives. That may be the case even when the child is placed or adopted as a baby. It is also the case when children are adopted from abroad, even in circumstances where there can be no contact. In one case, an adoptive mother of a Chinese child, where there had been no form of contact, described how on one occasion, on hearing the telephone ring, her 3-year-old child asked, "Was that my Mummy from China?"

In attachment terms, those original relationships have laid down the basis for the child's internal working model(s) of significant relationships.

Hence, acknowledging the significance of their family of origin to the child and carers is an important parental and often, in our context, a therapeutic task. This needs to happen even in the absence of any contact in reality through different conversations; at home with the substitute carers; with the allocated social worker and the child, with and without the carers; and frequently as part of the process in therapy. This means that as professionals we need to question our assumptions and beliefs about the ongoing role and meaning that birth families have in children's lives after permanent placement, so as not to pre-judge what may be in the child's best interest in terms of contact. Training and preparation of adopters and foster carers needs to address these considerations as well.

The definition of the birth family

We also need to draw a wide definition of birth family not confined to birth parents, so as not to exclude significant relations who may offer ongoing links, such as grandparents, uncles and aunts as well as siblings and cousins. Previous foster carers also may play an important role, especially in the early stages of placement and sometimes, an ongoing one. Thinking about the range of available birth relatives gives opportunities for children to remain in touch with their heritage and loved ones while, if necessary, avoiding potentially dangerous relationships with abusing relatives. However, there are often dilemmas posed by contact with members of the extended family, for example, with grandparents, who remain in touch, understandably, with their own son or daughter, who has been the source of the abuse of their grandchild. Similarly, the benefits of ongoing sibling contact that potentially lasts a lifetime seem self-evident. It may sometimes create anxiety for children when the sibling remains in the birth family and may seem not to be safe and/or may maintain the feeling of rejection in the placed child, who may have been the only one to be ejected from the family. The efforts involved in maintaining contact for sibling groups who have been placed separately can be considerable for the new parents.

In one case, where the mother had died and the father was unable to parent his children, a group of four children from a minority ethnic group were taken into care. Following assessment, it seemed that their considerable emotional needs and disturbing behaviour towards each other after years of privation and emotional neglect meant that placing them together would pose too many challenges for carers. Despite this, their links with each other and with their father meant that it was felt that they should continue to have meaningful contact. Social services and a local voluntary organization found four sets of foster carers from the same background who lived near each other but in another geographical area, who were prepared to work together. They went through individual and group assessments. They shared a belief in the importance of ensuring that the children held on to their cultural heritage and their relationships with each other. The foster carers drew boundaries round their family life so that the children had both the opportunities of continuity in important aspects of their lives, but also security and individual attention. This was achieved by intensive social work support to the couples as a group, which in time grew into a mutually supportive network. Often, however, resources to enable and support this degree of flexibility are lacking.

Research findings

In the last few years there has been an increasing amount of research attention paid to the question of the benefits to children of ongoing contact with their birth families, in an effort to underpin the significant change in attitude to and arrangements for post-placement contact (Neil & Howe, 2004). In the United Kingdom it is now usual for the majority of both fostered and adopted children to have some form of birth family contact (PIU, 2000). Grotevant, McRoy, and Ayers-Lopes (2004), in a study of children in the United States who were adopted in infancy and followed since the 1980s, found that contact between adopted children and their birth mothers, when children had no memories of living with their birth families, did not appear to be harmful for the children. Furthermore, contact may be helpful and child outcomes better when the adults involved interact collaboratively, with the child's best interests in mind. Taking into account that each type of contact arrangement presents particular challenges and opportunities, they concluded that the level of openness should be decided on a case-by-case basis, with the possibility of changes over time. We had already been influenced by the well-established research that has shown that children are more likely to return home when temporarily separated if contact is maintained with their families (Triseliotis, 1990). The placement of older children with already established family relationships, which they were reluctant to relinquish even if they could no longer live at home, required a different approach, and this was supported by the finding that most looked-after children eventually return to their birth families. Clinical experience showed that young adopted people in early adolescence or approaching adulthood without contact are frequently impelled to seek out their birth families, which may not then always be the most constructive experience. Other research has demonstrated that adopters may feel more entitled to parent with the ongoing knowledge and relationship with the birth parent that contact may bring. This all suggests that where it is possible for contact in some form—whether direct (face-to-face) or indirect (letter-box in some form)—to be maintained, it may ultimately be the most beneficial for all concerned.

The role of child and adolescent mental health services (CAMHS)

Perhaps inevitably, the situations most commonly presented to a child and adolescent mental health service working with this group of families are those where the question of contact has become problematic or challenging. They frequently fall into two categories: where professionals, courts, and families are in conflict about the question of future contact after placement and seek our advice about what is in the child's emotional interest, or where contact, having been agreed, appears to be creating ongoing psychological problems for the child and family. The children in the families whom we see have often had serious experiences of abuse and neglect in their families of origin at the hands of some, if not all, family members. The risk of re-evoking traumatic memories of abusive episodes with associated symptoms of post-traumatic stress disorder has to be carefully assessed in any consideration of contact. Howe and Steele (2004) have confirmed the risks inherent in contact with previously maltreating parents. Children may see their new parents as being unable to protect them in the context of the continuing contact. This then interferes with their ability to make a secure attachment to the new carers. These seriously abused children, who continue to feel unsafe, may behave in the aggressive, distancing, and controlling ways that they formerly used to protect themselves in their birth families. This may create huge strain in the placement. Making the child feel safe is the priority. When placed with carers who are able to foster secure attachments and promote resilience, sometimes it may eventually be possible for the child to deal with the level of emotional arousal that contact will trigger. This requires adopters who have high levels of sensitivity, empathy, and reflective attunement. Often we have found that the young people themselves want the contact to continue, irrespective of the quality of their previous experiences, about which they may be in denial. So we find ourselves in a position where we may have to listen to the children's wishes and feelings and filter them through our understanding of their desperate desire for the love of the abusing parent and concern for their well-being.

The legal context

In the current childcare context in England, an assumption is made within the legal system, arising both from the Children Act 1989 and the Adoption and Children Act 2002, that maintaining ongoing links with members of the birth family of a child placed away from home, in an adoptive, foster, or kinship care placement, is likely to be in the child's interests, unless this is clearly not the case. Section 34 of the Children Act 1989 states that "where a child is in the care of the local authority, the authority shall allow the child reasonable contact with his parents." In considering the child's welfare, the court, when making a decision about adoption, has to have regard to a number of issues including (4f, Adoption and Children Act 2002)

> the relationship which the child has with relatives and with any other person to whom the court or agency considers the relationship to be relevant, including:
>
> 1.   the likelihood of any such relationship continuing and the value to the child of its doing so;
>
> 2.   the ability and willingness of any of the child's relatives or of any such person, to provide the child with a secure environment in which the child can develop and otherwise to meet the child's needs;
>
> 3.   wishes and feelings of any of the child's relatives or of any such person regarding the child.

The legal provision for contact largely reflects the views developed and held in the childcare community over time. The concept of openness in permanent placements of whatever form as preferable, whenever possible, to closed structures is generally held to be in the child's interests. It is important not to see the support given to contact as simply being an imposition of the courts, although the way in which the system works implies that if there are doubts about the wisdom of ongoing contact, the onus is on those opposing it to provide the evidence.

The meaning of contact

Professionals working in the field of adoption and fostering hold beliefs about the value of contact based both on their own personal life stories and their professional training and practice. These all affect the decisions and recommendations that they make about contact. Many of us have experienced personal events in our lives which have a profound impact on the way we work as carers and professionals with families and children who cannot stay with their birth families. These experiences consciously and unconsciously affect the way we make decisions about contact, and we need to give thought to how we are being influenced, using various forms of self-reflective practice.

Anecdotally, many professionals who work in this field have been touched in some way by fostering or adoption in their personal lives. Information gathered informally in training courses suggests how, frequently, workers in this field have been adopted or have been part of a foster family as a sibling or a looked-after child, or are themselves adoptive or foster carers or are otherwise in family situations, for example, post-divorce, where there are issues of separation between parents and children. In all these situations, issues of contact have meaning for them personally, and it is important for the worker to practice in a self-reflective way to ensure that these life experiences contribute to their understanding but do not drive the decision making. Personal and professional life scripts may come together here with the worker wishing to utilize his personal story in the interests of other children. Professional training, which provides theoretical frameworks for thinking about practice, opportunities for supervised work, and reflective practice safeguard the worker from acting only on the basis of their personal beliefs.

A small-scale qualitative research study (Harris & Lindsey, 2002; Lindsey, Harris, & James, 2005) has shown that there are a number of key considerations that influence professionals' decision making about contact. This is in the context of there being no definitive rules or guidelines, despite the increasing understanding that comes from the research, which itself continues to emphasize the individual nature of each decision. In the first study, key themes relating to beliefs about contact held by experts, guardians, and judges, which, they said, influenced them in their decision making and recommendations included: identity formation, the wishes and feelings of the child, parental capacity, attachment, the developmental needs of the child, safety, and permanence. The professionals' individual personal and professional experiences influenced, in turn, how each of these themes was understood and employed in decision making.

Identity formation

The significance of contact for identity formation is multifaceted. It may provide information about the child's physical identity: "Who do

I look like?" It may signal their membership of the multigenerational family existing over time into which they were born, with its history and myths (Byng-Hall, 1995). It relates as well as to the cultural, ethnic, religious, and communal aspects of family identity. These are clearly likely to have even more significance if the young person has lived in the family for any length of time and has established relationships with family members. However, at the same time, it is important to see identity as an evolving process, not as stuck in time and only linked to birth family. Over time the young person has the potential for further personal identity development as a member of a new family. This is particularly relevant when considering the profound psychological difficulties that many fostered and adopted children have. There is hope that a new family may give them the opportunity for change, including a changed identity, for example, from the role of victim or rejected child.

A young boy from a criminal background settled in a middle-class adoptive home, where they tried to inculcate their values. In between contact visits, he appeared to identify with their way of life and views about education. Following each visit home he was drawn back into his birth family's beliefs, which included admiration for a relative who had committed murder. Despite the dilemma posed by the conflict between their two ways of life, the adopters decided to persist with the contact since it seemed so important for their son to remain connected to his mother and grandmother. They hoped that eventually he would choose their way of life for himself. Years of challenging behaviour ensued, but ultimately the young man acknowledged the devotion of his adoptive parents and achieved a stable way of life and a university degree.

The wishes and feelings of the child

The meaning of the child's wishes for contact has been alluded to already. Understanding these must include an assessment about on whose behalf the wishes are being expressed by the child. These wishes may at times be for the adopters or foster carers where the child has understood their ambivalence about ongoing contact, or on behalf of the birth parent. However, a frequent clinical experience is that when children are determined that they need to see their birth family, despite professionals' conviction that it is not to their benefit, refusal may result in the breakdown of the placement. It may be preferable for the child to experience the distress and disappointment that may arise from their unfulfilled hopes for the contact experience but make the decision themselves. The capacity of carers to hold the child through this experience is crucial.

A common experience for the team has been where professionals and family members have not spoken with particularly young children about their hopes for contact with their birth family, because of a lack of skills in communicating through language or play. This arises out of fears that children will be unable to understand the difficulty that adults have in being certain about what will happen. The children are then left without any knowledge or opportunity to share their feelings. The anxiety engendered compounds the separation and often leads to the child's withdrawal or to symptoms such as tantrums, oppositional behaviour, crying, and clinging.

> In one case, we were consulted by adoptive parents, whose three junior-school-age children were well established with them. The children had experienced poor and inconsistent care in their extended birth family, including some physical neglect and abuse. They wanted to discuss their dilemma that two of the three children were saying that they no longer wanted the face-to-face contact that took place every six months. They thought it would be helpful to give their children the chance of discussing this with professionals outside the family. These contact arrangements had been established by the court, and the parents were committed to continue them unless it was thought that it was not in the children's interest to do so. They told us that the arrangements were often not adhered to by the mother but maintained by the grandmother. The two older children were rebelling against the contact, in which they felt that little interest was taken in them. They felt betrayed and further damaged by the inconsistent behaviour of their birth mother. The youngest had been parented most of her life by the grandmother and so had a closer relationship with her than did her siblings. This was an example where it was important to consider the needs of the children separately, despite their membership of the same family, so that the wishes of the older two could be addressed without disadvantaging the youngest. It was possible to explore a change to indirect contact for all the children with the mother through discussion with the social worker, who was still involved, and to consider yearly contact for the little girl with her grandmother, which the others could join if they chose.

Listening to the children had a positive effect on their self esteem, which also manifested itself in other aspects of their daily lives.

Parental capacity

Parental capacity refers to the ability of the birth parents to allow the child to be cared for by others and to become what I have elsewhere termed "a non-parental parent" (Lindsey, 1995). If birth parents are able to make the extraordinarily difficult transition to seeing themselves as a significant other to their child but no longer involved in the day-to-day running of the child's life, relinquishing their parental role, then there is a chance that they will be able to cope successfully with contact without the risk of undermining the new family or threatening the placement with breakdown. At the point when decisions are made in the courts about contact, the birth parent may frequently not yet have had the chance to do the mourning work and come to terms with the loss of their child. Hence, contact with the parent may seem likely to be a future threat rather than supportive of a child's placement. It is therefore important to acknowledge the process that has to take place for birth families and to recognize that their capacity for contact may change and may respond also to sensitive therapeutic work. For contact to be successful, the parents also have to retain a belief in their value and importance to the child, which will have been fundamentally affected by the child's removal. It will also be affected by the parent's own history of parenting and whether, as is often the case, history is being repeated. Equally, it is important to recognize the parent for whom this transition is not possible and with whom ongoing contact is likely to be damaging and disappointing for the child. This is made more complex by the fact that the capacity for contact is not clear-cut. Parents with problems of addiction or mental illness may at times be fit for contact and at others incapable of meeting their child's needs. This puts the onus on the supervising social worker, adopter, or kinship carer to make a judgement on an episode-by-episode basis. This may not be feasible in the long term and certainly not without a supportive, formalized local infrastructure for contact arrangements and supervision.

Parental capacity also refers to the capacity of the substitute carers to see the value in ongoing connection with the birth family both for the child and for themselves in their task of bringing up the child. The adopter or foster carer who sees the contact with the birth parents as an integral part of caring for their child and values the contribution that the birth parent can still make in the child's life enables the child to begin to integrate their different family experiences rather than having to hold them separately in their mind. Assessments of carers and adopters need to explore their readiness to take the child plus the birth family on board. Even today, with the changed views about ongoing contact in adoption, there are adopters who may hope to create a new family free of the baggage of the previous connections to the birth parents. Their psychological preparation for the full task of adoption has not been complete. Since the child may respond to face-to-face contact in a disturbed or disturbing manner that the carers experience directly, they may have the understandable response of questioning why the child should suffer further and have his stability affected by the pursuit of contact. It will be important to be clear what the motivation is for the adopters in questioning the ongoing purpose of the contact: hence the need for careful pre-placement training about this issue. It may certainly be the case that the experience of contact is disturbing to the child, but there may be situations for some, especially older children, where the disturbance may nevertheless be a price worth paying for the maintenance of a relationship that is important. At other times, the price may clearly be too great, and a decision needs to be made that it should stop or be reduced in some way.

> In one case, a mother, who had been in care from a young age herself, had struggled to care for her young daughters. She had required ongoing support and respite care from social services with whom she had collaborated despite her serious mental health problems. She had shown herself to be consistently loving and concerned for her children, who reciprocated her affection. She had never allowed them to experience neglect or maltreatment. Finally, her fragile mental health led to a difficult decision to place the children together for adoption. She recognized the need for this but wanted to maintain contact with her children, whom she loved and had never rejected. It was necessary to do a great deal of work with the adopters, who had been given to understand that there would be no contact because of the mother's condition. They expressed their disappointment initially as "if contact continues, then they will never be our children". The answer to such a view had to be that if that was their definition of gaining a family through adoption, then they were right. Fortunately, it was possible for sensitive work to be done which resolved the dilemma and led to a moving conciliation between the adopters and the birth mother.

Attachment

In our research (Harris & Lindsey, 2002), we found that profession-als were sometimes using the concept of attachment as an issue to be taken into account when considering contact, but that this term was being used in a variety of ways including, but not exclusively, the definitions as given by Steele in chapter 3. When used loosely, it was taken to mean any relationship of significance between the parent and the child, and in particular to refer to the emotional tie that the parent has for the child. When seen in this way, there is a risk that the "attach-ment" that the parents have for the child is then proposed as a reason for ongoing contact, although attachment in the strict use of the term is not actually what is being described. It may only be describing the parent's wish for an ongoing connection to their child and may not reflect the pattern of relationship around security that the child has with this parent, or his emotional needs. On the other hand, the likeli-hood of the children whom we see in substitute care having secure attachments to their birth parents is very remote, and the chances that the pattern of attachment is more likely to be insecure, resistant or avoidant, or even disorganized is high. It is often just those children who have had an insecure attachment to the birth parent who so much want it to continue.

However, it could be argued that if the child is beginning to de-velop more secure patterns of attachment in their new placement, there may be an opportunity for change in their relationship to the birth parents mediated through contact, which may create some trust in the relationship. This may particularly be the case where the reason for the separation lies outside the parent–child relationship, as in acute psychiatric illness or addiction. Care must be taken, however, not to pull the child back into a dysfunctional way of relating as the price to pay for the ongoing relationship.

Developmental needs and safety

The changing developmental needs of children over time mean that arrangements for contact can never be fixed as a once and for all arrangement but must be seen as open to modification as they grow up.

Ultimately, the most important consideration has to be the chil-dren's physical and emotional safety, which must always be safe-guarded, and the need that they have for a secure and permanent placement.

The social workers' perspective

All these factors have to be balanced in what is often a complex decision-making systemic process. This was illuminated in our second study of 12 social workers (Lindsey, Harris, & James, 2005), for whom the main theme was "the interests of the child are paramount". The key factors influencing social workers in their thinking about contact were a balance between their personal life experience and professional contexts. The latter included their use of theoretical underpinnings from attachment theory, systems theory, and family history; the impact of their legislative duty; the availability of resources and practical considerations. One of the striking features that differed from the first study was the social workers' awareness of the need for flexibility in thinking and arranging for contact. They had a considerable sense of responsibility and anxiety in relation to the ongoing management and decision making about contact. This was often in situations where the plan for contact was a *fait accompli* that they were expected to put into practice and was very different from that experienced by the professionals in the first study. It clearly reflects the reality in practice. This connected with their appreciation of the importance of teamwork. They were very aware of the risks of lone working and isolation. They felt the need for shared understandings of the complex interrelationships involved in the contact triangle. They saw consultation with other professionals such as CAMHS as being beneficial, enabling them to share decision making within a complex system. These findings then confirm the importance of making opportunities available for consultation in services dedicated to work with looked-after and adopted children and their families.

It also stresses the need to see contact as an evolving dynamic process in the lives of all concerned.

> In one case, we were consulted during the process of Court Proceedings about the arrangements that should be made for post-placement contact for three children of the same mother but of two different fathers. The questions included the nature of contact that should take place between the children and the three parents as well as that between the siblings. The assumption being made by the court was that although the decision had been made that the children would be permanently placed, contact arrangements would surely be agreed, and all the parents were insistent on this. The work consisted of individual assessments of the parents and

the children, including observations in the foster home and observations of contact visits with their parents. We used a structured
observational setting to assess the quality of the relationships, including the process whereby the parent joined the child at the visit
and left again. The older teenage son was placed separately from
the younger pre-school and school-age children. He was desperate
that his sisters should not move on from the family to whom he
remained loyal. This made it very difficult to recommend ongoing
contact post-adoption because of the risk that he would seek to disrupt the placement. Although she was unable to care adequately
for him, he was determined to go home to his mother.

During our observations of contact, we saw the mother's inability
to keep the children in mind. She used the sessions to talk to the
supervising worker about her concerns, with little attention given
to the children and their needs. With careful supervision, the quality of her interaction with the children improved at times, but not
consistently. The father of the two eldest children was ambivalent
about taking on any additional responsibilities, despite having
the capacity to meet his children's needs emotionally. We saw
the ambivalent and at times anxious and resistant attachment of
the older girl in the contact sessions, attempting to engage with
her father who, in this context, could respond thoughtfully and
helpfully. We faced the sadness of seeing a parent who could offer
something constructive to a child who was attached to him finding it hard to make the commitment of having her to live with him
or even of very regular contact. The father of the younger child
was threatening to professionals and had a history of domestic
violence. Again, he proved to be a competent parent but one to
whom his child showed an avoidant pattern of attachment. In
the face of her behaviour, he became in turns seductive and cajol-
ing, using presents and sweets, or critical, angry, and dismissive.
Keeping these children in contact with their birth parents carried
a considerable emotional risk. At the same time, the chances of
successful adoptive placements were found to be very slim because of the nature of their learning and psychological difficulties.
We faced the dilemma of recommending a post-placement future
in which face-to-face contact would not be desirable while for
the foreseeable future these relationships represented all the significant family the children had, apart from their temporary foster
care. Their expressed wish was for their contact to continue. Since

the children showed evident problems, we were able to continue to provide psychotherapeutic support to the carers and to the children during the long process of court hearings. The intention was thus to enable them to become more available for an adoptive placement.

Very often, the task is to help professionals holding differing views to resolve these during a process of consultation.

In one case, a young girl whose father had died was still in contact with a psychiatrically ill and at times disturbing mother. She had been placed with an experienced foster carer after her father's death and was reported to show appropriate sadness and much resilience.

The questions that the foster carer, social workers, placements officer, and guardian could not resolve focused on the relationship both with the mother but also with an older married brother, who wanted contact and eventually to have his sister to live with him and his family. It seemed likely that the differences in view about the suitability of the married couple related to the beliefs held about the way in which placements should be made for a child in such a position. One view was that the girl deserved individual focus and that this was necessary because of her loss and her precarious relationship with her mother. This view would favour a placement outside the family—a fresh start. Another view was that since the sister-in-law was expecting a new baby, any contact and the home study should be delayed until after the baby was born. There was an idea that she would be an outsider in an already established family and that there would be insufficient ability to attend to her emotional needs. A further view was that although ultimately the contact with the brother and his family would give her a much needed sense of family identity, it was necessary to be sure about the commitment that they would be able to make to her at a time when they would understandably be preoccupied with a new baby. The view was that a slow introduction was needed in case she would be let down. The normative opinion was that the family was offering a settled, happy, and loving home for the girl to whom they wanted to make a commitment, and that there was no need for delay. The observation by the foster carer was that she was only sad when she had to return from visiting her brother's home. The other concern was whether they would be able to deal with the unpredictable nature of the mother's demands and manage any future contact in a protective way for their sister.

Exploration of the beliefs inherent in these differing positions allowed a consensus to emerge. This acknowledged the importance of contact and placement within her birth family for the girl's future identity, provided that the assessment of the brother and his family continued to prove as positive as it seemed at this initial stage. It also facilitated the more cautious position, which wanted an assessment of the state of the family following the birth of the new baby and to take the process at a slow enough pace to allow the new mother and baby's needs to be taken into account. A compromise was reached. She should be allowed to visit the family at the time of the new arrival's birth so that she could feel included as a family member at this important moment in their lives, rather than remaining an outsider. Following regular visits, a plan would be made for her to transfer to the family after the birth of the baby when it seemed that all the concerns about commitment and emotional availability were satisfied.

Conclusion

In the same way as it is psychologically healthy for the newly created foster, adoptive, and kinship care families to be open to awareness of the original birth family in their lives, even if physically they are not part of their ongoing existence on a regular basis, it seems essential that the therapeutic work that is done with these families and their professionals when they seek our help addresses the meaning of the birth family. This may not always be easy and timing is sensitive. The issues may sometimes need to be considered with the parents separately from the children, so as to give opportunities for voicing experiences of torn loyalties and memories that cannot yet be shared in the new family (see Barratt, chapter 12). Child and adolescent mental health services also need to give a lead by attempting to work with all the parties, including the birth parents, whenever this is possible and appropriate. Professionals need always to be mindful of the many personal and professional influences on their therapeutic work and decision making. They should try to ensure that they have opportunities for reflective practice and encourage those with whom they work in the multi-agency context to do the same.

PART V

WORK IN DIFFERENT SETTINGS

Both chapters in this section are written by child psychotherapists, who worked with the children they describe as well as consulting to their foster carers, children's homes, and the wider system. Both describe organizational and institutional dynamics and defences.

Louise Emanuel writes about a model of consultation and support within a community setting. She makes the important point that psychotherapy cannot, of itself, put right the dire situations in which many of the children find themselves. Unless support is provided for the carers and their workers, the children's placements will continue to break down, with catastrophic consequences for all involved.

Hamish Canham, in a chapter based on a 1998 article in the *Journal of Social Work Practice*, gives careful consideration to the danger that the dynamics involving the children may too easily become enacted in the children's homes created to care for them, a point also made by Emanuel. Although Canham died before he had added clinical examples to this chapter, the editors chose to include it as it gives strong support to the need for residential care for some children. Many of the children who are eventually able to live in families will have had episodes of living in residential care. Clinical examples have been provided as an addendum to the chapter from Canham's own writing and from Jenny Kenrick's work.

Jenny Kenrick

The contribution of organizational dynamics to the triple deprivation of looked-after children

Louise Emanuel

In this chapter I describe how the trauma and disturbance associated with severe deprivation and abuse by children and families can impact on the professionals involved in their care, interfering with their capacity to think about and provide containment for the children and their carers and thereby compounding their deprivation. The chapter title refers to the "double deprivation" as originally described by Henry (1974) together with a third level of deprivation, which can occur within the organizational setting. The first deprivation is inflicted by external circumstances and is out of the child's control; the second derives from internal sources as the child develops "crippling defences" (Henry, 1974) that prevent him from making use of subsequent offers of support, for example, by foster carers or adoptive parents (or a psychotherapist). The third refers to the ways in which, as Britton (1981) writes, " the profoundly disturbing primitive mechanisms and defences against anxiety" used by children and families get "re-enacted" in the system by care professionals, who are the recipients of powerful projections. These defences, including unconscious attacks on linking, can interfere with professionals' capacity to think clearly or make use of outside help with their overwhelming caseloads. A social services department may then replicate these children's original experience of neglect, allowing them to fall through a hole in the "net"work. This form of "re-enactment" as a substitute for

a thoughtful response by professionals within an organization, combined with the "double deprivation" described by Henry, can result in
a "triple deprivation" for children within the care system. (The concept
of "triple deprivation" was originally described by Sutton, 1991.)

I first describe the time-limited project on which I have based this
chapter—one that involved working jointly with a local child and
adolescent mental health service and social services department to set
up a therapeutic service for looked-after children. I show how I had
to change my approach to the task to take into account the context
in the community within which I was working. I then describe how
a package of consultation to the social services network and of support for the foster carers, as a prelude to individual psychotherapy,
helped to save the placement of a child who was already "doubly
deprived", thereby preventing further emotional deprivation—that is,
"triple deprivation".

Finally, I consider a further aspect of organizational deprivation,
that which relates to the situation of "drift" in relation to care plans for
children who have suffered serious abuse and neglect. I examine the
dynamic underlying these situations as I experienced it in my work,
which Britton (1981) describes as a "collapse of strategy" and Cooper
and Webb (1999) refer to as a "maze". I think the paralysis that can
occur in the system bears a striking resemblance to the "freeze" reaction of small children who display what Main (1995b) describes as a
disorganized/disorientated attachment to frightening or frightened
mothers on reunion during the Strange Situation procedure. The child
may freeze, caught between contradictory impulses, unable either to
approach mother for comfort or to flee. (See also chapters 3 and 8.)

One could use this as a metaphor to consider how a "disorganized" state of mind can be re-enacted in the care system, whereby
social workers become paralysed by the often conflicting emotional
demands of parents and children, as well as by the conflicting demands of their managers. Unless they are able to turn to their manager
to provide a "secure base" (Bowlby, 1980), these conflicts can become
intolerable for social workers and interfere with their capacity to think,
with serious consequences for the safety and emotional well-being of
the children in their care. I think it is possible that insecure ambivalent
as well as insecure avoidant patterns of attachment to cases—where
a professional can become over-preoccupied with or, conversely, detached from a case—may also arise. However, I shall focus on the more
extreme "disorganized" attachment pattern of professionals to their

work setting and to the part it may play in the "triple deprivation" of some looked-after children. An understanding of this dynamic may enable us to consider what support could be offered by child mental health professionals in this kind of setting.

Work context

The aim of the time-limited pilot project was to find a way of ensuring that children in the care of the local social services department, who are perceived as one of the most deprived and needy groups, are able to access child mental health services for assessment and treatment for emotional and behavioural difficulties, where appropriate. I was based in one of three local child and adolescent mental health teams within the area and attended regular meetings with the multidisciplinary staff team within my base clinic, as well as liaising with the other two clinic staff groups around cases involving looked-after children. I was managed by the Consultant Child Psychotherapist within the child mental health centre, and over time, as the complexity of the post became evident, a steering group was formed, comprising managers from the child mental health and social services departments.

The therapeutic service I was required to develop within the social services department from my base in the local child mental health clinic included offering intensive and non-intensive individual psychotherapy to a few of the most disturbed looked-after children, support for foster and adoptive parents, and consultation to the professionals in the local social services department, in that order of priority.

The social services department is divided into the field social worker teams, who support the children in care, and the fostering and adoption link worker teams, who support the foster and adoptive parents of children placed in their care.

Setting up a service that spans the health and social services departments is a complex and multifaceted task, and it became increasingly clear to me that a lot of work would be required with the professional network before I would be able to undertake individual psychotherapy work with any children. At the time I took up my post, I was reading *Into Thin Air* by Jon Krakauer (1997), which charted in raw detail the simultaneous attempts of at least eight separate expedition teams from around the world to reach the summit of Everest. Poor communication, competitiveness between teams, and language barriers meant that mutual cooperation and support were minimal, and, when weather conditions deteriorated, some teams withheld vital communication equipment from others. Krakauer suggests that the lack of mutual understanding, communication, and cooperation between expedition teams was the largest factor in the resulting deaths of seven experienced climbers within a few days.

I quickly realized, when I began meeting with managers from the social services teams, that I was faced with similar language and communication barriers, and that mutual misunderstandings abounded. I was met with hostility by managers who had not been consulted about my post and who resented my offer of individual psychotherapy for a minority of children when they were feeling so pressurized with an overwhelming number of difficult cases. It became clear to me that attending to the requests of referring social workers and their managers, and understanding the pressures on and expectations of them by the families, the media, and society as a whole were essential if I was going to be able to work alongside them in trying to help the children. Focusing exclusively on the child without attending to the needs of the carers can leave professionals, foster carers, and adoptive parents feeling neglected and misunderstood, and without their active cooperation and alliance any efforts to treat a child are likely to fail or be undermined in some way.

Keith

This view was confirmed when I took at face value a referral for psychotherapy of 10-year-old Keith, fostered with close relatives of his abusive birth mother. As I introduced myself at the initial meeting, the foster carers announced that they no longer wished to keep him, and the meeting ended in disarray. They had been angered by comments by his school about their care of Keith, which his social worker had reported to them the previous day. Although initially annoyed that this unscheduled visit by the social worker had undermined "my" therapy case, on reflection I realized that an actual offer of psychotherapy can precipitate a crisis in the child's placement, by stirring up both carers and case workers.

I offered to meet both the link and field social workers and their team manager, to discuss what had happened at the meeting and we came to an understanding together that it was not really psychotherapy for Keith that was being sought by the social workers, but an opportunity to air their worried feelings about this being a potentially unsuitable foster placement.

However, we could see what made it difficult to discuss these issues openly: as divisive conflicts emerged between the link social
worker, feeling "her" foster carers were being pushed to the limit
by a difficult child, and the field social worker, feeling the foster carers lacked understanding of "her" child's difficulties. These
conflicting yet necessary identifications with their own client group
could be discussed, and the dangers of unhelpful splitting could
be acknowledged. Attempts at further work with the foster carers
resulted not in the offer of psychotherapy, but in the decision to
remove the child from his placement, as it was felt that his former
abuse was being replicated to some extent in the family.

Developing a therapeutic approach to casework

The workers felt that this had been a helpful consultation exercise,
and I recognized that my role could include offering a forum for
discussion to facilitate communication between different agencies or
even between different sections of the same department. In this way,
a "therapeutic approach" to thinking about complex cases at a referral stage could be made available, prior to any formal psychotherapy
input to the child and/or family. If the fragmentation and splitting,
disagreements, conflicts of loyalty, and rivalry that often entered the
professional network via the troubled children and families could be
addressed within the network first by providing a thoughtful forum
for discussion, perhaps there would be a better chance of succeeding
in thinking clearly and planning for the real needs of the child.

This case also alerted us to the particular difficulties of working
with carers who are closely related to abusive birth parents. These
placements, often known as "kinship care", may rely on an unac-
knowledged split between the "bad abusive parents" and the "good
rescuing relatives". The very idea of attending the child mental health
clinic may have felt threatening to this family, as if they sensed that if
we scratched beneath the surface we could discover more similarities
than differences between the birth and foster carers.

As a result of this experience I changed my approach, redefining my
role with a strong emphasis on consultation, joint work, regular support for foster and adoptive parents, and a service particularly geared
towards children in transition, laying the least stress on the individual
psychotherapy vacancies. I made myself available at regular times
for consultation on the premises of the field social worker teams to
facilitate access and set up regular work discussion groups for the link

social workers, at the request of their manager. I encouraged managers to attend discussion meetings together with their field social workers, since an understanding of the meaning of children's nonverbal and verbal communications about their emotional needs can impact on the management strategy of a case and a combined perspective is helpful. I also made sure that the senior management staff were clear about my role so that they could, in turn, give clear information to their team leaders and endorse with some confidence the work I was undertaking jointly with them. (The detailed framework of the service offered has been described elsewhere—Emanuel, 2000.)

This change in emphasis met initially with some hostility, mainly from managers, and a suspicion that I was simply withholding the very resource that social workers most wanted. My suggestion of coordinating network meetings was at first felt to be time-wasting, particularly by hard-pressed team managers, who only occasionally attended these meetings. However, the painstaking telephone calls, hours of meetings, liaison, consultation, and joint work began to pay off, and I noticed a shift in attitude towards the service.

I was reminded of Krakauer's account again months later, when I was sending out an appointment arranging an assessment and copied the letter to eight different agencies. I thought about how difficult and time-consuming it is to maintain communication with the network surrounding looked-after children (like expedition teams, all speaking a different professional language), and yet how essential it is to do so, to ensure that these children experience the same kind of "holding" as would a child from a well-functioning birth family. These efforts to model the importance of close liaison were rewarded when a field social worker approached me requesting a case discussion involving the relevant link worker and their managers, offering possible meeting times that they had agreed in advance.

This seemed to be the major challenge of my post—to try to understand where and how obstacles to communication within different teams arise and to try to promote ways of thinking about children and families that would ensure close cooperation, in order to help the child feel safely held within the system. I have come to realize that, if a project of this kind is to succeed, it requires the endorsement and support of the senior management team, which can filter down to the professionals on the ground in the same way as parental values help to create a family culture. Staff turnover, understaffing, and lack of support for managers themselves appeared to militate against the development of this culture.

Social workers feel sometimes that they are serving many masters at once, working as professionals on behalf of the child, keeping an eye out for the press, and needing to cover their backs, being aware of the law and court procedure. Similarly, I had two masters and felt equally conspicuous as I tried to get things right for the children and the professionals, for the mental health team, and for the social services department. It was essential for me to have my own supervision and to feel supported by my manager.

Social workers are often subjected to painful experiences via their clients. Sometimes the lack of a stable senior management structure and support can leave them either feeling overwhelmed by the intensely disturbing projections they receive or using the same kind of second-skin type of defences (Bick, 1968) that we see in the children in their care, who are described as restless or hyperactive. Indeed, departments that are understaffed and faced with a high volume of demanding cases may be set up to maximize throughput and minimize sustained thinking about the painful dilemmas of the client group. It is often difficult for staff, unaccustomed to the opportunity to stop and reflect on their work, to remove themselves from the relentless pressure of work in order to think about a case. Being available to help professionals understand the powerful emotions communicated to them via the mechanism of projective identification can enable them, in turn, to be more available to the children and their carers. It can be a great relief to professionals to recognize that their feelings of distress or inadequacy may, in fact, be emanating from a child or a birth parent who is passing on unbearable feelings of upset or failure about their own parenting. The social worker has to tolerate these feelings on their behalf.

Kia

For example, a social worker, Sean, described to me a very "frightening" experience of supervising contact with Kia, aged 3, and his mother, who appeared to "flip into a terrifying psychotic episode" during a contact session. Mother bombarded Kia with incoherent information, to which he responded by smiling politely and appearing to cut himself off from the intrusive noise. Sean found himself feeling fearful of something dreadful happening to Kia when his mother took him to the toilet, becoming suddenly so panic-stricken when they went into the toilet together that he began banging frantically on the toilet door and shouting. He then went home, collapsed for 36 hours, and felt he was "going mad".

I suggested that perhaps Kia had no way of verbalizing his feelings of terror, confusion, and anxiety, so he projected them into others, in the hope that someone would understand his emotional states by being made to experience the feelings themselves. Perhaps that is what had happened when the social worker suddenly felt panic-stricken on Kia's behalf. Sean felt relieved that he did not need to take his feeling of "going mad" personally, but could understand it more as a communication from Kia about his panic and terror when with a "mad" mother. This could be important in recognizing just how frightening contact with his mother in her current disturbed state of mind could be. It may also have alerted Sean to a concern that, without protection from these disturbing episodes, a vulnerable part of Kia might soon be killed off emotionally, as he became increasingly cut off from his feelings.

Work with foster carers to prevent placement breakdown— and triple deprivation

The concept of "double deprivation" (Henry, 1974) again came to mind when I heard about 12 year old Jason, whose violent, unmanageable behaviour had led to the breakdown of his previous foster placements. His current placement—his last chance for family life before residential care was considered—was in serious difficulties because of his increasingly threatening and violent behaviour towards his foster carers, who were reaching breaking point with him.

Jason

Jason had experienced abuse and neglect since infancy and had therefore suffered a "primary deprivation" within his birth family. His current tough demeanour and his use of projection as a defence mechanism to rid himself of feelings of helplessness, lodging them in others, may once have been essential survival strategies but were now ingrained in his personality. In his current situation, within a benign foster family, these defence mechanisms, based on the projection of feelings of terror into others, were working against him, putting him at risk of rejection by his foster family. He was in danger of depriving himself of the very resource he so desperately needed, a secure loving foster family, thereby compounding his "primary" deprivation with "secondary" deprivation.

Jason used knives to terrorize others while appearing to be "devoid of feeling himself, unreachable like a 'brick wall'" (Henry, 1974). This defensive brick-wall attitude can result in the child losing the care he is most in need of, since foster carers have difficulty without regular support in coping with intolerable feelings of rejection, inadequacy, fear, and helplessness projected into them. Placements often break down, perpetuating the cycle of deprivation.

Since Jason's birth parents remained ostensibly cooperative although unable to care for him, he was voluntarily accommodated and could be withdrawn from his current foster placement at any time. The placement was in crisis when I was asked to become involved and attended a planning meeting. I noted in this first meeting that the link worker (with a role of supporting the foster carers), had not been invited, and I was alerted immediately to the theme of "exclusion" that would underlie this case, stirred up by this boy's profound feelings of exclusion. In this meeting, there was a suggestion from the child's social worker and her manager that the link worker was not doing enough to support the placement. I heard that Jason was verbally so abusive and rejecting to his foster mother that she had pretty much withdrawn, and foster father had taken over, unilaterally dealing with Jason in order to "protect" his wife.

At the time I was curious about this extreme situation, where one half of the couple appeared to be so completely flattened. I wondered to myself whether this clearly competent field social worker could be finding it difficult to make space for the more diffident-sounding link worker to take on his full role. I also wondered whether this dynamic could reflect in any way what might actually be happening between this foster-carer couple, whose capacity to work in a united way as carers appeared to be under fire from Jason. Could this foster father also be finding it difficult to make space for his wife to take on her full foster-mothering role? After a further meeting with both field and link workers it was agreed that the link worker and I would meet with the foster carers together, without Jason, since they sounded desperate about the situation and urgently needed support. There was no point offering individual psychotherapy if his placement was about to collapse (Sprince, 2000).

My initial thoughts were confirmed in our first meeting, where foster father described Jason's increasingly violent and disruptive threats to attack and destroy them. As he declared himself strong enough to cope with Jason single-handed, foster mother faded into the background, looking exhausted and utterly flattened by these assaults. We heard from foster father that Jason "hated mothers" as a result of his past experience. They were taken aback, but momentarily interested, when I suggested that perhaps Jason might miss foster mother's maternal care, as his verbal abuse of her usually came at the end of a long day of her absence at work. He might feel rejected and reverse the situation, giving *her* an experience of rejection. The couple's pattern was replicated in the relationship between me and my link worker partner—our first work together—where I talked almost exclusively and he faded quietly into the background.

Over the first few meetings, the foster carers described what sounded like an escalating series of threats and attacks on foster father, often in mother's absence, first with a sharp compass, then with kitchen knives, and one physical attack with kicks and punches. These were accompanied by taunts that foster father was "thick"—a reference perhaps to an unreachable "brick-wall object". They complained that Jason "felt nothing" and seemed to have "no memory" of the incidents, losing himself for hours in violent Playstation games.

I thought this was an extreme situation in which, in the interest of apparently protecting foster mother from attack, she was being pushed increasingly to the margins of the parental couple and was becoming increasingly ineffective, hardly daring to return home after work. Foster father, on the other hand, full of defensive bravado, claimed he could cope with it all. I suggested that successfully driving a wedge between his foster carers and disrupting their parental functioning might serve to increase Jason's anxiety and persecuted attacks.

There was intense anxiety about the case, and a realistic concern about the carers' safety, which I shared. At a meeting I agreed that, of course, their safety was a priority but suggested that, instead of ending the placement, it might be suspended, and temporary accommodation found for Jason with a view to his return to this family, while work continued with the carers and possibly with Jason. I felt that only work with the foster carers on the impact of such a disturbed child on their parental relationship could achieve a positive future outcome. Replacing Jason with another disturbed child would probably result in a repetition of this pattern. Losing them as a fostering resource would be a tragic waste, since they had much to offer.

I had noticed that as foster mother became increasingly anxious about the risk to their safety—would he murder them, set the house on fire?—foster father appeared to minimize his fears. I thought that the more Jason felt he was faced with an unreachable "brick-wall object", the more the attacks were likely to escalate in intensity as a way of trying to force into foster father some of his feelings of hurt, distress, and fear—possibly even terror. Foster father needed to allow some of Jason's feelings in through his defensive armour, or increasingly violent means to penetrate it would be used. If the parents could be helped to work together to understand and move towards sharing their feelings of vulnerability and redress the balance, so that foster mother could be less permeable to Jason's powerful projections and foster father could be helped to be more permeable, the placement could possibly be saved. A placement suspension was agreed by everyone in a remarkable leap of faith, and a local placement was sought but not found. However, the very act of suggesting an "out" for the carers while maintaining their support calmed the situation down considerably.

Work continued with the foster carers and, in addition, I offered to see Jason for an assessment, together with his social worker, for three sessions. These sessions revealed the extent of his distress and disorientation as he collapsed on the floor of the consulting-room like a baby one minute, then talked about being "the master of the house" the next. He also gave a graphic illustration of what must go on at home when he attempted to create a split between me and the social worker and to paralyse us as a couple: he began intrusively demanding personal information from us, putting pressure on us to break the boundaries of the session. We stood firm, neither one of us divulging inappropriate information, demonstrating that we would not allow ourselves to be split in this way. At the feedback meeting the foster carers were relieved that we recognized just what an emotionally troubled and damaged child they had to deal with. Unless foster carers can be offered a regular space where they can be helped to think therapeutically about the meaning of the children's communications and behaviour, we cannot expect them to remain receptive and thoughtful when under constant bombardment by projections of a most disturbing nature.

Stabilizing the foster placement was a priority before individual work could be considered, and to this end the link worker agreed to continue to join me in meeting with the foster carers on a fortnightly basis. He and I met for 15 minutes before the sessions, to touch base and exchange information. Gradually foster father became more able to acknowledge Jason's vulnerability, which touched on his own childhood experiences, and foster mother felt supported enough to play an active part in Jason's care. Very soon Jason's physical attacks ceased completely, and the placement stabilized. A wary truce set in, whereby, in order to avoid confrontation, the foster carers kept contact with Jason to a minimum. They were perturbed by his overly physical approach to school friends and agreed sadly that they had little physical contact with him. My co-worker and I had grown correspondingly closer and more united in our approach, and we tried to help them develop a more intimate relationship with Jason, bearing in mind the rules limiting physical contact of foster carers with children in their care. They acknowledged that the main reason for keeping their distance was that they had always felt he would reject their approaches, as he exuded a message not to get too close.

We explored how this brittle, unapproachable stance was Jason's only defence against disappointment in situations where he had always been rejected or expected, like an adult, to take the initiative. This is part of the "double deprivation" that he unconsciously brought on himself. His foster mother described how hurt she felt one day when Jason had ignored her and approached her husband for all the small maternal comforts that she usually provided. Later they mentioned that Jason, who had returned that day from a visit to his birth mother, had told them that she was planning to move in with her current partner and his children. I suggested that Jason may have felt unable to put into words how rejected and excluded he felt, so he gave foster mother an experience of feeling cold-shouldered, the least favoured parent, just as he may feel the least favourite of his mother's children. This time the foster mother could draw her husband's attention to the split and gain his support for her hurt feelings, and we discussed how they could begin slowly to verbalize for Jason some of their understanding of his emotional states.

They were shaken in the week of his birthday by a trivial event, which had escalated to such a pitch of aggression in Jason that the foster father had threatened to cancel his birthday party. Foster father had called on his wife to help calm Jason down, and Jason had gone to bed, narrowly avoiding the threatened cancellation of his party. They were resistant to my suggestion of a link between his birthday and his outburst. However, as they recalled with increasing anger that Jason had heard from neither of his birth parents, opening each birthday card expectantly, the connection became clear. It appeared that the neglect and deprivation he felt from his own parents were to be projected into his foster carers, almost provoking them into depriving him of his party, but prevented in time by the fact that foster father could call on his wife for support.

After several months, the foster carers expressed gratitude for the help they had had in understanding Jason's behaviour and wondered whether Jason, too, could benefit from this sort of help. Now that my link worker colleague and I had a good working relationship and a solid alliance with the family, individual psychotherapy was a viable option and could be considered.

Envious attacks on foster carers

Since many of the looked-after children I am involved with have been voluntarily accommodated, even though they have been neglected or rejected by their parents, birth parents exert a powerful presence on foster families. This can sometimes disrupt or sabotage the placement. Feelings of competitiveness and envy can get stirred up in birth parents, who discover that their children are receiving better parenting and material advantages in their foster home. If these are acted upon, they can disrupt good relationships that may be just beginning to form between the child and his foster carers, social worker, or child psychotherapist. Some birth parents, driven by their own unmet needs as children, may find it difficult to allow their children to receive something good from anyone else, particularly if they themselves feel unsupported and inadequate.

This was powerfully brought home to me when Jason's foster carers described to me how their first Christmas together had been ruined by Jason's birth father arriving unexpectedly at the foster home, verbally abusing him and threatening to withdraw him from the placement. Perhaps Jason's excitement about his Christmas presents on a recent visit to his birth father had evoked feelings of envy or inadequacy in Jason's father at the material and emotional care his son was receiving elsewhere.

Acting out of envious feelings in the network

This basic dynamic of families set against each other can be replicated in the network in a range of ways between different agencies and professional groups. Thinking about the sometimes envious undermining of foster placements by birth parents helped me to understand something that had been puzzling me for some time and which is linked with my earlier point about the need for endorsement from the highest level of management. I had noticed that with several cases I was about to take on, initial meetings had been set up and arrangements for meeting carers and child were in place, and at that moment something would come, like a bolt out of the blue, and disrupt the proceedings. In one case, the social worker had been sent by her manager to tell me that a duplicate referral had been made simultaneously to an out-of-borough specialist agency, and that they would be following that up instead.

The team managers, particularly when there are changes and re-organizations going on at a level above them, may themselves feel at times rather under-supported and under-resourced, always at risk of being blamed, and criticized—like the deprived birth parents and foster carers with whom they work. They may then find it difficult to see their social workers receiving support and thoughtful input from the consultant. This could stir up unconscious feelings of rivalry in managers, who may end up removing cases from other agencies, like the birth father who threatens to disrupt his child's foster placement. It can also lead to competitiveness between professionals and agencies, all striving to be the one with something valuable to offer.

In order to avoid rivalry between professionals and agencies, and to promote joint work, I tried to make a more active alliance with the team managers. I met them individually and suggested that they joined me in running the case discussion groups they had requested for their social workers, as a way of integrating our respective roles and approaches. I found that this increased attendance at the group and reduced conflicts of loyalty in social workers, who were unsure whether to turn to me or to their manager with a problem. The quality of observational detail brought to the discussion improved, as the manager could often highlight aspects of the case that complemented the material brought by the case workers. Material often pointed to splitting and fragmentation within the network.

Disorganized attachments in babies and the link to paralysis in the institution

As I hear, through consultation, about children in care, I have been struck by the fact that many children who have been severely neglected, emotionally and physically abused, sometimes born drug-addicted, still have access to their abusive birth parents, and there may be a reluctance to move towards permanency and adoption, with its implications for reduced contact.

This leaves the children living in limbo, with many short-term placements, filled with unbearable uncertainty. Social workers and their managers may neither commit themselves to seek court action to enable them to remove the child from birth families, nor yet do they feel they can in conscience return children to their families. I am aware that there are often legal and other external complications, but the basic dynamic is one of paralysis or "stasis" in the system.

Clinical observation would lead me to suggest that many of the most disturbed looked-after children display a "disorganized attachment pattern" towards a birth parent. Some of the main characteristics of the child's behaviour in the "D" category of attachment, on reunion after separation from mother, are a "freezing of all movement, with a trance-like expression, rocking or collapse" (Main, 1995b). The child appears to be caught in an "irresolvable paradox in which it can neither approach, shift its attention or flee, pulled between approaching his primary carer for comfort while simultaneously feeling the need to flee a frightening (or frightened) person" (Main, 1995b, p. 222).

In some cases this disturbed relationship may be reflected in the professional network, whereby social workers are faced with similar contradictory impulses, feeling they can neither turn away from and "flee" a potentially enraged birth parent, removing a child from a neglectful or abusive situation, nor fully engage in supporting the birth family, knowing that they may be leaving a child at risk. This can have an equally disorganizing effect on social workers' capacity to respond thoughtfully to children's needs, leading to a "collapse of strategy". This may result in placatory responses or denial of the serious damage caused to children by their parents, in the same way as abused children need to deny on some level the knowledge of their parents' abuse. This may lead to situations of "drift".

I have also noticed that, at the very moment when the organization moves towards taking steps to end the impasse, when the facts of a situation seem to be clear and indisputable, social workers report that the birth mother has "opened up" and has disclosed her own abuse and deprivation. Once again they feel pulled in two directions, torn between attending to the needs of an infant in the adult or to the child himself, a situation exacerbated by the under-provision of Adult Mental Health Services, another layer of deprivation in the care system.

The conflict between placing the child's needs first and attending to the often child-like needs of the birth mothers may become intolerable in situations where the support and "secure base" social workers seek from their own managers is not available to them.

Managers may be unable to provide a "secure base" to their social workers because of pressures on them from higher up in the organization and from society at large. In these situations the social workers may be more vulnerable to feeling overwhelmed by the powerful projections of frightening or frightened birth parents.

I would suggest that this paralysis in the system could be understood as a countertransference experience, a powerful communication via the mechanism of projective identification into the professional of the child's experience of collapse in the face of contradictory states. Unless this experience can be thought about in a containing setting, it can lead to re-enactment. However, this may also be a countertransference experience not only of the individual professional involved, but of the organization as a whole, and it may be reflected as an institutional dynamic on many levels.

My experience has been that it is the social workers who are exposed to the brunt of the emotional impact of these cases, while their managers distance themselves from the case, "to be able to make clear planning decisions". They, too, seem to realize that the overwhelming bombardment of intense feelings can interfere with thinking.

From my contact with the managers, I became aware of how they, too, were subjected to the same disorganizing forces from higher levels of management, politicians, and a society trying to cope with often unbearably painful dilemmas. They are equally faced with contradictory pressures—to ensure that children are not left to die of abuse and neglect with their birth parents, but also to work in partnership with birth parents. In essence, social and political opinion is itself paradoxical, posing an irresolvable dilemma about attending to the often conflicting needs of birth parents and children, particularly when faced with the unbearable truth about the cruelty and deprivation suffered by some children in our society. One can understand how, when support and containment ("a secure base") are not available from the highest political and social levels, senior managers may themselves become "disorganized", unable to formulate a strategy for coping or to support their workers.

Conclusion

During this period of work with the social services departments, it could be distressing to hear of the appalling experiences of some of the children, especially when their hopes and expectations would be cruelly dashed, and of the social workers, themselves subjected to abuse and criticism. This was replicated in my relationship to the organization, when I would find that at times my painstaking work to establish links between teams would be disrupted, destroying hopes of holding a case within the network. The uncertainty I experienced about the permanence of my post echoed the anxieties of many children who lived in unbearable states of uncertainty about their future. The deeper the emotional investment one makes, the more intense the anxieties about it all coming to nothing, and one can understand these children's need to defend themselves against such involvement. However, it seems important to recall that before the involvement of any other professionals, the catastrophe had occurred, in infancy or young childhood, usually within the birth family. This primary heartbreak, like deprivation, enters the care system, impacting on staff throughout the institution.

I have sought to describe how my experience of trying to set up a service for looked-after children helped me to understand the ways in which the professionals within organizations may be caught up in unconscious processes in relation to the troubled families they work with, which may, in turn, influence their responses. Drawing attention to these dynamics and providing support and containment to the professionals has, in some cases, enabled them, in turn, to work together with their colleagues and other agencies in a way that is more containing for the foster carers and children and has prevented further disruption and deprivation. I have also tried to explore whether the "disorganized/disorientated" attachment category for babies can help us to understand the paralysis experienced by social workers when faced with contradictory impulses and demands from needy birth parents and needy children.

I shall end by quoting Britton writing about organizational dynamics:

> It is the recognition of these provocative or paralysing effects in such cases which at least gives pause for reflection. Change as a *consequence* of 'realization', rather than change as an *alternative* to 'realization', may prevent patterns which cross not only individual but generational boundaries. [Britton, 1981, p. 54; italics added]

CHAPTER 19

Children who cannot live in families: the role of residential care

Hamish Canham

For many years now, the tide of opinion has been against placing children and young people in residential care, and there has been a commensurate burgeoning of fostering and adoption services. This opinion has been rooted in the feeling that children need to be in families, a well-founded desire to give children homes, and a prejudice against institutional care, reinforced by a constant flow of scandals in children's homes. In this chapter I outline why I feel there will always be a need for residential provision for certain children. I then look at some of the issues that besiege children's homes and make the work so demanding and difficult. Finally, I also reflect on what is needed in children's homes if they are to provide a containing and therapeutic environment for children to live in.

Why residential care is needed, and for whom

There is a large number of children and young people who, when things go wrong at home, are placed almost as a matter of course in foster care. Very often these children are not suited to family life, and there is a tragic mismatch between foster carers who want to provide children with a substitute home and the children whose level of disturbance means they place an impossible burden on any family where they go to live. There are, of course, exceptional foster carers who seem

to be able to tolerate very high levels of destruction, sexualized behaviour, and violence in their homes. However, for most foster carers,
the daily impact of living in close proximity to such distress, which so
often manifests itself in attacks on the foster home and indeed on the
foster carers, causes immense emotional strain and can lead to burnout
and breakdown.

There is disillusion, guilt, and anger for both foster carers and children as things begin to crumble. For the children, the existing feelings
about the disintegration of family life are compounded when things
go wrong again. And for some children this experience is repeated
through a trail of broken foster placements. It is not uncommon to
hear of children having lived in ten or more foster homes. It can reach
the point where it becomes abusive to put children and foster carers
through this experience, as the consequences for everyone can be so
damaging. The foster carers are put into the impossible situation of
having their homes and lives wrecked while the children grow more
and more frightened of the power of their destructiveness.

My argument is that this is neither the children's nor the foster carers' fault. The children or adolescents have been wrongly placed. Some
of the children or adolescents who come into residential care do so
because they need the solidity of containment that only an institution
can offer. There are some children who are simply so disturbed as a
consequence of the traumatic experiences they have been through, and
whose difficult behaviour is so relentless and exhausting, that shifts
of people, taking it in turns to do the looking-after, are needed. Sometimes these shifts are needed around the clock too, with night staff
taking over from the day workers. The opportunity for recuperation
and time away in a different environment is generally not available in
foster families in the same way.

I also do think that there are children and adolescents who may not
be acting out in this way, but for whom residential care may well be
the best option. One such category might be children who come from
their family homes into care and where a return home is a possibility. For these children, going into foster care can confuse the process
of rehabilitation, involving, as it does, forming new attachments and
getting used to a new style of family life, which may be very different
from that at home. In these circumstances, residential care provides the
possibility of a temporary space away from home, where work on the
issues that led to the family breakdown can take place. There is not a
rival family available for comparison, nor is the emotional energy re-

quired for forming relationships drawn away from the family of origin in the same way.

There is also quite a large group of children and adolescents whose experiences in families make the intimacy of substitute family life too close to manage. Included in this group might be the many abused and traumatized children for whom the slight distance of the staff and the anonymity that institutions can offer is very reassuring.

It may be that time spent in a children's home will lead to a settling-down in children as some of their difficulties are attended to, and they may then move back into family life. However, there will also be a number of children in every local authority where residential care of some kind—be this a children's home or a therapeutic community—seems to be the only way of containing them. The option of a therapeutic community may be difficult to get sanctioned, either because the local authority cannot afford it or because the child or adolescent will not be accepted or will refuse to go. This means that serious consideration needs to be given to how best to resource and sustain the work needed to look after these children in children's homes. Many of the ways of working developed in therapeutic communities can, I think, be usefully transferred to children's homes and other forms of residential provision (see, for example, Reeves, 2002; Sprince, 2002).

Group and institutional forces at play in residential care

A great deal of work has been carried out at the Tavistock Clinic in relation to how groups and institutions "behave". Perhaps the best-known examples of work in this area are those of Bion (1961) and Menzies Lyth (1959). The development of the work begun by these pioneers and others is lucidly described in Obholzer and Roberts (1994). What this work has shown is that whole groups, the culture of the workplace, the way management systems are organized, are influenced by unconscious forces in the same way that the individual psyche is structured according to particular anxieties and the defences which are erected to protect against these.

What Menzies Lyth (1959) showed was the way in which the prime anxieties in relation to the work being carried out effectively organize the way an institution and the staff within it work. In institutions and staff groups where there are large amounts of anxiety and the defences against them are likely to be more rigid, one may encounter a situation where the activity of the staff group is largely being carried out in the service of defending against the pain and anxiety evoked by the work rather than carrying out the designated task. In other words, the unconscious agenda has the upper hand to such an extent that the task for which the staff group consciously meet does not get carried out.

Working with children in the care system inevitably stirs up deep-seated anxieties, and many of the difficulties encountered in residential settings—and indeed in the wider social service field—often stem from insufficient attention being paid to the potentially corrosive effects of long-term anxiety within teams. The reality of most children's homes is that they contain some of the most vulnerable, damaged, and disturbed children in the community. My experience of consulting to children's homes and hearing about their residents is that many of them would probably fall into the category of the mentally ill, and this impression seems backed up by research (Meltzer et al., 2003).

This means that in residential homes the staff team and managers will be confronted by raw emotional states of the most painful and distressing kind. These will come not just from one, but from many of the children and adolescents in their care. The danger is that coming into close contact with such powerful and disturbing mental states can make individual workers feel emotionally battered and possibly ill. Working with this group of children inevitably evokes painful feelings in the workers, as Hoxter (1983) has so clearly described. Furthermore, each child brings to the children's home and the staff members a set of feelings and expectations from their previous experience, which can easily get recreated between the child and a particular worker, or within whole staff teams. This dynamic re-enacting of past experiences that have not been properly or fully understood and digested has, for a long time, been one of the key tools used in psychoanalytic psychotherapy for understanding the difficulties people experience in everyday relationships. It is what Freud called the transference, and it has been developed by all schools of psychoanalysis as the primary means for helping patients bring to light the way in which conflicts from the past colour relationships in the present. In a psychotherapy session, the feelings and fantasies that a patient has about his or her psychotherapist and the emotional responses to these are used as the way in which characteristic ways of relating, thinking, and feeling can be brought into greater consciousness and linked back to early childhood experiences.

Within children's homes, such scenarios are replayed all the time between individual workers and individual children or between groups of children and groups of staff. There are perhaps certain sets of feelings and experiences that the children living in residential care typically bring with them (Canham, 2000; Hoxter, 1983). It is useful to identify some of these in order that they can be understood and thought about rather than, as is the danger, being replicated in the system and clogging the effective running of the children's home in the same way as they can remain as undigested feelings in the minds of the young people in the care system. One cannot disentangle these feelings easily, and usually they overlap or coexist but may cluster in groups such as abandonment and shame, depression and hopelessness, despair and rage, deprivation and abuse.

At some level all children in residential care are likely to experience feelings of having been abandoned, and with this often come feelings of despair about the future, a sense of shame about their situation, and feelings of being of low importance. It also often brings, I think, an internal sense of nothing being certain or solid or fixed. After all, if a child's parents are unable to look after them this must lead to profound doubts in the child's mind about any adult's capacity to care for them, deep worry about the damage they have caused, and also doubts about their own capacities to sustain meaningful relationships. This sense of themselves that young people in care so often have is frequently demonstrated by a characteristic form of behaviour in children's homes: namely that the residents often seem to spend long periods of time on the doorstep of the house or repeatedly going out and coming back in again. This is what I have described (Canham, 1998) as a "doorstep life": where children concretely express their uncertainty about where they feel themselves to be—neither properly in nor out, of not feeling wanted and ambivalent about where they want to be.

Often the feelings that the residents are full of are dealt with by projecting them into the residential workers. The motivation for doing this may be in order to temporarily make the young people feel they have dumped their problems elsewhere; but there may also be a more helpful component, which is that the recipient of the feeling will appreciate what the young person is going through. If this second component is missing or is not appreciated by the recipient, then residential workers often end up feeling of low importance, second-rate in comparison to foster carers and social workers, and that children's homes are, at best, a necessary evil and would, in an ideal world, be closed down. This is part of the reason why in virtually every children's home I have encountered there has always been a rumour that it might be closed down. The perpetual threat of sudden abandonment has entered the culture of these homes and taken its place as an unconscious phantasy in much the same way that the reality experienced by children who have been abandoned haunts their lives. The other reason staff teams feel they might be closed down is because there is often a measure of reality to the idea. There has been widespread closure of homes, or selling off of residential provision to private or charitable organizations. My proposal is that this kind of action is rooted in the painfulness of accepting that some children cannot live with their parents and that the closure of homes is an attempt to deny the problem by eradicating its solution. It is rather like not making a will as a way of avoiding thinking about the prospect of death.

This is an example of a defensive strategy employed—in this case at an organizational level—to combat painful realizations. It is perhaps not surprising that it should be difficult—even impossible at times—for an organization like a social services department not to find ways of wanting to minimize the consequences of what children have been through when that is often the most horrific abuse and neglect. To maintain attention on some of the bleakest aspects of human nature and behaviour on a daily basis requires huge amounts of support (Briggs & Canham, 1999). It is further complicated because a similar set of feelings about the reality of parental abuse exists in society. Social services departments are in a conscious contract with society, which wants to turn a blind eye to what parents can do to children, to the point where it often seems that it is the social workers who are being blamed for the abuse. One might see this as the latter being blamed for not carrying out the role that society has given to them.

If it is a problem for society, social services departments, and residential staff to fully acknowledge what some of these children have been through, then the problem is often so much greater for the children who have actually experienced it and who, being children, do not have the same mental resources to work out what has happened. Henry (1974) has described a process by which an initial experience of abuse or deprivation is defended against internally by a shutting down of a part of the mind that can know about what has happened. This leads to a diminished capacity to relate, because the defences being employed are unusually rigid and tough and serve to keep at a distance potential reminders of intimacy and hope. The child is consequently depriving himself of an opportunity for using human relationships as the basis for development. Henry (1974) calls this "double deprivation". The risk that I wish to highlight is that the shutting off to painful experiences can all too easily happen in children's homes' staff groups too. This renders them all the more vulnerable to a cultural reacting to children's distress rather than finding ways of thinking about it.

Any staff group is likely to struggle to keep together in its task from time to time. I think there are particular forces at play in children's homes that make this task hugely difficult. As we have seen in earlier chapters, many children in care come from homes where there have been high levels of domestic violence and where there has been a basic failure between the parents to come together in the best interests of the child. This dynamic of warring, suspicious parents can get very powerfully recreated in staff teams—for example, with one shift feeling their work is undermined by another, or two workers having diametrically opposed and irreconcilable views of a child. (For further examples see Emanuel, chapter 18.)

Many staff groups seem to have difficulty in establishing a coherent and regular working practice. Different shifts can work in radically different ways. In staff meetings the same issues are discussed over and over, without any resolution. I think that this area of difficulty reflects the enormous struggle that most young people in care have in building a concept of a steady internal home after such disrupted early lives. However, my feeling is that if these dynamic issues in staff groups between staff members and between residential workers and clients can be thought about, they provide vital clues to the nature of the difficulties with which the young people are struggling and can therefore inform and deepen an understanding of the children for the residential workers. This means that the staff will be less likely to be pulled into the unhelpful recreation of past dynamics, and the young people can experience something new, and a way out of the cycle of endlessly repeating abusive experiences.

Providing a therapeutic environment in children's homes

To my mind, this is the central issue that needs attending to if residential care is to work. Menzies Lyth (1985) has written about the operation of "social defences" in residential establishments in her paper "The Development of the Self in Children in Institutions". In this she stresses how young people need the opportunity to model themselves on the people in the institution and the institution's whole way of functioning. Children need to have an experience of an organization that tries to create a culture in which what is going on between people is discussed and thought about, and where the adults struggle to do so despite the pressures I have described to do otherwise. Children also need to have the experience of adults who are not overwhelmed by the pain of what they have been through, but who can bear to think about and imagine what it must have been like. It is this capacity to keep on thinking and to tolerate psychic pain that determines the success of any children's home. It is this capacity that determines whether or not a unit is therapeutic. This is the crux of the matter. If children have a sustained experience of living in an organization where the staff are capable of continuing to think about painful issues, then they are more likely to develop this capacity in themselves. Without an experience of this kind of processing, children and adolescents are unlikely to be able to relate to their own experiences, and present and future relationships will be contaminated by what happened in the past.

Containing anxiety in children's homes will always be difficult. Menzies Lyth writes (1986): "I have come to the depressing conclusion that institutions have a natural tendency to become bad models for identification" (p. 42). She explains that this is because of the difficulties that human beings have in cooperating effectively together, the anxiety the work arouses, and the defences against these anxieties. I think that this is true and is the reason why there has been opposition to residential care with its risks of institutionalizing children.

However, there is a more positive way of looking at the possibilities that an institution can offer. A well-functioning group is able to tolerate higher levels of anxiety than any one individual or couple. It must be remembered that foster carers and adoptive parents are subjected to the same projections and are likely to resort to similar defensive strategies. Some of the children and adolescents who come into residential care do so because they need the solidity of containment that only an institution can offer. In order to do this, as I have emphasized, the institution needs to be capable of providing a space for the individual working in it to think about the impact of individual children and the resident group as a whole on them as individuals and as a group. Thinking about the painful experiences that young people in the care system have been through is hard work for young people and staff alike. It requires an organization in which members can open themselves up to emotional experiences. Not only is this taxing on an individual level, but it is also often not encouraged by organizations where "opening up" seems a sign of weakness or lack of professionalism. However, without this willingness in the staff team, young people will have the model that their experiences are just too much to contemplate and that they will overwhelm people.

In the same way that the children need adults around them in a supportive way, so, too, do the workers. My experience is that it is almost inevitable that in any children's home staff group there will be some kind of enactment between staff members related to the internal conflicts young people bring with them, which are then played out in this new setting. In order for these to be used in the way I have described, as a way into understanding the nature of the children's experience, often requires someone who is outside the force field that this dynamic creates. It may be possible for managers to achieve this vantage point, but it may require someone coming from outside to disentangle what is going on. Sprince (2002) gives a detailed description of this kind of consultancy. A consultant coming regularly to the home can enable staff groups and individual workers to be interested in the dynamics rather than becoming a victim to them. An understanding that the feelings of despondency, uselessness, and anger, so common in residential work, might reflect the despair and frustration of the young people can be liberating and help sustain people in this enormously difficult work. With this kind of input, children who have come to doubt the value of human society may begin to appreciate family life again.

Addendum: Examples of children in residential care

Anxiety about Terry who seems to "fit in" too easily

> Terry is white and from Ireland. He says he is 16, but the staff in the home are very sceptical about whether this is his true age. His story is that he was born in Ireland in a squat and moved around with his parents until he was 11. He says his father sexually abused him from the age of 5 and his mother physically abused him. When he was 11, they just abandoned him. He was then looked after by two men until he was 16. They taught him to read and write. When 16, he decided to come to London to "find himself".

> However, Terry has no proof of identity and therefore cannot claim any benefits, and he ended up in the children's home because he was homeless. Prior to this, he says he made money by begging.

> Terry does not waver in any detail from this story about his past, but he has no way of being identified and claims not to know his

parents' surnames. The staff in the home feel highly sceptical of Terry's story and have the feeling that he may have been in care somewhere else. He was quickly at ease in the home, learning all the rules swiftly, always up early and complaining to the officer in charge if staff did not wake him on time.

In the home Terry is one of those children who cannot leave the staff alone. He constantly wants to be with them. He is very helpful, wanting to make cups of tea and set the table, but also very suffocating. There is concern among the staff group that Terry may be prostituting himself because he goes out and returns with quite a lot of money, looking as if he has been taking drugs.

How can staff manage, knowing so little of his true history or what he is really up to in his present life? They, after all, carry responsibility for his care. To share this burden and to attempt to resolve ongoing dilemmas, the staff's need for support and consultation can well be appreciated. It was to such a consultation group that Terry's case was brought to Canham.

Jo—a young child who could thrive in residential care after the vicissitudes of foster care

Jo, a 7-year-old boy of African–Caribbean/white UK heritage, had been in the care system since he was a baby, and had suffered many vicissitudes while in different foster families: physical abuse and neglect, death of a foster carer, sudden moves precipitated by foster carer's needs rather than his own. Now he needed a home immediately following the discovery that he had been physically abused by his foster carer. It happened that that night there was no foster place within the local authority's provision, and he was moved to a small voluntary children's home. There they found him hard to manage but were dedicated to supporting his established weekly psychotherapy.

One week the tubes were delayed. Jo knew that he was late for his session. He jumped over the ticket barrier and ran to the clinic, crossing two major roads on his way. He did not want to miss his session. The escort arrived later, very distressed. The response of the children's home was to extract a mini-van from their managers so that they would, in future, be able to bring him safely and on time. This success was not only because there was a benign management. The workers in the home had worked as a team to get to know Jo. His key worker was a huge, gentle African–Caribbean—a new model of a black male for Jo, who became deeply attached to him. The escort, a young white woman, now coming by van, had long discussions with Jo about dinosaurs, God, what families could be like. Sometimes he just slept, from a position of ease it seemed rather than as an escape from anxiety.

A year later the local authority found a long-term foster family. They, the children's home, and the clinic worked together to pre-pare Jo for this family. In the therapy he and I thought about the losses involved in the move. Almost for the first time Jo, who had already gone through so many precipitate moves in his life, was able to think about this issue before it happened.

In the children's home the intensity of relationships was less than in the families he had previously been with. He had been helped in his relationships with his peers. He had also, slowly, found confidence and a measure of trust in the adults who looked after him. With hindsight, and over that year, I could see how Jo, backed by the reflective environment of the home, had been able to use his therapy sessions more thoughtfully, and that thoughtfulness had extended to all his relationships. He had also quickly learnt to read and write after he went to the home. This timing is very striking. Because he felt more emotionally contained in the home, he effectively had more energy to apply to learning. He also now wanted to find out about the world around him, and his endless curiosity was responded to by the staff. Moreover the capacity to read and write helped him to extend his expressive and emotional language—and with me he seemed safer to explore his more un-comfortable feelings and to find names for them.

At the time of the move into his new family, Jo seemed to have more chance of allowing the family to provide him with the long term care he so badly needed.

Tom—who found breathing space in residential care

Tom, an older adolescent boy, had spent the past four years out of school looking after his father, who was slowly dying, and also tending to his mother, who had a severe psychiatric illness marked by suicidal depression and violent outbursts directed at others.

When this boy's father died, the family disintegrated. An older sister left home, and the mother's mental health declined to the point where she required hospital admission. Initially, almost as a matter of course, this boy went into a foster home. However, here he seemed to feel intensely claustrophobic and spent most of his time on the streets with his friends, increasingly getting into trouble with the police. It was then decided to place Tom in a children's home. Here he flourished: having been a chronic asthma sufferer, he said that for the first time in his life he could breathe properly. Although Tom is talking concretely about a physical symptom, at another level one can see the reference he is making to the breathing space afforded to him in the less closed-in world of the children's home

Tracy—whose forceful projections into her key worker were thought about in a staff consultation group in such a way as to increase the understanding of the staff of Tracy's particular difficulties

Tracy, aged 10, came from a large family where all the children were neglected and physically abused. They were sexually abused by their parents and parents' friends and, as they grew older, by one another, almost like an extended form of sibling play. Tracy was finally placed in a children's home. Her key worker brought, initially rather reluctantly, her complex feelings about Tracy to the staff discussion group. She had over the six months that Tracy had been in care become very attached to her. But she had been disturbed by three dreams. In each dream she was with Tracy and was sexually aroused and excited in the dreams and afterwards on waking. It distressed her greatly to report these dreams. She was a thoughtful and sensitive person, steady in all her relationships with the children in her care. Unravelling the dreams and thinking about the day-to-day context and the relationship between her and Tracy, it became clearer that Tracy was projecting aspects of her self and her sexuality forcefully into the worker. She, in her turn, was acting as a container for these feelings, which were safe with her as there was no risk that she would become the seduced seducer of Tracy. She was a container, as described by Bion (1962), and used the work group to work out how feelings that were so powerful that they even entered her dream life could be thought about and understood. Then the risk of actually acting out the role in which she found herself from the force of the projective identification was removed.

One can see how if the same feelings had been projected onto a less well-supported foster carer, for example, she might have been so alarmed that she might have wanted to end the placement. Worse, an enactment could have taken place in either foster or residential care that could have severely damaged all involved, specially confirming for the child her expectations of sexuality in relationships with adults. In the residential home the staff group was able to use the powerful information brought by the dreams to understand Tracy better and just how overwhelmed she had been by her sexual experiences. Her key worker had the support of the staff group to encourage her continuing thoughtful care of Tracy.

A FAMILY'S PERSPECTIVE

CHAPTER 20

"Then there were four": learning to be a family

Jason Andrews

> A hundred years from now it will not matter what my bank
> account was, the sort of house I lived in, or the kind of car I drove.
> But the world may be different because I was important in the life
> of a child.
>
> Dr Forest E. Witcraft (1950)

A curly-haired girl with big brown eyes stared at me, a puzzled, yet intrigued, expression on her face.

Only days before, her foster carers had explained to the 9-year-old that she was going to be adopted. She had grasped the concept, understood she was going to live with a new Mummy and Daddy who would be her "forever parents".

But hearing it and believing it were two different things, and, based on her experience to date, a new Mummy and Daddy was not on her "must-have" list.

She seemed eager, too keen to please, but her underlying fear was palpable. For she was still grieving over her forced separation from her birth mother. Katie wanted *her,* not us.

Sophia, her younger sister, appeared. She was 3 years old and her hair, like Katie's, butchered by the Jack the Ripper of the hairdressing world.

She was tiny, cute, had mischievous dark eyes, and talked like Mickey Mouse.

She cocked her head to one side, as if calculating what our buttons were. She made straight for my £500 camera, and, being the complete pushover that I was, I let her play with it.

Both girls turned me to mush.

Adoption was meaningless to Sophia, and the changes in her life, like the multitude of traumatic disruptions she had experienced, were to bring her to the edge of mental collapse before she began a healing process.

Katie was, emotionally, the stronger of the two, had more "bounce-back" in her, and had experienced an element of positive bonding with other people.

Sophia had not experienced any positive bonding, apart from the special relationship she had with her sister, sometimes explosive, but loving nonetheless.

Katie was a "child–mother" to Sophia, and the dynamics of this relationship needed to change. She had tended to Sophia when their birth mother left them for days without food, changed her soiled clothes, and tried to protect her as best she could.

We were the fifth home for them in two years. The most recent had lasted a year—a bad placement that further damaged an already traumatized Sophia and one that made Katie feel lonely and unloved.

Sophia was terrified of the most basic park apparatus when she first came to live with us because she had not had the opportunity to explore her world in the safe way that most toddlers do.

When we gave her the safety to explore, she went to the other extreme and rode her scooter like a bat out of hell, disregarding little old ladies in our local high street who thought Dennis the Menace's kid sister had moved in.

Both girls' worlds had been dangerous and violent.

In a safe environment, both would need to learn to be sisters to each other and, if possible, to be children.

Katie and Sophia had been bits of paper up until this moment, a mass of statistics and life history supplied by social workers that told of neglect, abuse, and starvation.

What could possibly qualify us to help such needy children?

Our only qualifications were big hearts and an unshakeable determination to help them.

Neither of us had had much experience of children, except we had once been children ourselves and played with the offspring of relatives and friends, whom, at the end of the day, we could give back.

But Sophia and Katie were not children we could return when we were exhausted and at the end of our tether.

And believe me, we were frequently exhausted and at the end of our tether in the first couple of years.

Several months after the children came into our care, prior to the Adoption Order, our social worker from the Adoption Society asked us to describe the experience so far.

My wife, Tara, said: "It's like we've been put inside a milkshake maker and it's not stopped shaking."

It is not that we were naive. But we were desperate to have children. We would have accepted the little girl from *The Exorcist* if she had been offered. Indeed, there were occasions when we thought we had been.

Two lost babies pre-term had led us to adoption. It is not something we had considered before.

But after we lost our second baby, we could not get pregnant again. "Unexplained infertility," they called it.

The choice was to remain childless but spoil ourselves rotten: four holidays a year, no financial worries, do what we wanted when we wanted.

Or adopt: fewer, or no, holidays, financial struggles, and lose our freedom and ability to live life on impulse.

It was an easy choice!

But the process was far from easy, and sometimes it felt like social workers were living under our bed.

This was necessary, of course. You just cannot give needy kids out willy-nilly. It is only right that prospective parents should have to prove themselves. But it is stressful.

I had a particular reason to worry we would not be allowed to adopt. I had had a dysfunctional and abusive childhood.

I did not want to hide this from the social workers, and I managed to successfully argue that I was not, in turn, a prospective abuser, but a compassionate, loving man, not in spite of my experiences but because of what I learned from them and my determination to break the chain.

"It stops with me, guys", I had proclaimed to the universe many years ago.

As survivors, I don't think we ever completely heal, but it is possible with hard work and, in my case, the love of a special person, for us to get to a point where we find joy in living and where our adult selves are able to nurse the fragments of the hurt children within us, love them, and protect them.

It would be easy, of course, for me to identify with Katie and Sophia, but I do not do this, and it would be a mistake to do so. Their experiences were different from mine, we are very different people, and we respond to our environment in different ways.

But I can empathize, because I remember what it was like to feel loveless, unlovable, rejected, and bad and how, with the help of therapy, I learned to think of myself as loved, lovable, accepted, and good.

This is what Tara and I want for our children, too. I waited until my 20s to get help. But we can help these children *now*.

Thanks to the Tavistock, that is exactly what we are doing.

Parenting embraces an element of selfishness, because most people are looking for something back. At best, this will be their love, joy in their company, a sense of fulfilment. At worst, it can be a validation of one's self, a need to realize one's own lost dreams through that child, and that is a terrible burden for children to carry.

Tara and I want their love. Of course, we do. It is a basic human need, but parenting is also a vocation for us.

Okay, so most of us like to feel to a lesser or greater extent we are making our mark on the world. Some of us do it by becoming big in business, in politics, or in the arts.

But making one's mark does not depend on material achievements. One kind word to an ostracized child at the right time in the right way can move mountains, can set in train a sequence of events that have infinite echoes far greater than we can ever imagine.

Yes, it is true, Tara and I wanted to be parents. We wanted children who would call us Mummy and Daddy, whom we could share our lives with. But we also consciously set out to change the destiny of two children who had everything against them.

And with all the support we have had from the Tavistock, we are doing so.

Katie, in particular, is now changing her *own* destiny. Many of the shackles from her past are still there, but they've loosened. Some have dropped off.

In the last year, particularly, she has found a degree of self-motivation that she had never had before.

We are the catalyst, the Tavistock provide some of the tools, now Katie is becoming empowered.

The opportunity to avail ourselves of the Tavistock was offered one minute and could have been gone the next. Our social worker told us about the Fostering and Adoption team in the Child and Family department. We were not obliged to seek their help, but she strongly advised us not to let what she said was a golden opportunity pass us by.

We knew the children would need long-term psychotherapy, and we welcomed the offer.

I do not believe the Tavistock on its own or we on our own could have helped our children but, rather, it is the combination of the two that has worked.

It is a two-way partnership, and both sides have to be willing. It is no good if adoptive parents feel pressured into getting such support and therefore are not enthusiastic participants.

The team could have given advice forevermore, but without our commitment and compassion, our ability to act on that advice, and our own instincts, nothing would have come of it.

Sometimes just having their reassurance helped enormously.

There have been numerous times when Katie has had heart-to-hearts with us, both as a couple and individually.

It is painful to see children hurting so much, and it is easy to question your own abilities, their issues seem so enormous.

"What am I doing wrong? Isn't there more I can do? Would other parents have been able to help them more? Maybe I'm not up to the job."

These are the things that frequently went round our heads.

But our workers never judged us—at least, if they did, they never let on. They were encouraging, and they really understood the difficulties we faced.

They spoke to us in such a way that when we left sessions with them, we did feel as if we were good parents, that we were the right couple for the children, and that we were doing the right things to help them.

Under the guidance of the Tavistock, I feel we evolved from being nervous new parents to confident, forthright, seasoned parents who instinctively make good choices.

When the politically correct brigade talk about adoption, it is always about the children, what is in their best interests, but our therapists understood that it was not just about the children. It was about "the family". The well-being of all of us was important.

If Mum and Dad were knackered or distressed, they were not going to be as effective as they could possibly be: if one tyre on a car is punctured, you're not likely to make it from London to Scotland, are you?

The team included a child and adolescent psychiatrist, social worker, child psychologist, child psychotherapists, and family therapists.

When we needed help in getting Statements of Special Educational Need, they helped us in what was a battle against establishment red tape and hindrance and a system that, I believe, puts financial prudence over and above the welfare of children; when we needed respite care, they endorsed our application; when we felt the schools did not adequately understand our children and therefore the best way to support them, they met with their teachers; when local authority social workers were hell-bent on maintaining damaging birth family contact with Sophia merely because it was in their constitution, they used their expertise to support us in our argument that some of these contacts were harmful; when Sophia was stealing repeatedly from school, one of our therapists came up with creative solutions that we would never have thought of . . . and they worked.

The two professionals, Dr A and Mrs B, with whom we worked on a regular basis, were people who understood and appreciated what we and the children were going through.

They gave helpful opinions, which made a huge difference to our lives when we felt like we were groping in the dark. They have been a light for us.

We would never have come up with some of the effective strategies for helping the children without our regular meetings with them and the children's individual therapists.

They gave us hope, and the more we talked to them, the better we became at parenting.

When we had family meetings, we were all able to learn more about our interactions with each other, gently guided by the therapists, and we worked particularly hard on the issue of sibling rivalry. Like many issues the children had, their jealously of each other was at the extreme end of extreme. Each wanted our undivided attention, and woe betide their sibling if she competed.

And when we were worried about anything at all, Tara and I could write to the therapists, seeking their advice, or meet with them to discuss current difficulties.

When, at one stage we feared Sophia's behaviour might be exacerbated by a possible brain abnormality arising from circumstances surrounding her birth, they organized the necessary medical procedures so that we could rule that out.

Both children, especially Sophia, hit us with everything they had in the first couple of years. Imagine the worst, and you can be sure, that is what we had to deal with.

At times we felt like throwing in the towel. But that is precisely what Sophia wanted us to do. What could she do to prove that we didn't really love her after all? What could she do to reinforce in her own mind and everyone else's that she was essentially "bad"?

It could have been so tempting to give it up, hand them back, and say, "Look, guys, we made a mistake. You never told us it was *this* bad." But we could not do that, for the simple reason that none of it was their fault.

And I think we loved them from the moment we read about them. When we set eyes on them, they had us, hook, line, and sinker.

They were our girls then, and they'll be our girls for ever.

I don't know why we felt this love so quickly. Maybe it was just meant to be.

Fathering is not about physically creating a baby. It is about parenting. And just because a child is not of your flesh does not make them any less deserving of your love.

With adoption, if you make the child *your* child, then they are yours, and it makes no difference how they came into your life. Being a parent is an attitude—not a condition.

But love is not enough for our children. They need much, much more. The Tavistock has worked with us to provide them with the things they need other than love, the techniques and the creativity to help us nurture children who are capable of learning to be at ease with themselves.

And it is working.

If you ask Katie and Sophia do they like going to the Tavistock, they will say "no". But both will acknowledge they have benefited.

Katie writes that she does not enjoy going to the Tavistock and insists she does not need to, any more.

Yet, within the space of a few paragraphs, she also says:

"I think that all children and adults who have had a difficult start to their lives should be offered therapy, because it will give them a chance to talk and express their feelings about what has happened to them.

"To me, I prefer the one-to-one sessions [to family meetings] because it enables me to talk about issues that I might not be able or might not want to discuss at home or to the family."

Katie has always argued she does not need therapy or even want it. But we have the proof of the pudding.

Katie has turned into a wonderful young lady, resilient, strong, and proud. At 15, she has a close circle of friends, where not all that long ago she had none.

She is a confidante to her friends. They go to her with their problems because they know she cares, they know she understands their pain, and she offers sensible advice.

But she still has a lot of problems—as her parents, we can see this better than friends and family, who see her socially and only see the self-assured, confident façade that Katie chooses to present.

As her parents, it is necessary for us to ensure Katie continues with therapy. That way, she can continue building on what I consider to be nothing short of the phenomenal progress she has already made.

I asked Sophia, nearly 9, a set of questions I had prepared about the Tavistock. She said:

"I think the Tavistock has helped me a little. I can explain how I feel sometimes. It makes me feel a bit better. Sometimes I don't like to talk . . . I don't know why. When I go there I'm always grumpy . . . it's annoying, I miss Golden Time at school.

"I think in a few years I will be glad I've gone. When I play Mummies and Daddies, she [the therapist] says the baby needs a lot of looking after because she hasn't been here for a while. That annoys me a lot.

"I go there to help me talk about things that happened in the past and what has been happening, if I've arguments at school. I think all children who have had a hard life should be able to go to the Tavistock because it helps them sometimes.

"I found the family meetings more helpful than my therapist because she says I mean things that I don't mean . . . she gives me a headache. Sometimes I got embarrassed at family meetings. I don't get embarrassed anymore. The last two family sessions I didn't get embarrassed much. I get shy and embarrassed going to people's houses but then after five minutes I talk to them like I've known them all my life.

"I'm happier now than when I first came here because I used to be very nervous. We had only just met you. Now I'm not nervous because I've been with you for five years. I had been to so many homes, I wondered if I was going to be moved again.

"I feel that the Tavistock is there for children because some children were brought up in ways they shouldn't have been and need help to talk about it. I was thinking about it in bed one night and thought that's a good thing. . . . I go to the Tavistock twice a week. When I finish going I hope I won't find it hard to talk about my feelings, things that happen at school and about the past."

I didn't prompt Sophia, didn't load the questions—this is what she said verbatim.

I was staggered at her level of understanding relative to just six months ago, and this really speaks volumes for the good work that the Tavistock has done and continues to do with her.

This is thanks, in great part, to the working chemistry between all the members of the team.

Dr A and Mrs B were an insightful force for good that helped us over the most difficult stages of parenting Katie and Sophia.

We did not always agree with their suggestions, but even when we did not, they respected our views and our right to make the final decision.

Dr A once suggested putting Sophia on Ritalin. Tara was dead against from the off, fearful it would dampen the spark that *is* Sophia. I did not dismiss it out of hand but wanted to research the pros and cons and possible long-term effects.

I do think all the evidence we presented to Dr A probably indicated that Ritalin could be helpful, but it just did not feel right to us.

Dr A did not make us feel railroaded into trying Ritalin, and we did not feel judged for declining her suggestion, even though I think she felt strongly Ritalin was the best way to go.

She continued to help us feel empowered, guided to be better parents, and understood. When we made errors, she did not make us feel like awful parents. She gave us good ideas, and we were always open to creative solutions.

Like the balance between Dr A and Mrs B, Tara and I have a special balance. Tara's strengths lie where mine do not, and vice versa

We do have criticisms of the Tavistock. No sooner did Katie get used to one therapist, she moved on. Now she's just got used to another therapist who has done really good work with her, and that therapist, too, is leaving.

Continuity is important in this kind of work. Once you work well with one person, it is hard to start up again with someone else, especially for children who do not handle change well.

However, this does have a positive angle: a change of therapist and the discovery that another person can be trusted with their "stuff" is a good thing.

Life changes, it moves on. Even us adults can find that difficult sometimes.

Tara and I will continue to be grateful for the support staff at the Tavistock give us.

We feel strongly that everyone who adopts should have access to the sort of facilities the Tavistock provides if they are willing to seek it whole-heartedly. I understand not everyone accepts such offers of help. That is a shame for the children.

Sophia's on the mend now. She's got a longer road to travel than her sister, but she has bucketloads of charm. If she tames her demons, there'll be no stopping her.

I think Katie and Sophia now understand they've got us for keeps. It doesn't matter what they throw at us, we will never stop being their Mum and Dad.

They're like the delphiniums in our back garden—when we got them, they were a flowerless mass of grubby leaves with jagged edges. They are now growing into beautiful flowers, tall and proud.

We'll keep adding the water.

REFERENCES

Aber, J., Slade, A., Berger, B., Bresgi, I., & Kaplan, M. (1985). "The Parent Development Interview." Unpublished manuscript, City University, New York.

Ainsworth, M., Blehar, M., Waters, E., & Wall, S. (1978). *Patterns of Attachment: A Psychological Study of the Strange Situation*. Hillsdale, NJ: Erlbaum.

Alvarez, A. (1992). *Live Company*. London & New York: Tavistock/ Routledge.

APA (2000). *Diagnostic and Statistical Manual of Mental Disorders, 4th edition (text revision; DSM-IV-TR)*. Washington, DC: American Psychiatric Association.

Andersen, T. (1987). Reflecting teams: dialogue and meta-dialogue in clinical work. *Family Process, 26*: 415–428.

Andersen, T. (1991). *The Reflecting Team: Dialogue and Dialogues about the Dialogues*. New York: W. W. Norton.

Anderson, H., Goolishian, H., & Windermere, L. (1986). Problem determined systems: Towards transformation in family therapy. *Journal of Strategic and Systemic Therapy, 5*: 1–11.

Archer, C. (1996). Attachment disordered children. In: R. Phillips & E. McWilliam (Eds.), *After Adoption: Working with Adoptive Families*. London: British Association for Adoption and Fostering.

Argent, H. (2003). *Models of Adoption Support: What Works and What Does Not*. London: British Association for Adoption and Fostering.

Bandura, A. (1977). *Social Learning Theory*. Englewood Cliffs, NJ :Prentice-Hall.

Bateson, G. (1979). *Mind and Nature: A Necessary Unity*. London: Wildwood House.

Beck, A. T. (1976). *Cognitive Therapy and the Emotional Disorders*. New York: Guilford Press.

Beebe, D., & Lachman, F. (2002). *Infant Research and Adult Treatment*. Hillsdale, NJ: Analytic Press.

Bick, E. (1968). The experience of the skin in early object relations. *International Journal of Psychoanalysis, 49*: 484–486.

Biehal, N., Clayden, J., Stein, M., & Wade, J. (1995). Moving on: Young people and leaving care schemes. *Social Services Review, 73*: 401–420.

Bion, W. R. (1952). *Experiences in Group*. London: Tavistock..

Bion, W. R. (1959). Attacks on linking. In: *Second Thoughts*. London: Karnac.

Bion, W. R. (1961). *Experiences in Groups*. London: Routledge.

Bion, W. R. (1962). *Learning from Experience*. London: Karnac.

Bishop, E. (1983). One Art. In: *The Complete Poems: 1927–1979*. New York: Farrar, Straus & Giroux.

Bohman, M., & Sigvardsson, S. (1980). A prospective, longitudinal study of children registered for adoption: A 15-year follow-up. *Acta Psychiatrica Scandinavica, 61*: 339–355.

Boston, M., & Lush, D. (1994). Further considerations of methodology for evaluating psychoanalytic psychotherapy with children: Reflections in the light of research experience. *Journal of Child Psychotherapy, 20* (2).

Boston, M., & Szur, R. (Eds.) (1983). *Psychotherapy with Severely Deprived Children*. London: Routledge & Kegan Paul.

Bowlby, J. (1951). Maternal care and mental health. *World Health Organisation Monograph Series No.2*. Geneva: WHO. [Reprinted New York: Schocken Books, 1996.]

Bowlby, J. (1969). *Attachment and Loss, Vol. 1: Attachment*. New York: Basic Books.

Bowlby, J. (1973). *Attachment and Loss, Vol. 2: Separation, Anxiety and Anger*. New York: Basic Books.

Bowlby, J. (1980). *Attachment and Loss, Vol. 3: Loss, Sadness and Depression*. London: Hogarth Press.

Bowlby, J. (1988). *A Secure Base: Clinical Applications of Attachment Theory*. London: Routledge; New York: Basic Books.

Briggs, S., & Canham, H. (1999). Editorial article. *International Journal of Infant Observation, 2* (2): 2–11.

Britton, R. (1981). Re-enactment as an unwitting professional response to family dynamics. In: S. Box, B. Copley, J. Magagna, & E. Moustaki (Eds.), *Psychotherapy with Families: An Analytic Approach*. London: Routledge & Kegan Paul.

Britton, R. (1998). *Belief and Imagination*. London: Routledge, New Library of Psychoanalysis.

Broad, B. (Ed.) (2001). *Kinship Care: The Placement Choice for Children and Young People*. Lyme Regis: Russell House.

Broad, B., Hayes, R., & Rushforth, C. (2001). *Kith and Kin: Kinship Care for Vulnerable Young People*. London: Joseph Rowntree Foundation/National Children's Bureau.

Brodzinsky, D. M. (1987). Adjustment to adoption: A psychological perspective. *Clinical Psychology Review, 7*: 25–47.

Brodzinsky, D. M, Smith, D. W., & Brodzinsky, A. B. (1998). *Children's Adjustment to Adoption: Developmental and Clinical Issues*. Thousand Oaks, CA: Sage.

Buchanan, J. (2000). An adoptee's thoughts on adoption. *Context, 52*.

Burr, D. (1995). *An Introduction to Social Constructionism*. London: Routledge.

Byng-Hall, J. (1995). *Rewriting Family Scripts: Improvisation and Systems Change*. London: Guilford Press.

Cairns, K. (2002). *Attachment, Trauma and Resilience: Therapeutic Caring for Children*. London: British Association for Adoption and Fostering.

Campbell, D., & Grønbæk, M. (2006). *Taking Positions in the Organization*. London: Karnac.

Canham, H. (1998). Growing up in residential care. *Journal of Social Work Practice, 12* (1): 65–75.

Canham, H. (1999). The development of the concept of time in fostered and adopted children. *Psychoanalytic Enquiry, 19*: 160–171.

Canham, H. (2000). Exporting the Tavistock model to social services: Clinical, consultative and teaching aspects. *Journal of Social Work Practice, 14* (2): 125–133.

Cecchin, G. (1987). Hypothesising, circularity and neutrality revisited: An invitation to curiosity. *Family Process, 26*: 405–413.

Chamberlain, P., & Rosicky, J. G. (1995). The effectiveness of family therapy in the treatment of adolescents with conduct disorders and delinquency. *Journal of Marital and Family Therapy, 21* (4): 441–459.

Chandler, L., & Johnson, V. (1991). *Using Projective Tests with Children: A Guide to Clinical Assessment*. Springfield, IL: Charles C Thomas.

Cohen, J. A., Deblinger, E., & Mannarino, A. P. (2004). A multisite, randomised controlled trial for children with sexual abuse related PTSD symptoms. *Journal of Academic Child and Adolescent Psychiatry, 43*: 393–402.

Cohen, J. A., Mannarino, A. P., & Knudsen, K. (2005). *Child Abuse and Neglect, 29*: 135–145.

Cohen, N. (1996). Parents' sense of "Entitlement" in adoptive and non-adoptive families. *Family Process*, 35 (4).

Collishaw, S., Maughan, B., Goodman, R., & Pickles, A. (2004). Time trends in adolescent mental health. *Journal of Child Psychology and Psychiatry*, 45 (8): 1350–1362.

Cooper, A., & Webb, L. (1999). Out of the maze: Permanency planning in a post-modern world. *Journal of Social Work Practice*, 13 (2): 119–134.

Cooper, G., Hoffman, K., Powell, B., & Marvin, R. (2005). The circle of security intervention: Differential diagnosis and differential treatment. In: L. Berlin, Y. Ziv, L. Amaya-Jackson, & M. Greenberg (Eds.), *Enhancing Early Attachments*. New York: Guilford Press.

Cowan, P. A., Powell, D., & Cowan, C. P. (1998). Parenting interventions: A family systems perspective. In: I. E. Sigel & K. A. Renning (Eds.), *Handbook of Child Psychology, Vol. 4: Child Psychology in Practice* (pp. 3–72). New York: Wiley.

Cronen, V. E., Johnson, K. M., & Lannamann, J. W. (1982). Paradoxes, double-binds and reflexive loops. *Family Process*, 21: 91–112.

Crumbley, J., & Little, R. (Eds.) (1997). *Relatives Raising Children: An Overview of Kinship Care*. Washington, DC: Child Welfare League of America Press.

DfES (1997). *When Leaving Home Is Also Leaving Care*. Department for Education and Skills, Social Services Inspectorate.

DfES (1998). *The Quality Protects Programme: Transforming Children's Services*. Department for Education and Skills.

DfES (2000). *Adoption: A New Approach* (White Paper). Department for Education and Skills.

DfES (2005). *Statistics of Education: Children Looked After in England: 2003–2004. National Statistics Bulletin, 1*. Department for Education and Skills.

DoH (2004). *National Service Framework for Children, Young People and Maternity Services*. Department of Health. Norwich: TSO.

Dockar-Drysdale, B. (1993). *Therapy and Consultation in Child Care*. London: Free Association Books.

Dozier, M., Higley, E., Albus, K. E., & Nutter, A. (2002). Intervening with foster infants' caregivers: Targeting three critical needs. *Infant Mental Health Journal*, 23 (5): 541–554.

Dozier, M., & Sepulveda, S. (2004). Foster mother state of mind and treatment use: Different challenges for different people. *Infant Mental Health*, 25 (4): 368–378.

Dozier, M., Stovall, K. C., Albus, K. E., & Bates, B. (2001). Attachment for infants in foster care: The role of caregiver state of mind. *Child Development*, 72: 1467–1477.

Ellis, A. (1962). *Reason and Emotion in Psychotherapy*. New York: Lyle Stuart.

Emanuel, L. (2000). *Looked-After Children Project*. Unpublished manuscript.

Emde, R. N., Biringen, Z., Clyman, R. B., & Oppenheim, D. (1991). The moral self of infancy: Affective core and procedural knowledge. *Developmental Review, 11*: 251–270.

Evan B. Donaldson Adoption Institute (2004). *What's Working for Children: A Policy Study of Adoption Stability and Termination*. New York (available as pdf file).

Fairbairn, W. R. D. (1952). *An Object Relations Theory of the Personality*, New York: Basic Books.

Falicov, C. (2002). "Migration, Ambiguous Loss and Resilience Through Rituals." Clinical Scientific Lecture, Tavistock Clinic, London (11 February).

Fergusson, D. M., Lynskey, M., & Horwood, L. J. (1995). The adolescent outcomes of adoption: A 16-year longitudinal study. *Journal of Child Psychology & Psychiatry & Allied Disciplines, 36* (4): 597–615.

Field, T. (2004). Prenatal depression effects on the fetus and neonate. In: J. Nadel & D. Muir (Eds.), *Emotional Development: Recent Research Advances*. Oxford: Oxford University Press.

Flaskas, C. (1996). Understanding the therapeutic relationship: Using psychoanalytic ideas in the systemic context. In: C. Flaskas & A. Perlesz (Eds.), *The Therapeutic Relationship in Systemic Therapy*. London: Karnac.

Forehand, R., & Long, N. (1988). Outpatient treatment of the acting out child: Procedures, long term follow-up data and clinical problems. *Advances in Behaviour Research Theory, 10*: 129–137.

Forehand, R., & McMahon, R. J. (1981). *Helping the Noncompliant Child: A Clinician's Guide to Parent Training*. New York: Guilford Press.

Fraiberg, S. (1980). Ghosts in the nursery: A psychoanalytic approach to the problems of impaired infant–mother relationships. In: *Clinical Studies in Infant Mental Health*. London: Tavistock.

Fredman, G. (1997). *Death Talk: Conversations with Children and Families*. London: Karnac.

Freidberg, R. D., & McClure, J. (2002). *Clinical Practice of Cognitive Therapy with Children and Adolescents*. New York: Guilford Press.

Freud, S. (1909c). Family romance. *Standard Edition*, 9.

Freud, S. (1912b). The dynamics of transference. *Standard Edition*, 12..

Freud, S. (1920g). *Beyond the Pleasure Principle. Standard Edition*, 18.

Gerhardt, S. (2004). *Why Love Matters: How Affection Shapes a Baby's Brain*. London: Brunner-Routledge.

Green, H., McGinnity, A., Meltzer, H., Ford, T., & Goodman, R. (2005). *Mental Health of Children and Young People in Great Britain, 2004*. Norwich: HMSO.

Greenspan, R. (1997). *Developmentally Based Psychotherapy*, Madison, CT: International Universities Press.

Grotevant, H. D. (1994). Adoptive family system dynamics: Variations by level of openness in the adoption. *Family Process, 33* (2): 125–146.

Grotevant, H. D., McRoy, R. G., & Ayers-Lopes, S. (2004). Contact after adoption: Outcomes for infant placements. In: E. Neil & D. Howe (Eds.), *Adoption and Permanent Foster Care: Research, Theory and Practice*. London: BAAF.

Groze, V., & Rosenthal, J. (1993). Attachment theory and the adoption of children with special needs. *Social Work, Research and Abstracts, 29* (2): 5–12.

Hamilton, V. (1987). Some problems in the clinical application of attachment theory. *Psychoanalytic Psychotherapy, 3*: 67–83.

Hardy, K. V., & Lasloffy, T. A., (1995). The cultural genogram: Key to training culturally competent therapists. *Journal of Marital and Family Therapy, 21* (3): 227–237.

Harris, R., & Lindsey, C. (2002). How professionals think about contact between children and their birth parents. *Clinical Child Psychology and Psychiatry, 17* (2): 147–161.

Hartman, A., & Laird, J. (1990). Family treatment after adoption: Common themes. In: D. Brodzinsky & M. N. Schechter (Eds.), *The Psychology of Adoption*. New York: Oxford University Press.

Hebb, D. (1949). *The Organization of Behavior*. New York: Wiley.

Henderson, K., & Sargent, N. (2005). Developing the Incredible Years Webster–Stratton parenting skills training programme for use with adoptive families. *Adoption and Fostering, 29* (4).

Hengeller, S. W. (1999). Multisystemic therapy: An overview of clinical procedures, outcomes and policy implications. *Child Psychology and Psychiatry Review, 4* (1): 2–10.

Henry, G. (1974). Doubly deprived. *Journal of Child Psychotherapy, 3* (4): 15–28. [Reprinted as "Double deprivation". In: *Internal Landscapes and Foreign Bodies*. London: Karnac, 1997.]

Henry, G. (1983). Difficulties about thinking and learning. In: M. Boston & R. Szur (Eds.), *Psychotherapy with Severely Deprived Children*. London: Routledge & Kegan Paul.

Herman, J. (1992). *Trauma and Recovery: From Domestic Abuse to Political Terror*. New York: Basic Books.

Hildebrand, J. (1998). *Bridging the Gap: A Training Module in Personal and Professional Development*. London: Karnac.

Hodges, J., & Steele, M. (2000). Effects of abuse on attachment representations: Narrative assessments of abused children. *Journal of Child Psychotherapy, 26* (3): 433–455.

Hodges, J., Steele, M., Hillman, S., & Henderson, K. (2002). *Coding Manual for Story Stem Assessment Profile.* Unpublished manuscript, The Anna Freud Centre, London.

Hodges, J., Steele, M., Hillman, S., & Henderson, K. (2003). Mental representations and defences in severely maltreated children: A story stem battery and rating system for clinical assessment and research applications. In: R. Emade, D. Wolf, & D. Oppenheim, (Eds.), *Revealing the Inner Worlds of Young Children* (pp. 240–267). Chicago, IL: University of Chicago Press.

Hodges, J., Steele, M., Hillman, S., Henderson, K., & Kaniuk, J. (2003). Changes in attachment representations over the first year of adoptive placement: Narratives of maltreated children. *Clinical Child Psychology and Psychiatry, 8* (3): 351–367.

Hodges, J., Steele, M., Hillman, S., Henderson, K., & Kaniuk, J. (2005). Change and continuity in mental representations of attachment after adoption. In: D. M. Brodzinsky & J. Palacios (Eds.), *Psychological Issues in Adoption: Research and Practice.* Westport, CT: Praeger.

Hodges, J., & Tizard, B. (1989). Social and family relationships of ex-institutional adolescents. *Journal of Child Psychology and Psychiatry, 30*: 77–97.

Hodges, S. (2003). *Counselling Adults with Learning Disabilities.* London: Palgrave Macmillan.

Howe, D. (1996). *Adopters on Adoption: Reflections on Parenthood and Children.* London: British Association for Adoption and Fostering.

Howe, D. (1998). *Patterns of Adoption: Nature, Nurture, and Psychosocial Development.* Oxford: Blackwell Science.

Howe, D., & Steele, M. (2004). Contact in cases in which children have been traumatically abused or neglected by their birth parents. In: E. Neil & D. Howe (Eds.), *Contact in Adoption and Permanent Foster Care: Research, Theory and Practice.* London: British Association for Adoption and Fostering.

Huxley, S. (1983). Some feelings aroused in working with severely deprived children. In: M. Boston & R. Szur (Eds.). *Psychotherapy with Severely Deprived Children.* London: Routledge & Kegan Paul.

Hunt, J. (2003). *Family and Friends Carers.* Scoping paper prepared for the Department of Health. Crown Copyright.

Hunter, M. (1993). The emotional needs of children in care: An overview of 30 cases. *Association of Child Psychology and Psychiatry Review, 15* (5): 214–218.

Hunter, M. (2001). *Psychotherapy with Young People in Care: Lost and Found.* Hove: Brunner-Routledge.

Hurry, A. (Ed). (1998). *Psychoanalysis and Developmental Therapy*. Psychoanalytic Monographs No. 3. London: Karnac.

Joseph, B. (1989). *Psychic Equilibrium and Psychic Change*. London: Routledge.

Kazdin, A. F. (1997). Practitioner review: Psychological treatments for conduct disorder in children. *Journal of Child Psychology and Psychiatry, 38*: 161–178.

Kelly, C., Allan, S., Roscoe, P., & Herrick, E. (2003). The mental health needs of looked after children: An integrated multi-agency model of care. *Clinical Child Psychology and Psychiatry, 8* (3): 323–335.

Kenrick, J. (2000). "Be a kid": The traumatic impact of repeated separations on children who are fostered and adopted. *Journal of Child Psychotherapy, 26*: 3.

Klein, M. (1940). Mourning and its relation to manic-depressive states. In: *Love, Guilt and Reparation*. London: Hogarth Press & The Institute of Psychoanalysis.

Klein, M. (1946). Notes on some schizoid mechanisms. In: *Envy and Gratitude*. London: Hogarth Press & The Institute of Psychoanalysis.

Krakauer, J. (1997). *Into Thin Air*. New York: Doubleday.

Lang, W. P., Little, M., & Cronen, V. (1990). The systemic professional: Domains, action and the question of neutrality. *Human Systems, 1*: 39–55.

Laub, D., & Auerhahn, N. C. (1993). Knowing and not knowing massive psychic trauma: Forms of traumatic memory. *International Journal of Psychoanalysis, 74*: 287–302.

Laws, S. (2001). Looking after children within the extended family: Carers' views. In: B. Broad (Ed.), *Kinship Care: The Placement Choice for Children and Young People* (pp. 115–126). Lyme Regis: Russell House.

Lear, J. (1998). *Open Minded: Working out the Logic of the Soul*. Cambridge, MA: Harvard University Press.

LeDoux, J. (1998). *The Emotional Brain*. New York: Phoenix.

Lieberman, A. (2003). The treatment of attachment disorder in infancy and early childhood: Reflections from clinical intervention with later adopted foster care children. *Attachment and Human Development, 5*: 279–282.

Lieberman, A. (2004). Traumatic stress and quality of attachment: Reality and internalization in disorders of infant mental health. *Infant Mental Health Journal, 25*: 336–351.

Lieberman, M., Doyle, A., & Markiewicz, D. (1999). Developmental patterns in security of attachment to mother and father in late childhood and early adolescence: Associations with peer relations. *Child Development, 70* (1): 202–213.

Lindsay, W. R. (1991). Psychological therapies in mental handicap. In: W. Fraser, R. MacGillivray, & A. Green (Eds.), *Caring for People with Mental Handicaps*. London: Butterworth.

Lindsey, C. (1993). Family systems reconstructed in the mind of the family therapist. *Human Systems*, 4: 299–310.

Lindsey, C. (1995). Systemic and developmental aspects of contact. In: H. Argent (Ed.), *See You Soon: Contact with Looked-After Children*. London: British Association for Adoption and Fostering.

Lindsey, C., Harris, R., & James, R. (2005). "A Study of the Meanings Given by Social Workers to Contact with Birth Families." Unpublished manuscript, Tavistock Clinic, London.

Losel, F., Bender, D., & Blinsender, T. (Eds.) (2003). *Psychology of Law: International Perspectives*. Berlin: de Gruyter.

Lyons-Ruth, K., & Jacobvitz, D. (1999). Attachment disorganization: Unresolved loss, relational violence, and lapses in behavioural and attention strategies. In: J. Cassidy & P. R. Shaver (Eds.), *Handbook of Attachment*. New York: Guilford Press.

Lyons-Ruth, K., Yelin, C., Melnick, S., & Atwood, G. (2003). Childhood experiences of trauma and loss have different relations to maternal unresolved and hostile–helpless states of mind on the AAI. *Attachment and Human Development*, 5: 330–352.

Macdonald, G., & Turner, W. (2005). An experiment in helping foster carers manage challenging behaviour. *British Journal of Social Work*, 35: 1265–1282.

Main, M. (1995a). Discourse, predication, and recent studies in attachment: Implications for psychoanalysis. In: T. Shapiro & R. Emde (Eds.), *Research in Psychoanalysis: Process, Development, Outcome*. Madison, CT: International Universities Press.

Main, M. (1995b). Recent studies in attachment: Overview. In: S. Goldberg, R. Muir, & J. Kerr (Eds.), *Attachment Theory: Social, Developmental and Clinical Perspectives*. Hillsdale, NJ: Analytic Press.

Main, M., & Cassidy, J. (1988). Categories of response to reunion with the parent at age six. *Developmental Psychology*, 24: 415–426.

Main, M., & Hesse, E. (1990). Parents' unresolved traumatic experiences are related to infant disorganised attachment status: Is frightened and/or frightening parental behaviour the linking mechanism? In: M. T. Greenberg, D. Cicchetti, & E. Cummings (Eds.), *Attachment in the Preschool Years* (pp. 161–182). Chicago, IL: University of Chicago Press.

Main, M., Kaplan, N., & Cassidy, J. (1985). Security in infancy, childhood, and adulthood: A move to the level of representation. In: I. Bretherton & E. Waters (Eds.), *Growing Points of Attachment Theory and Research*.

Monographs of the Society for Research in Child Development, 50 (1–2, Serial No. 209): 66–104.

Main, M., & Solomon, J. (1990). Procedures for identifying infants as disorganized disoriented during the Ainsworth strange situation. In: M. Greenburg, D. Cicchetti, & E. M. Cummings (Eds.), *Attachment in the Preschool Years: Theory, Research, and Intervention*. Chicago, IL: University of Chicago Press.

Main, M., & Weston, D. (1981). The quality of toddler's relationship to mother and to father. *Child Development, 52*: 932–940.

Mason, B. (1993). Towards positions of safe uncertainty. *Human Systems, 4*: 189–200.

Maturana, H. R. (1988). Reality: The search for objectivity or the quest for a compelling argument. *Irish Journal of Psychology, 9* (1): 25–83.

Maughan, B., & Pickles, A. (1990). Adopted and illegitimate children growing up. In: L. N. Robins & M. Rutter (Eds.), *Straight and Devious Pathways from Childhood to Adulthood* (pp. 36–61). New York: Cambridge University Press.

McFadden, E. J. (1998). Kinship care in the United States. *Adoption and Fostering, 22* (3): 7–15.

Meltzer, D. (1975). Adhesive identification. *Contemporary Psycho-Analysis, 11*: 289–310.

Meltzer, H., Gatward, R., Corbin, T., Goodman, R., & Ford, T. (2003). *The Mental Health of Young People Looked After by Local Authorities in England*. London: Office for National Statistics.

Menzies Lyth, I. (1959). The functioning of social systems as a defence against anxiety. In: *Containing Anxiety in Institutions*. London: Free Association Books, 1988.

Menzies Lyth, I. (1985). The development of the self in children in institutions. In: *Containing Anxiety in Institutions*. London: Free Association Books, 1988.

Menzies Lyth, I. (1986). A psychoanalytic perspective on social institutions. In: *The Dynamics of the Social*. London: Free Association Books, 1989.

Monck, E., Reynolds, J., & Wigsall, V. (2003). *The Role of Concurrent Planning: Making Permanent Placements for Young Children*. London: British Association for Adoption and Fostering.

Neil, E., & Howe, D. (2004). Conclusions: A transactional model for thinking about contact. In: E. Neil & D. Howe (Eds.), *Contact in Adoption and Permanent Foster Care: Research, Theory and Practice*. London: British Association for Adoption and Fostering.

NICE (2005). *Depression in Children and Young People: Identification and Management in Primary, Community and Secondary Care*. National Institute for Health and Clinical Excellence, Practice Guideline Number 28.

NICE (2006). *Methylphenidate, Atomoxetine and Dexamfetamine for Atten-tion-Deficit Hyperactivity Disorder in Children and Adolescents.* National Institute for Health and Clinical Excellence, Technology Appraisal (March).

Obholzer, A., & Roberts, Z. V. (1994). *The Unconscious at Work.* London: Routledge.

O'Connor, T. (2000). The effects of global severe privation on cognitive competence: Extension and longitudinal follow-up. *Child Development, 71* (2): 376–390.

O'Connor, T., & Rutter, M. (2000) (with the English and Romanian Adop-tee Study Team). Attachment disorder behaviour following early se-vere deprivation: Extension and longitudinal follow-up. *Journal of the American Academy of Child and Adolescent Psychiatry, 39* (2): 703–712.

O'Connor, T., & Zeanah, C. (2003). Attachment disorders: Assessment strategies and treatment approaches. *Attachment and Human Develop-ment, 5*: 223–244.

ONS (2000). *Mental Health of Children and Adolescents in Great Britain.* Of-fice for National Statistics (available at http://www.statistics.gov.uk/downloads/theme_health/ChildAdol_Mental_Health_v1.pdf).

ONS (2003). *The Mental Health of Young People Looked After by Local Authori-ties in England.* Office for National Statistics (available at http://www.statistics.gov.uk/downloads/theme_health/ChildrensMentalHlth.pdf).

ONS (2005). *Mental Health of Children and Young People in Great Britain, 2004.* Office for National Statistics (available at http://www.statistics.gov.uk/downloads/theme_health/GB2004.pdf).

Pallett, C., Blackby, K., Yule, W., Weissman, R., & Scott, S. (2005). *Fostering Changes: How to Improve Relationships and Manage Difficult Behaviours.* London: British Association for Adoption and Fostering.

Pally, R. (2000). *The Mind–Brain Relationship.* London: Karnac.

Park, K., & Waters, E. (1989). Security of attachment and preschool friend-ships. *Child Development, 60* (5): 1076–1081.

Parke, R. D., Cassidy, J., Burks, V. M., Carson, J. L., & Boyum, L. (1992). Familial contributions to peer competence among young children: The role of interactive and affective processes. In: R. D. Parke & G. W. Ladd (Eds.), *Family–Peer Relationships: Modes of Linkage* (pp. 107–134). Mahwah, NJ: Lawrence Erlbaum.

Patterson, G. R. (1982). *Coercive Family Processes.* Eugene, OR: Castalia.

Pearce, B., & Cronen, V. (1980). *Communication, Action and Meaning: The Creation of Social Realities.* New York: Praeger.

Perry, B. D., Pollard, R. A., Blakeley, T. L., Baker, W. L., & Vigilante, D. (1995). Childhood trauma, the neurobiology of adaptation and "use-dependent" development of the brain: How "states" become "traits". *Infant Mental Health Journal, 16*: 271–291.

Phillips, R., & McWilliam, E. (1996). *After Adoption: Working with Adoptive Families.* London: British Association for Adoption and Fostering.

Pickens, J., & Field, T.(1993). Facial expressivity in infants of depressed mothers. *Developmental Psychology, 29* (6): 986–988.

Pitcher, D. (2002). Placement with grandparents. *Adoption and Fostering, 26*: 6–14.

PIU (2000). *Prime Minister's Review of Adoption.* Performance Innovation Unit Report, Cabinet Office.

Priel, B., Melamed-Hass, S., Besser, A., & Kantor, B. (2000). Adjustment among adopted children: The role of self-reflectiveness. *Family Relations, 9*: 389.

Quinton, D., Rushton, A., Dance, C., & Mayes, D. (1998). *Joining New Families.* Chichester: Wiley.

Ramchandani, P., & Jones, D. P. H. (2003). Treating psychological symptoms in sexually abused children: From research findings to service provision. *British Journal of Psychiatry, 183*: 484–490.

Reeves, C. (2002). A necessary conjunction: Dockar-Drysdale and Winnicott. *Journal of Child Psychotherapy, 28* (1): 3–27.

Reinecke, M. A., Dattilio, F. M., & Freeman, A. (2003). *Cognitive Therapy with Children and Adolescents: A Casebook for Clinical Practice.* New York: Guilford Press.

Reyes, M., Buitelaar, J., Toren, P., Augustyns, I., & Eerdekens, M. (2006). A randomised, double-blind, placebo-controlled study of risperidone maintenance treatment in children and adolescents with disruptive disorders. *American Journal of Psychiatry, 163*: 402–410.

Reynolds, D. (2000). The ties that bind: A personal view. *Context 52, Association for Family Therapy.*

Robertson, J. (1989). *Separation and the Very Young.* London: Free Association Books.

Roy, P., Rutter, M., & Pickles, A. (2000). Institutional care: Risk from family background or patterns of rearing? *Journal of Child Psychology & Psychiatry & Allied Disciplines, 41* (2): 139–149.

Runyon, M. K., Deblinger, E., Ryan, E., & Thakkar-Kolar, R. (2004). An overview of child physical abuse: Developing an integrated parent-child cognitive–behavioural treatment approach. *Trauma, Violence & Abuse, 5* (1): 55–85.

Rushton, A., Mayes, D., Dance, C., & Quinton, D. (2003). Parenting late-placed children: The development of new relationships and the challenge of behavioural problems. *Clinical Child Psychology and Psychiatry, 8* (3): 389–400.

Rushton, A., Monck, E., Upright, H., & Davison, M. (2006). Enhancing adoptive parenting: Devising promising interventions. *Child and Adolescent Mental Health, 11* (1): 25–31.

Rustin, M. (1997). Rigidity and stability in a psychotic patient: Some thoughts about obstacles to facing reality in psychotherapy. In: M. Rustin, M. Rhode, A. Dubinsky, & H. Dubinsky (Eds.), *Psychotic States in Children* (pp. 245–266). Tavistock Clinic Series. London: Duckworth.

Rustin, M. (1999). Multiple families in mind. *Clinical Child Psychology and Psychiatry, 4* (1).

Rutter, M. (1998) (with the English and Romanian Adoptees Study Team). Developmental catch-up, and deficit, following adoption after severe global early privation. *Journal of Child Psychology and Psychiatry 39* (4): 465–476.

Rutter, M. (2000). Recovery and deficit following profound early deprivation in inter-country adoption. *Adoption and Fostering.*

Rutter, M., O'Connor, T., Beckett, C., Castle, J., Croft, C., Dunn, J., Groothues, C., & Kreppner, J. (2000). Recovery and deficit following profound early deprivation. In: P. Selman (Ed.), *Inter-Country Adoption: Developments, Trends and Perspectives* (pp. 107–125). London: British Association for Adoption and Fostering.

Ryburn, M. (1994). *Open Adoption: Research, Theory and Practice.* Aldershot: Avebury.

Sameroff, A. J., & Emde, R. N. (1989). *Relationship Disturbances in Early Childhood.* New York: Basic Books.

Schore, A. N. (2003). *Affect Regulation and the Repair of the Self.* New York: Norton.

Schuengel, C., Bakermans-Kranenburg, M., & van IJzendoorn, M. (1999). Frightening maternal behavior linking unresolved loss and disorganized infant attachment. *Journal of Consulting and Clinical Psychology, 67*: 54–63.

Schuengel, C., Van IJzendoorn, M., Bakermans-Kranenburg, M., & Bloom, M. (1999). Frightening, frightened and/or dissociated behaviour, unresolved loss, and infant disorganization. *Journal of Consulting and Clinical Psychology.*

Schwartz, J., & Begley, S. (2002). *The Mind and the Brain.* New York: Harper Collins.

Scott, S., & Lindsey, C. (2003). Therapeutic approaches in adoption. In: H. Argent (Ed.), *Models of Adoption Support.* London: British Association for Adoption and Fostering.

Scott, S., Spender, Q., Doolan, M., Jacobs, B., & Aspland, H. (2001). Multicentre controlled trial of parenting groups for childhood antisocial behaviour in clinical practice. *British Medical Journal, 323*: 1–7.

Siegel, D. (1999). *The Developing Mind*. New York: Guildford Press.

Silverstein, D., & Demick, J. (1994). Towards an organisational-relational model of open adoption. *Family Process, 33* (2).

Sinason, V. (1992). *Mental Handicap and the Human Condition: New Approaches from the Tavistock*. London: Free Association Books.

Slade, A., Aber, J. L., Fiorello, J., DeSear, P., Meyer, J., Cohen, L. J., & Wallon, S. (1994). *Parent Development Interview Coding System*. New York: City University of New York.

Solomon, J., & George, C. (1999). *Attachment Disorganization*. New York: Guilford Press.

Sprince, J. (2000). Towards an integrated network. *Journal of Child Psychotherapy, 26* (3): 413–444.

Sprince, J. (2002). Developing containment: Psychoanalytic consultancy to a therapeutic community for traumatised children. *Journal of Child Psychotherapy, 28* (2): 147–161.

Sroufe, L. A. (1990). An organizational perspective on the self. In: D. Cicchetti & M. Beeghly (Eds.), *The Self in Transition: Infancy to Childhood* (pp. 281–307). Chicago, IL: University of Chicago Press.

Steele, H., Steele, M., & Fonagy, P. (1996). Associations among attachment classification of mothers, fathers and their children. *Child Development, 67*: 541–555.

Steele, M., Henderson, K., Hodges, J., Kaniuk, J., Hillman, S., & Steele, H. (2006). In the best interests of the late-placed child: A report from the Attachment Representations and Adoption Outcome study". In: L. Mayes (Ed.), *Developmental Science and Psychoanalysis*. London: Karnac.

Steele, M., Hodges, J., Kaniuk, J., Hillman, S., & Henderson, K. (2003). Attachment representations and adoption: Associations between maternal states of mind and emotion narratives in previously maltreated children. *Journal of Child Psychotherapy, 29*: 187–205.

Steele, M., Steele, H., Woolgar, M., Yabsley, S., Fonagy, P., Johnson, D., & Croft, C. (2003). An attachment perspective on children's emotion narratives: Links across generations. In: R. Emde, D. Wolf, & D. Oppenheim (Eds.), *Revealing the Inner Worlds of Young Children* (pp. 163–181). Chicago, IL: University of Chicago Press.

Stenfert Kroese, B., Dagnam, D., & Loumidis, K. (1997). *Cognitive Behaviour Therapy for People with Learning Disabilities*. London: Routledge.

Stern, D. (1985). *The Interpersonal World of the Infant*. New York: Basic Books. [Reprinted London: Karnac, 1998.]

Sutton, A. (1991). Deprivation entangled and disentangled. *Journal of Child Psychotherapy, 17* (1): 61–78.

Sykes, J., Sinclair, I., Gibbs, I., & Wilson, K. (2002). Kinship and stranger foster carers, how do they compare? *Adoption and Fostering, 26* (2): 38–48.

Tavistock Training Publications (2006). *Care Stories: A Training Package for Those Working with Looked-After Children and Adolescents.* London.

Taylor, E., Dopfner, M., & Sergeant, J. (2004). European Clinical Guidelines for Hyperkinetic Disorder, first upgrade. *European Child and Adolescent Psychiatry, 13* (Suppl. 1).

Tizard, B., & Hodges, J. (1978). The effect of early institutional rearing on the development of eight year old children. *Journal of Child Psychology and Psychiatry, 19*: 99–118.

Tomm, K. (1987). Interventive interviewing, Part II: Reflexive questioning as a means to enable self healing. *Family Process, 26*: 167–183.

Trevarthen, C. (1979). Communication and cooperation in early infancy: A description of primary inter subjectivity. In M. M. Bullowa (Ed.), *Before Speech: The Beginning of Interpersonal Communication.* New York: Cambridge University Press.

Triseliotis, J. (1990). *Foster Care Outcomes.* Highlight No. 96. London: National Children's Bureau.

Triseliotis, J. (1993). Whose best interest? In: M. Humphrey & H. Humphrey (Eds.), *Intercountry Adoption.* London: Routledge.

Triseliotis, J. (2002). Long-term foster care or adoption? The evidence examined. *Child and Family Social Work, 7* (1): 23–33.

Triseliotis, J., & Russell, J. (1984). *Hard to Place: The Outcome of Adoption and Residential Care.* London: Heinemann.

Tsiantis, J., Kolvin, I., Anastasopoulos, D., Trowell, J., Tomaras, V., Miles, G., Papadopoulos, R., Soininen, M., Bostrom, C., & Almqvist, F. (2005). Psychotherapy for early adolescent depression: A comparison of two psychotherapeutic interventions in three European countries. In: E. D. Hibbs & P. S. Jensen (Eds.), *Psychosocial Treatments for Child and Adolescent Disorders: Empirically Based Strategies for Clinical Practice* (2nd edition). Washington, DC: American Psychological Association.

Van IJzendoorn, M. H. (1995). Adult attachment representations, parental responsiveness and infant attachment: A meta-analysis on the predictive validity of the Adult Attachment Interview. *Psychological Bulletin, 117*: 382–403.

Van IJzendoorn, M. H., & Bakermans-Kranenburg, M. J. (1996). Attachment representations in mothers, fathers, adolescents and clinical groups: A meta-analytic search for normative data. *Journal of Consulting and Clinical Psychology, 64* (1): 8–21.

Watson, J. B., & Raynor, R. (1920). Conditioned emotional responses. *Journal of Experimental Psychology, 3*: 1–14.

Webster-Stratton, C. (1992). *The Incredible Years. A Troubleshooting Guide for Parents of Children Aged 3–8.* Toronto: Umbrella Press.

Webster-Stratton, C., & Hancock, L. (1998). Training for parents of young children with conduct problems: Content, methods, and therapeutic processes. In: C. E. Schaefer & S. Breimeister (Eds.), *Handbook of Parent Training* (pp. 98–152). New York: Wiley.

Webster-Stratton, C., & Herbert, M. (1993). What really happens in parent training? *Behaviour Modification, 17* (4): 407–456.

Wechsler, D. (2004). *Wechsler Intelligence Scale for Children, Fourth Edition.* London: Harcourt Assessment.

WHO (1993). *The ICD-10 Classification of Mental and Behavioural Disorders: Diagnostic Criteria for Research.* Geneva: World Health Organization.

Winnicott, D. W. (1952). Anxiety associated with insecurity. In: *Through Paediatrics to Psychoanalysis.* London: Hogarth Press.

Winnicott, D. W. (1964). *The Child, the Family and the Outside World.* London: Penguin Books.

Winnicott, D. W. (1971). *Playing and Reality.* London: Tavistock Publications.

Witcraft, F. E. (1950). Within my power. *Scouting Magazine,* October (available at: http://www.scoutingmagazine.org/resources/webex/power.html).

Yeats, W. B. (1933). A second coming. In: *Collected Poems of W. B. Yeats.* London: McMillan.

Youngblade, L. M., & Belsky, J. (1990). Social and emotional consequences of child maltreatment. In: R. T. Ammerman & M. Hersen (Eds.), *Children at Risk: An Evaluation of Factors Contributing to Child Abuse and Neglect.* New York: Plenum Press.

Zahn-Waxler, C., & Smith, K. D. (1992). The development of prosocial behaviour. In: V. B. Van Hasselt & M. Hersen (Eds.), *Handbook of Social Development: A Lifespan Perspective. Perspectives in Developmental Psychology* (pp. 229–256). New York: Plenum.

Ziminski, J. (2004). *Negotiating Entitlements in Kinship Car Doctoral Thesis.* London: Tavistock Clinic.

INDEX